WALLED
GARDENS

WALLED GARDENS

Scenes from an Anglo-Irish Childhood

•

ANNABEL DAVIS-GOFF

Barrie & Jenkins
1990

This edition published in Great Britain in 1990 by
Barrie & Jenkins Ltd
20 Vauxhall Bridge Road
London SW1V 2SA

British Library Cataloguing in Publication Data
Davis-Goff, Annabel
Walled gardens: scenes from an Anglo-Irish childhood.
1. Fiction in English, 1945–. Biographies. Collections.
I. Title
823'914'09

ISBN 0-7126-3823-7

Printed by Mackays of Chatham

THIS EDITION PUBLISHED BY ARRANGEMENT
WITH ALFRED A. KNOPF, INC.

For
Susanna Moore

In an old house there is always listening, and more is heard than is spoken.

And what is spoken remains in the room, waiting for the future to hear it.

And whatever happens began in the past, and presses hard on the future.

—T. S. ELIOT, *The Family Reunion*

ACKNOWLEDGMENTS

It would not have been possible to write this book without the assistance of my entire family, and the book itself is a form of acknowledgment. I would, however, like to thank my uncle Frank Woodhouse and my sister Julia Barker for their photographic research, and my brother, Robert Davis-Goff, and my grandmother Mary Frances Woodhouse for permission to use photographs from their collections.

Mark Bence-Jones very kindly let me use information from his book *Twilight of the Ascendancy*, and the Ashmolean Museum, Oxford, provided a photograph of their portrait of William Goffe.

I also owe thanks to Robert Gottlieb and Lillian Hellman for help and encouragement with this book in its early stages.

CONTENTS

GLENVILLE

T H E D A Y on which my father should have been
buried turned out to be Grand National day. We knew that many
of his old racing friends would attend and that my father, more
than anyone, would have been shocked by the thoughtlessness of
holding a funeral on a racing or fox-hunting day.

The postponement gave us an extra day of family reunion in
Dublin. Although my parents had been divorced for twenty years,
it was at my mother's house that we started to congregate. My
brother's wedding had been the last time we had all been together.
And before that the weddings of my two sisters.

I am the eldest and had had the farthest to travel to come
home. The telephone had rung in the middle of the night in my
house in Connecticut. First there had been a pause, allowing me to
register a transatlantic hum, and then my brother's voice. "How
are you?" he asked, and I could read his mind as clearly as if I had
been awake and sitting in the same room as he was. He knew that
as soon as I heard his voice I would know something terrible had
happened and yet he couldn't, as an opening sentence and without

identification or greeting, start by telling me that my father was dead. That our father was dead.

The Irish are graceful about bereavement. They meet you on the street, put a hand on your arm and say, without embarrassment, "I'm sorry for your trouble. Will you have a jar?" And draw you into the nearest pub which is, inevitably, close at hand. This grace and ease and those good manners, which cannot be learned and come only from genuine kindness, began on the airline with the first Irish stewardess and with it came the realization that I was going home.

I have chosen to live my adult life away from my own country. Despite nostalgia and even occasional homesickness, it is not a choice I regret. But there is a deep feeling of peace which starts when the airplane gets close enough to the land for me to see not only the essential damp greenness of Ireland but that the trees grow lopsided, their irregular shapes formed by the prevailing wind. Recognition and memory. Going home. It would be sentimental and untrue to say that I have more in common with my average countryman than I have with my friends in New York. Not more or even as much, but something. Something small and important. Memory and knowledge. Knowing what an Irish country summer evening sounds and looks and smells like. A memory of a December morning with a light frost—frozen mud white-crested underfoot and pale sunshine. New-mown hay or apples slightly overripe after their winter in the slatted wooden storage racks. Some of this occurs in the exact form I remember only in Ireland. Most of it, of course, can happen anywhere. But the smell of tomatoes every year in our garden in Connecticut reminds me, not of the previous summer, but of my father in the greenhouse nipping off the small, pungent, green shoots between a stained thumbnail and forefinger. There is a feeling of relief which, I suppose, comes from knowing that I am among people who make the same associations with the sea, a gentle rain and the sounds of corncrakes and crows. Sea pinks and Christmas roses. The Angelus. Cowslips and salmon ladders. Crumbling Georgian houses and solid ancient ruins. Overgrown canals and miles of empty wide golden beaches. Fuchsia growing wild in the hedges of West Cork—a deeper, richer red than any fancy New York florist can ever offer. The other side of the same dusty August road a hedge of honeysuckle and wild roses. A gap—through a crooked handmade gate—shows a pond covered with water lilies. Giant oak trees, soft green beeches with nuts below on the moss, horse chestnuts with shiny conkers, mountain ash but also the treeless solid green and rock headlands out into the Atlantic with the occasional ruin breaking the flat line. Wild orchids. Fairy rings and hedgehogs. Turf fires. Sweaters made of unwashed wool—waterproof, slightly greasy and smelling a little of sheep until washed. Irish coins, each with a harp on one side and an animal on the reverse—a hen on the vast copper penny—a pig, a hare, a greyhound, a bull, a horse and a salmon on the silver. And so on.

I was the first to arrive; soon after, my younger sister, Alice, joined us. She'd had to make arrangements at short notice for someone to look after her two small children, and she was always odds-on to miss a train or plane. My mother had noticed, when Alice was still at school, that in any moment of pressure, particularly those which involved hurrying or the risk of being late, Alice would dash upstairs to wash her hair. Any phrase like "We should leave now if we want to catch that plane" or first race, or curtain, would guarantee her reaching out for the shampoo bottle. But this time she arrived when expected, which didn't prevent my mother and me each taking a quick sidelong glance to check for dampness.

My second sister, Julia, was the only missing member of the family. We were to meet her in Waterford the next day, before the funeral. My brother, Robert, and his wife, Sheelagh, heavily pregnant with their first child, spent the afternoon and evening with us. Sheelagh's baby was due any moment, and Robert, while fully occupied with the arrangements for the funeral, was terrified she would go into labour during the service. Or before, which would in a way be worse, presenting him with symbolic choices.

Sheelagh insisted that, if necessary, she would be fine on her own, and Alice and I insisted, without ever budging from our position that childbirth was nothing to fear, that Robert should stay with her.

My mother fed us at regular intervals. There was a fair amount of drinking, quite a lot of laughter. At the time, I thought the laughter came from the drinking and maybe from nervousness. Now I understand it came from shared memories.

"And time remembered is grief forgotten." Swinburne is not, perhaps, the first poet who leaps to mind in connection with my father (a man on whom one could not necessarily count to let an admiring reference to Oscar Wilde go unchallenged), but that evening, in my mother's house on the outskirts of Dublin, we became elated remembering moments we had for a time forgotten. The sense of loss diminished with every familiar story or joke retold, every moment relived, every memory repolished. Shared memories are the rock on which my kind of family is built. There is no substitute; blood counts for nothing in comparison.

The morning of the funeral, Alice and I got dressed. We'd both left home in a hurry and I, at least, had not given much thought to what clothes would be appropriate. I'd brought a dark coat and skirt and assumed that it would do. My mother, very tentatively, having long ago stopped giving advice, said she didn't think the piece of jewelry I had on my lapel was appropriate for a funeral. Her diffidence reminded me of an admirable quality shared by both my parents. From the time I reached the age of eighteen neither of my parents interfered with or criticized me. They would go out of their way to be loyal and supportive, even when my actions might have caused them more pain and embarrassment than they did me. My mother would praise me for my bravery in the face of some disaster largely of my own making but would never say, "If you hadn't been foolish enough to do such and such in the first place the whole thing never would have happened." Both were happy for me when I married and never suggested that if I'd done so four years earlier, rather than just before the birth of my second child, it might have been easier for them. It seemed to me then, and still does now, that they got it just right. Few are able to make the transition from a parent-child relationship to one based on mutual respect, or even tolerance, without a grinding of gears. Certainly my friendship with both my parents is better than that of almost anyone else I know. In some ways, my father's death did not interrupt every aspect of my relationship with him. The idea that I can still make my father laugh, and the certainty that memories of him can make me smile, takes some of the pain out of the loss and makes it a gentler kind of sorrow. The tiny incidents and ironies which I used to collect for my letters to him are no longer committed to paper, but they are still collected. We used to write to each other regularly, even during the transitional years just after I had left Ireland, when my frequent changes of address reflected my inability to find a comfortable place for myself on any level. Tact and reserve did not permit him to comment, but he once casually wrote that he hoped I would not change my abode again before it was time for him to renew his gun licence, on the back of which he was in the habit of keeping my current address.

Robert drove us from Dublin to Waterford down the Naas road. He retained his sense of humour and Sheelagh her serenity though every mile took us farther from Dublin and her obstetrician.

I was fascinated by the glimpses of beautiful Georgian houses, often half ruined, through the trees. After ten years of Manhattan skyscrapers and New England wooden houses I looked at them in a different way. It was not only a new awareness of their architectural beauty and perfect proportions but a feeling— experienced even in childhood, but stronger now—that each ruined Georgian house and each even older stone wall and every unaccounted-for rock, standing timeless in the middle of a field, had a message for me. Robert knew the names of the houses and of their owners. He knew the architecture, the history and, often, what paintings or other works of art each contained. I loved him for his intelligence and knowledge, undiluted by prurient curiosity.

We met Julia and her husband at an hotel. Julia, my sister and closest childhood companion, is a year and a half younger than I am and is the one with whom I most shared childhood experiences. Her present life in West Cork is about as far removed from mine in Manhattan as is possible. I left home when I was seventeen; Julia still lives in the South of Ireland. It is more than twenty-five years since we spent three consecutive days together, but we are bound by shared memories. She is the only person who also remembers what it feels like to sit, only just tall enough for one's chin to make it over the edge of the vast polished wood of the dining-room table, in a house which burned down thirty years ago. Or to stand by the kitchen table, its surface scarred by years of scrubbing with a hard brush, the grooves retaining a white residue of soap which we could pick out with our fingernails as we watched the cook make butter balls by expertly rolling small pats of butter between two damp, ridged, wooden paddles.

The hotel where we met Julia was new to me, on the other side of the river from the house where I'd spent my childhood. We crossed the river and took our flowers to the cathedral. It stood at the top of the hill, beside the school which Julia and I had attended as small children, part of which, in turn, had once been the Bishop's Palace where my grandmother had spent a winter as a young woman. We had passed the large and graceful cathedral every school day of our early childhood, its size and position overshadowing everything around it.

As a little girl, sitting between my parents on Sunday mornings, my legs dangling over the edge of the hard pew, during a sermon I couldn't follow, I had had plenty of time to observe the cathedral. It had seemed immense and beautiful and cold. But it had never seemed more so than when our small group, carrying bunches of spring flowers, advanced up the aisle. The church was empty and silent, except for our footsteps on the stone. My father's coffin dominated the transept. I was shocked and I sensed that the others shared my feelings. I had understood that he was dead, that I would never see him again, and I grieved for his loss, but I had failed to accept emotionally that a corpse lay inside the carved, wooden, and mercifully closed, coffin. My sisters and I began to weep while the others looked on helplessly, too sensitive and tactful to attempt comfort. I sensed also that in Julia's and Alice's grief, as in mine, there was a dangerous quality, that we would have been more likely to produce a savage, rather than a grateful, reaction to anyone attempting to comfort us.

We left our flowers and went outside and, without much discussion, decided to drive to where Glenville, our family house, had once stood. We were drawn by a morbid curiosity, a need to indulge our loss. It was certainly against all our better judgments.

After Glenville had burned down, the land had been sold and a dairy plant had been built on the site, but no one had bothered to demolish those parts of the stables and outbuildings that stood in areas not required for construction. We should have been able to work out where the house used to stand, since the weeping ash, which had once dominated the lawn, still remained, but we were unable to. Julia and I tried to reconcile our memories, which matched each other's, to the reality, but we couldn't. I still cannot reconstruct it, since, although intellectually I know that the tree and the stables were still there, I have no visual memory of what any of it looked like that afternoon. If I could remember that I would have to stop believing that Glenville still exists. Front doors open, camellias in bloom beside the steps. I would have to admit that it is no longer possible to run up those steps, enter the hall, dark after the summer afternoon sunlight, and go into the library, where the whole family would be waiting for me, coming in a little late for tea.

Alice and Robert don't remember Glenville. Robert hadn't been born when we lived there and Alice had been a very small child when we moved. It isn't just the house they don't remember—there is other information not available to them. Most of Julia's and my childhood memories are set there and the stories that my father would tell us could be imagined, in our mind's eye, in places we could remember, layering his memories over ours. And yet Robert, I imagine, must have been told things by my father that I don't know—memories evoked by walking together over a marshy field on a frosty morning hoping to put up some snipe, or discussed in a boat on the way back from a day's fishing. My father had a gift for making his memories ours and we were tied to him by what he remembered—sometimes events which had taken place before we were born. Robert, I believe, has deliberately made a place for my father's memories in the life he has chosen for his family.

Everything about Glenville was, of course, smaller than Julia and I remembered it. That was to be expected. We knew that things seemed larger to children and we had made allowances for that, but we hadn't understood that the proportions would also seem different.

It should have been depressing, but we experienced it more as being confusing. It was some time afterward that I understood why I couldn't work out where the house used to be. There was not a trace of the greenhouses or the walled garden.

THESE are some of the things I remember growing in the walled garden at Glenville: black figs—the tree was in one corner of the garden and sturdy enough for a child to climb, either to get to the ripe fruit or to reach the top of the aged red brick wall; pears, both the normal-sized ones and the large heavy ones which were picked green and left to ripen in drawers all over the house; plums, which we ate warm from the afternoon sun; loganberries; raspberries; strawberries—these grown first under frames and then, when it became warm enough, under nets to protect them from the birds (either way, we ate the berries by crawling, on our stomachs, in one end and emerging muddy, fruit-stained and full at the other); gooseberries—they used to give Julia a stomachache if she ate them, which led, despite her sincere promises before we embarked on forbidden overindulgence, to confessions halfway through lunch; red and white currants; peas, also best eaten raw in the garden; carrots, the baby ones, irresistible, if a little gritty; spring onions; broad beans; French beans; scarlet runners; sea kale, grown in the dark under terra-cotta cloches whose tiny-handled lids could be lifted off to peer in at the pale sunless vegetable below.

Flowers were not grown in the walled garden except for a solitary clump of peonies and a few Christmas roses casually placed beside the horseradish, which we dug up every Sunday morning to make sauce for the roast beef. If a Christmas rose grew in the lush green of an Irish spring it would disappear like a shabby genteel spinster, but emerging as it does from the cold, bare, brown, winter earth, it seems incongruous, mythic, symbolic and infinitely valuable.

The greenhouses at Glenville were full of even more delicious things to eat. On the walls, peach trees were espaliered against the peeling white brick, planted in the days when the garden and greenhouses were used only to grow produce for the family and their guests. The large silver fruit baskets which stood on our sideboard had once been filled with these and more exotic fruits, candlelit on polished wood at Edwardian dinner parties. Vines grew opposite the peach trees, on the slanted glass side of the smaller greenhouses. In the corner of the largest greenhouse, which had been built to accommodate larger tropical plants and trees, there was a sparse patch of Cape gooseberries.

But it is smell, not taste, that evokes those memories shocking in their intensity and clarity. Carnations and tomatoes. My father grew them both in one of the smaller greenhouses. Apart from the vines and peaches, the greenhouses were used to grow lettuce. Every bed in the large greenhouse and the smaller ones was filled with small heads of Boston lettuce each summer. My father planted out the seedlings, weeded and watered them, then, when they were fully grown, pulled them up and packed them in boxes and took them to Waterford. But even while doing this hard work, in the evenings, after a day at the office, he characteristically found an area of impractical, long-shot fun; in raised troughs, standing above the tiled floors, he grew tomatoes and carnations in something he called "the invention." The plants were put into a substance called Exflor and they were fed with pills dissolved in a gutter of water which provided irrigation. The carnations were magnificent, the tomatoes bore a surprising amount of fruit, and my father enjoyed himself. I don't know whether the value of the flowers and tomatoes ever exceeded the cost of the initial investment, but I know that one of my clearest childhood memories is of my father tending "the invention." I can smell the distinctive, unsentimental scent of carnations on a bar of soap in an expensive department store on Fifth Avenue and, for a moment, find myself three thousand miles away and over thirty years ago, a skinny little girl with long blonde hair staring up at her smiling blue-eyed father, the question on his lips long forgotten, but the lines on the skin at either side of his eyes part of my memory forever. Recently, my mother and I were visiting my brother at his house near Dublin and walking through a tiny greenhouse. I reached out to a tomato plant and nipped a shoot between my thumbnail and first finger, the way my father did to prune out the small redundant leafy growths which sprout between the main trunk and the branches of the plant. Without showing it to her, I held the strong-smelling leaves close to my mother's face.

"What does this remind you of?" I asked.

"Glenville," she said, without a moment's pause or any sign of surprise at my question.

It made me feel close to my mother, as though I hadn't left home so long ago or gone so far away. On a warm July afternoon in Dublin she thinks the same thing, when she catches the scent of tomato plants, that I do in my garden in Connecticut.

The bunch of carnations which I buy in New York at the Korean market on my corner brings with it a memory of the warm damp air of the greenhouses—the glass, grimy and a little green around the edges, the grapes pilfered off the vine (to my mother's despair, since we would pick them randomly from any available bunch like small destructive apes); peaches eaten off the tree and the stones disposed of in the dirt below (a shallow dent made with the heel, the return pendulum movement of the toe covering the pit with earth); the lily pond with the frogs and the giant grandfather goldfish, an unhealthy, old-aged, pale pink; my father, on the roof, painting, watching Julia and me sharing a looted chocolate bar, unaware of his amused presence above. The old grey gardening trousers, held up with a dilapidated, old school tie, and the open collarless shirt carried the evocative smell of tomato plants into the house with him at the end of the day.

The smell of tomato plants and carnations suited my father; although they were strong and distinctive, they were not sweet. My father had an acute sense of smell, and we were all—the children certainly, my mother perhaps less so—more than slightly proud of the time when he threw a vase of auratum lilies out of the library window. Their scent suggests something overblown, decadent. They are the lilies I imagine Shakespeare had in mind as "festering." To my father they seemed excessive, and I know that his dislike of the colour red and his refusal to allow any of us to wear it came from the same but unnamed source.

His distaste for excess was reflected in his appearance. None of his family was tall and, though strong and physically fit, he had a small frame. I never saw him a pound overweight. Nor, I think, did I ever see him take a snack between meals or eat anything if he weren't hungry. It took years after I had left Ireland to overcome the illogical belief that eating dessert is slightly unmasculine, and I am still not able to listen to a man discuss his weight or diet without some loss of respect.

My father's face was formed by his bone structure and softened by his wit. It had no spare flesh, no additional colour. I don't even know what colour his hair had originally been—by the time I remember him it was somewhat faded and thinning and a little grey. Even his name had been pared down. He had been christened Ernest, but all his life he had been known by his nickname, Sammy.

Children are supposed to wish their parents conventional, to conform to a standard which renders them invisible to the next generation. Since this was, in our case, clearly not possible, we aimed at the next-best thing: an acceptable stereotype. Once my father was established as a bona fide eccentric we would all be on safer ground, so we delighted in his habit of always using a smaller than normal fork and were proud of his allergy to fish.

(My own children approach their version of the same problem with infinitely more aplomb and skill. I discovered, with mixed feelings, sometime after the event, that my thirteen-year-old son had won the gratitude of his schoolmates by diverting a French class from a grammar test with his account of being what he calls "an ex-bastard"—his status resulting from, in his words, his parents having been "massive hippies." His instincts are the same as Julia's and mine were, but the execution far surer than anything we could ever have aspired to.)

IT IS POSSIBLE, without stretching the imagination over-much, to think that we had found, in the factory-desecrated ruins of our home, a kind of open coffin. A contrast to my father, sealed in a stark, pale wooden box. Everything at the cathedral neat and controlled, everything at Glenville random and jumbled and broken, with the uncontrolled illogic of a daytime nightmare.

Glenville was an Italianate mid-nineteenth-century house about a mile and a half outside Waterford, overlooking the river Suir. It was not architecturally beautiful in the way many Irish houses are. Its date was wrong for that, but it was large and pleasant. Apart from the main house and the walled garden, there were two lodges—one at the front gate, one at the back—a couple of fruit gardens, good stabling, small kennels and enough paddocks and grazing for a few hunters and a cow or two. It was not an estate or even a farm. It was a carefully thought-out, upper-middle-class residence for a family that had had civilized tastes and plenty of money to indulge them. A gentleman's property, but one which bore none of the responsibility which went with the estates of the landowning aristocracy. An estate in Ireland means a house set on a piece of land large enough to support a working, though not necessarily commercial, farm. It implies tenants and some position of authority held by the owner of the house, which would have been built considerably before Glenville was. Glenville produced nothing which was not consumed by its owners and any land not used for horses, cows, poultry and tennis was landscaped.

The comparatively mild climate of those parts of the southwest of Ireland touched by the Gulf Stream and North Atlantic currents, combined with an inherent preference for activities which take place out of doors, a cheap labour force and a comparatively affluent moment in the fortunes of the Anglo-Irish around the turn of the century, resulted in an enthusiasm for landscaping, often executed with a combination of knowledge and taste which had dramatic and beautiful results.

As the period of affluence ended (virtually overnight in our family), even the cheap labor became unaffordable and the imported plants and shrubs were left to become both a metaphor for the new, drastically reduced and unprotected state of the Anglo-Irish and a short-term experiment in Darwin's theory. By the time I was a child the result had a dreamlike quality. We played in woods containing eucalyptus trees and rhododendrons which had grown big enough for a child to climb up into and which still blossomed in bright improbable colours. The three ponds were another favorite playground. There had been two large oval ponds with a small round one between them. One of the oval ones had leaked and was full of marsh plants. It had a tiny island in the middle. The other two ponds were still intact and beside the larger one, on warm summer afternoons, we would sometimes have a family picnic. Three generations would gather on an overgrown grassy patch beside the water, surrounded by oversized plants whose inappropriate tropical lushness created a scene somewhere between a photograph from a Russian family scrapbook and a minor Rousseau. The water from this pond poured over a waterfall which took it underground for a while, then into a stream, another waterfall, a large ornamental pool, another waterfall, then down to the river below. Bamboo, which had been planted many years before, had proliferated and provided a tall dense jungle with just enough space between plants to allow children to creep sideways. A field of daffodils which had taken over in the same way was an even more beautiful backdrop to our games but contained fewer possibilities. Among the daffodils there was a walnut tree and a large chestnut, and in autumn we would roast chestnuts in the glowing embers and grey ash of the library fire.

In front of the house was a lawn, part of which had once been a tennis court. Closer to the house stood the large and beautiful weeping ash. Between the driveway and the lawn was a short but steep bank down whose grassy slope we would slide on tea trays or roll down and lie, dizzy, at the bottom, in the sweet smell of newly cut grass. My father used to mow this lawn. It was hard work; the lawn was large and lawn mowers were not the sophisticated machines they have now become. Nevertheless, he used to buy and then abandon quite a large selection of mowers. Mowing the lawn to keep up the appearance of the house and working in the greenhouses to pay for it took a large part of my father's leisure time and also a good deal of energy. He must have been all too well aware of the contrast between the life he then led and his memories of childhood. I never heard him make the comparison. "The good old days" was a phrase I often heard as a child, but never from my parents. We knew that the cheap and plentiful labour came not only from the poor working class but, in the original upkeep of the grounds at Glenville, through an arrangement with the local insane asylum. One of the first clues I had as a small child that the world could be cruel was the sight of truckloads of men from the asylum pulling sugar beets from a local farmer's wintery field and my mother's expression of pity when she explained to us who they were.

The climate and the rich earth and the constant rain helped keep up appearances in the gardens and grounds of large Irish houses long after the houses themselves had started to disintegrate.

Glenville was not the house in which my father had been born. His family had lived next door in a similar house called Maypark (which wasn't the family home either; that had been Horetown in County Wexford, built on land given to an ancestor by Richard Cromwell). Maypark was divided from Glenville only by fields and the immediate grounds and lawns of both houses. It had become a nursing home run by nuns. We used to meet the nuns during our afternoon walks. They, too, would take a little stroll after lunch and were the occasional source of boiled sweets which would be unwrapped from handkerchiefs taken out of secret pockets in their habits. They were quiet, calm, patient women and I was a little surprised that, having made the momentous decision they had, there was not a greater sense of conviction or aura of passion about them.

Glenville had a front gate and a back gate. The front-gate lodge was where the gardener lived. The driveway came from the front gate directly up to the house, where there was a gravel area large enough for a car or a pony and trap to turn, then continued past the ponds, the bamboo, the rhododendrons, overgrown patches of lawn with York and Lancaster roses struggling through the grass and weeds, to the stables and the coachman's house. The driveway continued, on one side the stable buildings, henhouses and, on the other, a large black-currant garden, to the back gate. Both gates opened out onto the lane.

The Little House, as the coachman's house was called after the last coachman moved out and our family moved in, was where my parents lived when I was born. The main house had been closed up as an economy measure some time before. The Little House was two stories high and built out of brick. The house, stables, barn and kennels were all part of one large, square, fortresslike construction. Except for the coachman's house, which occupied one corner and had a normal front door and windows, the rest faced inward. There were no windows on the ground level and the only access was from the front, through two separate sets of solid wooden double doors. The house and stables had been built during a time of political unrest, and while it had been impossible to build a house that was both pleasant to look at and secure, measures had been taken to protect horses, dogs, grooms and motorcars.

The best thing about the house was the magnolia tree, which grew on the courtyard side. Its heavy dark greenness against the red brick gave a feeling of absorbed and retained warmth, unusual and sensuously luxurious in so northern a climate. The worst thing was the layout of the house, although perhaps the way we utilized it added to the problem. At some time, probably when it had ceased to be servant accommodation and became the family home, it had been expanded and a bathroom and two other rooms had been added. Since the house was not freestanding, it had been necessary to add the new rooms on the ground level and to attach them to the existing kitchen. The main bedroom, dressing room and bathroom were behind the kitchen and the nursery quarters were upstairs. It is possible that there were good reasons for allocating space in this way, but it is also possible that using the top floor for nurseries (as belowstairs was used for kitchen activities) prevented anyone indulging in lateral thinking when deciding who should sleep where.

This added a complication to my mother's already harried existence when, at some unsatisfactory moment in his life, one or the other of my father's two younger brothers would come to stay and have to sleep in the dressing room of the main bedroom.

Most of my adult life has been spent in or near the theatrical community. Show-business people pride themselves on their temperament and sensitivity. It is generally accepted that to succeed in this curiously structured and transitory line of work one has to have a taste for intrigue and competition, to understand betrayal and to possess nerves of steel and a poker face. My guess is that the emotional temperature or the neurotic possibilities of high-powered behind-the-scenes life never come close to those of a household which includes: a marriage, two or more generations of family members, and a sprinkling of unrelated personnel whose terms of employment require them to live under the same roof.

If downstairs was full of worries about brothers-in-law, money, domestic staff and my father's business problems, life abovestairs was also not without dramatic possibilities. In a modest way I, too, was able to make a contribution toward the emotional temperature of the Little House. I was a morbid child. The British tradition of reserve was well instilled in me by the age of four and I found it impossible to communicate or voice my fears. These repressed feelings would occasionally burst out in appalling tantrums. My mother still well remembers, as I do, a tantrum which manifested itself in a hysterical rage ostensibly because my nanny had gone upstairs before me. No one ever inquired or, as far as I know, wondered what it was really about, possibly because it had an unpleasant hint of assumed social superiority, which would have been embarrassing and hard to deal with.

My nanny's name was Nelly. I knew even then that she wasn't a healthy influence, but of course at the time I never discussed her with my parents. Julia, being first a baby and then a small child during Nelly's reign, was even less likely to blow the whistle. Discipline was maintained by a series of threats and promises, none ever being fulfilled. If we were naughty or bold, as she, Nelly, would have said, she would threaten to lock us in the black closet at the top of the stairs. In fairness, the threat was clearly an idle one and carried little weight.

At some stage, Nelly became emotionally disturbed and it became apparent that she would have to go. My father took the position that firing nannies was women's work. It seems a little unfair. He was fifteen years older than my mother and would have been able to perform the deed with a fraction of the anxiety and—not too strong a word—the fear my mother felt. It had to do with the way he'd been brought up. He was more comfortable dealing with employees or servants than she was. He perceived the relationship in a different and less personal way. Oddly enough, his distant attitude often worked better than her more humane approach. Both parties appeared to feel more comfortable, or at least to recognize the ground rules.

My mother later told me that my father calmly continued to read a book while she took a stiff drink and fired Nelly. Tears, I imagine, ensued. Mine certainly did. "Nelly's gone" were soon, my father said, the saddest words in the English language. Despite experiencing a strong sense of loss, I don't remember feeling much, if any, affection for her. But I do remember an awful visit to her family. They lived in a cottage on the road to Woodstown, where she used to bicycle on her day off. Once when we were staying with my great-grandmother and great-great-aunt, who lived in Woodstown, she took me to see her family, incorporating the visit into our afternoon walk. It was a small cottage for a large Catholic-sized family. I only saw the main room, but I doubt if there were many more. Certainly not an indoor bathroom. The main room was a combined kitchen and living room. Her father sat at the hob beside the kitchen fire. The room was murky, lit by oil lamps. He told me that they were poor. I don't know if he wanted to make me, a junior member of the so-called privileged Protestant upper class, guilty, or whether he thought I would pass on this information to my father, who would do something for them or give Nelly a pay rise. Or maybe I was just a fresh audience for a running complaint. With that clarity reserved for childhood incidents horribly outside one's control, I remember his clinching argument. He took me to a cupboard where they kept their supplies and showed me an almost empty sugar bowl, not entirely clean—someone had helped himself to sugar with a tea-wet spoon—and said that that was all the sugar they had. I was used to the idea of shortages because of rationing, and used to the idea that almost no one we knew had enough money, but this was something different.

I have no memory of the move from the Little House to Glenville proper, or of the reasons for the move; still less did I understand that we were fulfilling some kind of Anglo-Irish destiny. I suppose we moved because our circumstances had improved slightly, or because the crowded atmosphere of the coachman's house had become impossible. Or a combination of the two. It was a very Anglo-Irish choice—to move into a large house without the means to make it comfortable or to live in it with comparative financial peace of mind. It was certainly not an ignorant choice. We were surrounded by examples of people stuck in large impossible houses when we voluntarily moved into ours. We didn't, of course, do anything as foolish as buying one. Glenville stood empty and in fairly good repair and the space must have seemed like a rationale for the move.

It is not a choice I would now make. The thought of all those not-quite-met responsibilities gives me a knot of anxiety, but I operate on a different value system, one geared toward freedom through simplification, whereas the society in which my parents (or at least my father) lived looked constantly over its shoulder. Few did it more gracefully than my father.

Glenville was built facing the lawn with its large and beautiful weeping ash. To the right of the house were the greenhouses and beyond them the walled garden. Each of the main rooms—the drawing room, dining room and library and, on the next floor, my parents' bedroom and the other two largest bedrooms—had a gently curved wall, into which regular, not bay, windows were set. In each, the window which sat square to the room looked out over the row of ornamental ponds and behind them, some way below, the river. The curved wall allowed a slightly different view from the secondary windows, so that the library also looked over one end of the lawn, edged with a row of red-hot pokers (Kniphotia Uvaria), and the dining room had one window facing an unusually large and beautiful laburnum, behind which lay the densely packed bamboo jungle, which seemed too dense, exotic, threatening. Vandals at the gates of Rome.

The house had a double hallway, the inner part double-height, and, on the upper level, there was a gallerylike landing and a corridor off which lay the main bedrooms. The layout of the house, topped off with a glass dome, made it impossible to heat.

At one point, a large stove was installed in the hall. We called it Pingo. Pingo was the Edwardian nickname of Sir Terence Langrishe, whose real name carried all the weight of literary and upper-class associations one man could be expected to bear. He was a friend of my parents' and had been, in some way, instrumental in our acquiring the stove. He may actually have sold it to us. Unless one was standing within a radius of four feet, the heat, which shot upward to the icy glass roof, eluded one entirely.

The cold and the dark shadows and the orange-red glow which came through the transparent but, to me, miraculously uninflammable windows on the front of Pingo were all part of one winter scene I remember. Julia and I were very small, Alice not yet born, when a party of carol singers from the Waterford Protestant cathedral came to Glenville. They had been expected all evening, and Julia and I had become more excited and more anxious as the evening wore on, our bedtime approached, and the carolers did not materialize. Our bedtime, never late, was slightly postponed and still no lights appeared on the driveway and there was no sound of cars on the gravel. Eventually, disappointed but not complaining, we allowed ourselves to be shooed up the stairs. We were far too excited to sleep, but lay in bed alert, with ears strained for the sound of visitors. Eventually they arrived and our mother came upstairs and told us to put on our dressing gowns and to watch from the gallery. It was too late and too cold for us to get dressed again and I suppose also that, although we were not sleepy, we must have been tired. Julia and I both had pink dressing gowns, each with a white bunny rabbit stitched on the pocket, and, wearing them over our nightdresses, we crouched in the dark gallery peering through the banisters, able to see and hear everything below. There is no rational explanation why two children, covered from neck to ankle in conventional nightclothes, should not have been able to go downstairs and join their parents to listen to Christmas carols, but the conventions of the time made it impossible. Two separate conventions came into play here; I am not sure which was the dominant. One had to do with dress. No one ever came downstairs in a dressing gown. Breakfast was eaten, fully dressed, in the dining room. In a well-run house a tray would have earlier been sent up to one's bedroom with a pot of tea and couple of slices of toast. This snack was called "early morning tea." The other convention was left over from the almost complete separation of adults from children a generation before. In those days, parents who could afford to do so had their children cared for by nannies and governesses and would frequently see them for less than half an hour a day. Phrases like "Children should be seen and not heard," not necessarily said as a joke, were common even when I was growing up. (When Robert Gregory, about whom Yeats wrote "An Irish Airman Foresees his Death," went off to war in 1917, his wife and a maid watched him leave from outside the hall door, while his two small daughters watched from an upstairs window.) As occasionally happened, these conventions worked in our favour that night. My mother, whose most dominant emotion was probably slight embarrassment, remembers nothing of that evening. Julia and I, benefiting from the dim light, the distance, the atmosphere of secrecy as we concealed ourselves, remember it as magical, theatrical, beautiful. It is almost certainly Julia's earliest memory. When the singing ended my parents gave the carolers money and mugs of hot tomato soup (from a can, not homemade, which in Julia's and my eyes made it a luxury). The scene's resemblance to a Christmas card was further enhanced since, very wisely, none of the carolers took off his coat or muffler.

We all dressed warmly, with lots of home-knitted sweaters. I didn't suffer much from the cold, but my mother, who has poor circulation, was wretched during the winter, as was Julia, who used to develop the kind of incapacitating chilblains one wouldn't expect to meet outside a polar expedition.

Although it was not possible to keep a house such as Glenville warm, it was necessary to keep it dry and in winter we varied the rooms in which we sat so that the study and library alternately had the benefit of our fire. Heating throughout the house, to the extent it existed at all, was provided on a room-to-room basis, and it was a mad dash at mealtimes from living room to dining room. All the main rooms, however, had large old-fashioned and unused radiators—another relic of an age of cheap labour and cheap fuel.

The furnishing of the house was varied. Most things left over from the past were fine and, I suppose, valuable. China, silver, glass and furniture were often old and beautiful, although I don't remember any good paintings. What had been added in the way of beds and other household furniture was inexpensive department-store stuff—I don't think there was much in the way of good modern design then, and if there had been, we couldn't have afforded it.

Today, spending part of my time in rural Connecticut, I sometimes see my nursery plates for sale as valuable antiques, or a soap dish identical to those I remember from a maid's bedroom at Glenville priced at two hundred dollars, and I have a fantasy involving time and space. If I could have gone forward in time and sideways across the Atlantic bearing almost any everyday house-hold object, sold it and returned with the money, it would have accomplished more than a year's worth of market gardening.

Julia and I, like most children, gravitated to the kitchen, not in search of delicious morsels—the kitchen did not have provisions for picking and snacking. We did not have a refrigerator or a biscuit tin and most edible treats were found in the garden or the greenhouses. What we were after was gossip and drama, women's magazines and the wireless, as we called the radio. My father disliked the wireless, and used to say that most people played it at a volume in inverse proportion to their intelligence, so the only source of music as light entertainment was in the so-called servants' hall. (All my childhood rooms had grander names than the functions they had come to serve. When my father had been a boy it had been a servants' hall and no one had ever thought to change the name even though the only remaining trace of old-fashioned service was a numbered board with a bell and indicators to show in which room the summoning bell had been rung.) If one of us were ill and confined to bed for several days, the wireless would be moved across to our bedroom, but the rest of the time it was tuned to Radio Eireann and used only by the maids and any child who might be lurking about eavesdropping. The two exceptions were Christmas afternoon, when we listened, liverish and faintly embarrassed to, in early childhood, the King's Speech and, later, the Queen's Speech, and the great sporting events of the year, the English and Irish Grand Nationals and the English and Irish Derbies. The horse races evoked less complicated emotions, but while I can remember no highlights from the Queen's speeches, I am still familiar with the winners of the races from the time I was six until I left home. My father might have had a small bet on these occasions, but the importance and excitement of the races far transcended personal gain. One year, when I was eight, a local horse called Freebooter was entered in the English Grand National and the level of excitement was higher than ever before. It was discovered that Madigan, the gardener, had placed a substantial bet on the local entry. Protocol, his shyness and muddy boots did not allow him to join us in the library while we listened to the race, but a happy compromise was reached. The library window was opened, the volume turned up, and Madigan stood outside among the camellias, overjoyed as his horse won.

We loved to listen to kitchen gossip, though I, at least, instinctively knew that, however fascinating, it wouldn't travel as far as the dining room. I would never have asked, as did Julia, still saucer-eyed from a belowstairs crash course on miracles: "What is Lourdes?" My father, his thoughts and maybe even his conversation elsewhere, replied without a moment's hesitation: "It's where they play cricket in London." This tiny incident illustrates the distance between kitchen and dining room but should not be taken as a suggestion that there was a gap in understanding, only in interests. We all read *Some Experiences of an Irish R.M.*, an entertaining novel in which a well-meaning but slightly pompous English Resident Magistrate is constantly, but not unaffectionately, made a fool of by the Irish, but the joke wasn't on us. Lourdes or Lord's, you took your pick. The difference was based on background and choice, not misunderstanding.

My mother accepted our childish wish to hang around the kitchen, but my uncle Charles (one of my father's two brothers, who sometimes behaved as though the difference between the way the house was run by my mother and the way it was when their father had been alive and rich was due only to her inept grasp of household management) was shocked by it. He used to call us "the Kitcheners" in tones of such sarcastic disapproval that I would see my mother press her lips together to stifle an angry rejoinder. To some extent my uncle was right. Certainly Julia and I were not exposed to any folklore, poetry, peasant wisdom, picturesque ways of speaking or expressions that Synge missed out on. The young women who came to work as maids were country girls longing to get to the city. They had cheap frizzy perms and Woolworth's makeup and read *Woman's Own* as voraciously as I did. They were not necessarily either clean or honest. I remember my mother dealing with both these problems with a mixture of slight irritation and extreme embarrassment. Trying to quell outbreaks of petty thieving and to find the gentlest way to tell a girl who'd never before lived in a house with running water to take a bath.

Despite a continuing state of financial anxiety, we always had a cook. The level of cuisine in Ireland then, in all but the grandest houses, was very low. The average cook automatically put the cabbage for lunch on to boil very shortly after breakfast. My mother, soon defeated by this attitude and, I suspect, not then knowledgeable enough to teach cooking, established a set menu: roast beef on Sunday, cold on Monday, shepherd's pie on

Tuesday, ending up with steak and kidney pie on Saturdays. I hated almost any form of meat. There was supposed to be an explanation for this. I once overheard my mother telling a friend that as a smaller child I'd "seen something nasty in the wood-shed." This aroused my curiosity, especially since we had a dark sinister woodshed haunted by stray cats, but Freud was not a name you heard bandied about in Ireland at that time and I was never encouraged to recognize my trauma, if indeed there had ever been one. Needless to say, when I was old enough to question my mother about it, she'd forgotten the whole incident.

Eavesdropping became a minor skill. In the kitchen, it was easy, or at least uncomplicated. The maids tended to be indiscreet, but when they wanted to talk about something which their instincts for self-preservation told them should be private, they would tell me to "run along to your own part of the house." I would leave, embarrassed by having overstayed my by no means certain welcome. I knew there was no way of manipulating them.

With my mother, it was a different matter. Deviousness could pay dividends. Not the exotic, dramatic dividends of kitchen stories, which were exciting, although I knew enough not to believe most of them and understood that they were meant as entertainment, not news, rather like the tabloids which transfix one's eye waiting in line at the supermarket checkout. Even so, to this day I believe it to be a sin to kill a spider or burn bread. On the other hand, I never doubted the accuracy of the information I gleaned from drawing-room stories and, although lacking in lurid events, they were a little scarier. I knew that my future was unlikely to depend on a miraculous cure at Lourdes but suspected that it might be affected by most of the four main topics touched on by my mother: marriage, death, money and drink. I never actually stood with my ear to the keyhole—the thickness of the doors, my own cowardice, the icy temperature of the hall made that impractical. But I developed a knack of being in the same room as my mother whenever she was talking to one of those rare people with whom she exchanged personal confidences. Early on in these conversations I would be told to go outside to play. I used to resist, although not too passionately, for that would be a giveaway. Instead I would whiningly complain that it was cold outside; I had nothing to do; I was reading. It was necessary to do this from the far end of the room, demonstrating that I was absorbed in whatever I was doing and well out of earshot anyway. At the beginning there might be a glance or two in my direction but gradually I was forgotten. Since they didn't often talk about things which concerned me directly, they assumed I didn't understand. But I soon had a complete picture of every family skeleton in a variety of surprising cupboards and a fairly accurate picture of the marriage of at least one of my mother's friends. Some of the gaps could be filled in during the summer months when we went to visit my grandmother Woodhouse. If I got her going at the right speed on the right subject she sometimes forgot that she was talking to a child.

The possibility of getting this information by asking a direct question never occurred to me and I doubt that the answers, if given, would have been nearly so revealing as those I gleaned by stealth.

A lifetime of listening and watching and wondering and being unable to ask questions about anything important has given me a heightened ability (as those deprived of one of their senses often develop the remaining ones to compensate) to see a whole and accurate picture. To be able to fill in the missing ninety-eight percent if I have the crucial other two. It was the start of my understanding that, as a whole frog can be constructed from a cell taken from a leg, within some tiny insight the whole picture is stored. It is, unfortunately, a bystander's art and it served only to distance an already remote child.

Most of the time, my pickings were slim: mother-in-law tensions; financial embarrassments; kitchen versus drawing room resentments. But occasionally I would hit a jackpot.

His name was Creed and hers was Scottie. They came to stay sometimes during the summer. Creed had been a friend of my father's from the time when they'd both been bachelors on the racing, hunting and dancing circuit. She was a friend of my mother's and less guarded in conversation than anyone I had then encountered.

I kept them both under surveillance. Creed was the easy one to observe since he was devoid of discretion and children ate the first three meals of the day with adults (tea was a real meal, as was breakfast, and lunch and dinner were given slightly less emphasis to compensate). He was an alcoholic in a quite advanced stage, but with a certain charm. He had been brought up in one of the more beautiful great houses of Ireland, but by the time he came to visit us he lived abroad close to a business which he had inherited and which kept him very comfortable.

After the first few drinks of the day (and only the early bird had any opportunity of observing him before) he went into mourning for his family house and the life that went with it. I listened wide-eyed, amazed to hear an adult speak so openly of feelings and more than slightly nervous at this suspension of all previously observed conversational rules. I sometimes understood events, behaviour and emotions even though I did not then know how to name them. Phrases like "self-censoring mechanism" or even the concept of alcoholism as a disease required information, and even a vocabulary, I did not yet possess. Sometimes I sensed what was important before I understood it, often from the tense, silent reaction of more knowledgeable or sophisticated adults, and sometimes because I knew there was a lesson, specifically for me, to be learned. Despite Creed's lack of inhibition, I understood that he was not telling the whole story and knew that what would have seemed to be the obvious solution—for him to sell his beautiful villa in Madeira and his profitable business and to invest the proceeds in a drafty Irish property with a leaky roof—would neither guarantee happiness nor address the subtext of his complaints. Although I had never heard the pain of nostalgia openly expressed before—all Anglo-Irish references to the past were funny at best and matter-of-fact at worst—I realized that he grieved not only for a house but for a way of life long gone, that even if he reconstructed it, complete with a stableful of Irish hunters, he was not the same man; that the years and too much Irish whiskey had killed the enthusiastic boy he had once been just as surely as death duties had taken his family "place."

Scottie was a large, cheerful, courageous woman. I was fascinated by her. She was noisier and more colourful than I was used to, with blonde hair and red lipstick and a genuine good nature. Both she and Creed used to make reference to a racier way of life than I ever hoped to witness in the South of Ireland. His anecdotes were bitter, savage and somewhat shocking, partly because of his barely buried rage, and partly because I knew that he had lost what I would now call his self-censoring mechanism. In contrast, her stories were funny. She had a series of catch-phrases which seemed wonderfully sophisticated to me. For instance, she would refer to any real estate benefit which might have been accrued through a sacrifice of a sexual nature as "a silk-lined sewer" and told us about a fortune-teller who had referred to her, Scottie, as "the broken blossom." I had no experience of humour as a defence and it was not until I later overheard her tell my mother, with her usual jolly laugh, that she'd left her first husband when he'd become insane and didn't think her reputation would survive leaving a second, that I understood that she was trapped. Years later when I came on the line in *The Importance of Being Earnest*: "To lose one parent . . . may be regarded as a misfortune; to lose both looks like careless-ness," I thought of Scottie.

Her outgoing nature and her inability to keep up any kind of convincing pretence in the face of her husband's uncontrollable alcoholism and unpredictable behaviour gave her an openness which made her a natural confidante for my mother.

My father and Creed used to go fishing on the Blackwater, the one sport Creed was still able to enjoy. Later, when I was seventeen and a school friend of Scottie's daughter, I spent a summer in Madeira with them. I realized then that Creed had an idealized view of my father, a mild form of hero worship, and that this hero worship was tinged with envy. My father had remained in Ireland, had won the steeplechases, had kept the faith.

I was, at that time, gathering information but not yet drawing conclusions. Getting ready to make a plan. Watching and waiting. And already aware that my parents' generation was the last one which could—and only just could—survive under the old Anglo-Irish format. Creed and Scottie were valuable, as were the maids, not only because most of the information they offered was relevant but because it was presented out in the open, in words. Occasionally one of my parents' other friends would say something telling, but only by accident, and it required a great deal of attention to gather even these small dividends.

I don't remember either of my parents having friends in the sense that I now have. The inherent reserve of Irish society made that impossible. My father's friends were the men with whom he had grown up; their friendship was based on humour, shared adventures, memories and interests—all firmly rooted in the past. I am sure that these friendships were devoid of intimacy, but I would not underestimate the strength of their camaraderie. Almost without exception, meetings between my father and his friends took place on the hunting field, the racecourse or a piece of marshland which might put up a few snipe or duck. Food never had an important place in these activities, although drink sometimes did.

My father would sometimes talk of other friendships in his past, although not with the sentimental attitude of his expatriate friend. The way he remembered them and the way he spoke of them allowed me greater access to their characters than I should perhaps have had if I had actually known them. I drew some important conclusions from my father's memories (apparently and admirably untainted by any trace of regret) of larger-than-life people many of whom seemed to have ended tragically.

From them I learned something about taking chances. Not the short-term, long-odds, unnecessary chance so dear to any Irishman. ("I'll chance it," he cries while he leaves the milk on the stove, or sets off with a flat spare tyre, or leaves the water running in the bath, the door unlocked, the car parked on the double yellow line.) They taught me about taking a chance when the odds are against you. The Anglo-Irish that I knew—the ones who had survived—played out their lives rather like punters at a roulette table betting with the minimum stake. They may last a long time, but eventually they must lose. Assuming that one's life is such that without taking a gamble one will not survive, it is surely better odds and more courageous to place your whole stake on one bet. Better, as I have heard gamblers say, when faced with a scary but mathematically correct decisive play, to be trampled to death by elephants than to be pecked to death by ducks. My father's attitude toward those who had demanded a little more from life, had played for higher stakes and lost, was such that I never doubted that they had made the right choice.

I fared less well watching my mother's friends. Because she fared less well. Women's lunches and the telephone as a social instrument had not reached Waterford. I never saw my mother chat on the telephone. Its location—in the hall, cold, dark, and public—ensured that it was used only for brief, important communications of a non-intimate nature. It seems sad to me that my mother had no one to call, as I do each day, for a nightly roundup and sign-off. Brothers-in-law, marital tensions, child-rearing inadequacies and the small doubts that eat away at our souls seem a little less permanent and more manageable when they can be related with humour instead of resentment to an intelligent and generous friend.

The gardener's lodge was a three-room cottage. It was there that I observed an alternative and more practical approach to life. I watched a working-class Catholic family who, although they had a much lower standard of living than we did, seemed to have a stronger control of their fate. The gardener, Mr. O'Shea, and his family lived in two bedrooms and a main room with an open fireplace over which hung a large black pot. Bread was baked on the inverted lid; bacon and cabbage boiled within. To wash, water had to be brought into the house and heated in the pot. The lavatory was a small privy at the back of the house.

Julia and I used to spend a fair amount of time in the gardener's cottage. Our welcome was more sure there than in the kitchen, partly because we played with the O'Shea children and partly because both Mr. O'Shea and his wife had the kind of good manners that are based on impeccable instincts. These instincts, I can't help noticing, are more often found in the native-born Irish than the Anglo-Irish.

The O'Shea boys, Jerry and James, were each slightly older than Julia and I. Their companionship was a relief after the complications of school, where I was always an outsider, short of friends and usually unsure of where I stood with other people. Not so when the four of us played Cowboys and Indians in the woods at Glenville, or in the deserted part of the stables, or pretended to drive the Ford Standard, up on blocks until petrol rationing ended. They brought no opinions or judgments with them. They accepted our lives for what they were and regarded new information and people with interest, but no curiosity. No one scored points for being a boy instead of a girl, or for being older or stronger or a Catholic or a Protestant or having a father with a title or a governess who spoke no English. Like their parents, Jerry and James had the natural good manners which come with kindness. If you didn't look at them slowly and with interest, you might have thought them simple country people, a little unimaginative. But what seemed like literal-mindedness was really common sense and a firm grip on reality. The O'Sheas' beliefs and values seemed simple only because they were clearly defined. I found it admirable then and enviable now when I constantly need to reexamine my beliefs and alter them to fit what logic and experience have shown me to be closer to the truth. Both the boys went to school with the Christian Brothers. Jerry became a bandleader and James is now a professor at a Canadian university. It is ironic that in my family, only one of us (not I) completed the equivalent of a high school education and that none of us went to university.

I remember visiting the O'Sheas' cottage late one afternoon. Mr. O'Shea, after work, sat at the oilcloth-covered table in the kitchen, reading *The Irish Independent*. On the wall, as in most Catholic homes, there was a lurid picture of the Sacred Heart. Even the choice of newspaper underlined the difference between his family and ours. *The Irish Times* was what the Anglo-Irish Protestant families read. *The Irish Independent* was what the Catholic Irish read. Both newspapers are independent of a political party, and the events they cover are, necessarily in a small, sparsely populated country, essentially the same. Both papers employ competent, thinking, entertaining journalists, but the readership is separate and rarely overlaps. *The Irish Times* is more likely to describe events at the Royal Dublin Society, while *The Irish Independent* is where you would look for a fuller coverage of the hurling match at Croke Park. *The Irish Times* did not provide a Sunday edition and on that day the Anglo-Irish switched over to the English Sunday papers, which gave them a slightly different view of world politics and a weekly dollop of gossip, book and theatre reviews and the crossword puzzles. Catholics took *The Sunday Independent* and it was at the O'Sheas' that I was introduced to my first syndicated comic strip. I used to enjoy—a fine example of the past habitual, one of the few aspects of Irish grammar I still remember, employed to convey the sense of "I used to be in the habit of"—I used to be in the habit of enjoying the Phantom serial cartoon on Sundays. So did both the gardener's sons. It was an eagerly awaited treat each Sunday after we had returned from church and they from Mass. I realize now that the Phantom was an American syndication but the associations were so strong that for many years I believed it to be Irish in origin. Each week the Phantom would be left in a cliff-hanger situation from which no escape seemed possible. Each new installment, of course, would rescue him from that particular peril only to hurl him into fresh jeopardy. I used also to enjoy discussing the Phantom with Mr. O'Shea, who, even if he didn't follow it as avidly as I did, clearly read it and was able to give commonsense if, it seemed to me, unnecessarily pedestrian opinions. This was a unique experience. Neither of my parents could be engaged in discussions of this kind and the maids had more sense than to venture quotable opinions on the romance columns on which both they and I relied so heavily for information about the outside world.

I can remember the moment at which I began to lose interest in the Phantom. Mr. O'Shea, presumably only to tease me, although possibly attempting to encourage a touch of realism, said, "Looks like he's had it this time." Weighted down and bound hand and foot, the Phantom had been left to die at the bottom of the ocean. I argued, fully and justifiably confident of his survival, but was unable to come up with a reasonable solution to his predicament. The Phantom did, as usual, live to star in the following week's installment, but I no longer cared. Mr. O'Shea had shown me that what I had admired had no real value. Not with a blanket dismissal of the genre or a laugh at a childish enthusiasm which might have been the Anglo-Irish way, but by giving the subject his full attention and giving me a thoughtful reaction. It occurs to me now that working-class Irish people, though by no means lacking in imagination or poetry, choose very carefully where they are going to suspend their disbelief. "The Emperor's New Clothes" is not a fable which could be set in Ireland. I think that the native Irish could not afford to entertain illusions and that it is very likely that the Anglo-Irish could not afford not to do so.

A gardener was not, for us, a luxury. The walled garden and Victorian greenhouses, with their blancmange-shaped roofs, provided enough fruit and vegetables to feed the house, and the surplus, when sold in Waterford, paid a gardener's wages, about three pounds a week. This selling of produce put my father in an unusual position. The relationship between the Irish Catholic shopkeepers and the Anglo-Irish gentry, to use an old-fashioned but accurate word, had always been subservient. Grandiose behaviour on one side and deferential treatment from the other lived on for some time after the Anglo-Irish upper class had become a little slow in paying their bills. Patronage was taken away from one tradesman in favor of another and this withdrawal was considered to be as effective a punishment as it might have been if the account were fully paid. Butchers, in particular, were always being "left," the very choice of word, usually denoting a more intimate relationship, underlining the gravity of the action. I remember one of my grandmothers, in a pony and trap, driving up to a butcher's shop. He came out, pleased and a little surprised, to greet her. After a moment, she realized, then told him, that she'd forgotten that she'd left him and drove off. (As a would-be vegetarian child I thought this rather funny, but later as an adult, faced with ten for dinner and a loin of pork which smelled slightly off, I experienced a feeling of rage which I like to think had some aspects of racial memory in it.) A family we knew got so far in debt to their butcher that they were "reduced" to asking him to dinner. Whether he found the dinner an adequate compensation for carrying their account for months or was disappointed by the conversational and culinary standards they had to offer, one will never know. Nor does history relate whether they served him some of his own unpaid-for meat.

Anyway, my father found himself on the other side of the fence, negotiating, if not actually haggling over, the wholesale price of a head of lettuce. These small shopkeepers were fiercely competitive and jealous and there would be endless complications about what my father had sold to a neighbouring shop and for how much. He often had to rely on tact and was sometimes reduced to barefaced lying.

After a few years, Mr. O'Shea developed an allergy to some kind of plant, never identified, and he and his family moved into

Waterford City, where he started a greengrocer's shop. We got a new gardener and I imagine my father found a relatively uncomplicated outlet for his produce.

R O O F S and driveways were where most large Irish houses first started to disintegrate. They seemed to be in constant need of repair and these repairs were very expensive. Our move to the larger house, entailing not only these expenses but the need for an additional maid or two, a gardener, a generally higher standard of living, mild entertaining and appearances to be kept up, plunged us into the usual Anglo-Irish trap.

The financial problems of the Anglo-Irish as opposed to the Catholic Irish were not greater, but they were newer and lacked simple solutions. When Ireland became a Free State in 1921, two-thirds of the Anglo-Irish population left—not driven out, but aware that the future held little for them in Ireland. For the remaining third, there was no dramatic or immediate reason for them to emigrate, and that possibility never occurred to many of them. They were no longer English and many thought of themselves as Irish. My family, for instance, had been there since 1680.

Taking a broader view, almost an evolutionary one, this was a moment in history when a group of people—something more than a class but just less than a race—were forced into a state of transition. As history has shown us, the faster the transition, the clumsier its execution. These people, the Anglo-Irish Protestant upper class, were not displaced. The opposite, really: they remained the same but everything around them changed. It was a society which had lived a life of privilege, not by earning it, but through an artificial maintenance of a social order which was then suddenly removed. (Privilege tends not to be absolutely consistent; many people who would consider two hunters in the stable a luxury would think themselves very hard done by if they had to bathe and dress in a drafty Irish bathroom with inadequate hot water.) The Anglo-Irish were not discriminated against by those newly in power, but left to their own inadequate devices. If a family were rich, or had enough land to farm and enough energy and know-how to do so profitably, there was no reason why their lives shouldn't have remained virtually the same. This rarely proved to be the case.

Very few of the Anglo-Irish we knew were employed, and the obvious solutions to the almost universal money shortages didn't apply. There were no promotions, pay rises, bonuses or even, for that matter, employment agencies or career consultants. Government jobs were not open to most Protestants since a proficiency in the Irish language was required. Those educated at English public schools obviously weren't qualified.

Most of the Anglo-Irish tried to bridge the ever-widening gap between rising prices (we didn't call it inflation in those days) and a fixed income, or rents and revenue from too small farms, or a combination of both. Plenty of imagination went into finding ways to earn more and spend less. Very few of these schemes made much difference to actual standards of living but they never lost their interest value. The more popular enterprises were market gardening and the keeping of a couple of dozen extra hens. Occasionally a family, already living in gloomy Protestant discomfort, would add to their problems by taking in a paying guest. Such a person would be jocularly referred to as "our P.G."

On the other hand, many of the ideas designed to save money gave us items which would now be considered luxuries. We wore hand-knitted sweaters and ate homegrown and freshly picked fruit and vegetables, homemade cakes and bread, fresh eggs and free-range chickens, pheasant, duck and snipe in season and our own honey. My father shot the game, but my mother was the one who, dressed as though she were going fox hunting in a riding habit, boots, gloves and a bowler hat with the addition of a veil over the hat and tied at the neck, would brave the bees, invade their hives, and bring back delicious squares of honeycomb.

There was a difference between the Anglo-Irish Protestants

and the Irish Catholics in their attitude toward poverty. The Catholic working class was poor and used, if not resigned, to that state. Their earnings were meagre and so was their existence. There was no shame attached to this state. Everyone was in the same situation and the standard was marginally higher than it had been. The Anglo-Irish upper class was, of course, considerably better off than the real poor but they were usually far from comfortable. Nearly all of them, drained by the upkeep of impractical, large houses, lived on a lower standard than they had a generation earlier. My mother did some voluntary work for a charity to aid Irish distressed ladies. These Protestant gentlewomen were probably less poor than their Catholic counterparts, but their genteel, shabby lot seemed more cheerless, certainly more lonely.

When I was a child we judged things by a standard set by the previous generation. Protestants and Catholics kept apart; the gulf seemed immense. Protestants continued to be the upper class but they no longer had any political power. The country was run by a Catholic government and the Catholic Church. Businesses were Catholic and so was the light industry that was growing up. Now, a generation later, the power of the Church seems to have modified a little and some Protestants, taking an evolutionary lurch forward, have been, to an extent, assimilated.

During the years I was growing up there was an atmosphere of decay, the native Irish being better equipped to deal with it. The Anglo-Irish often fell to pieces. They couldn't go completely "native" because their religion kept them separate, so their deterioration took place largely alone. Somerset Maugham's short stories of island life often remind me of our Irish neighbours. They often became eccentric and sometimes physically dirty. One thought little of visiting a house which contained too many dogs and had a sheep's head boiling in the kitchen, the combined smell of which the owners of the house had long since grown accustomed to. Members of quite distinguished families looked unkempt, the women having given up any effort with their appearance in the attempt to keep warm. And, of course, most of them drank a good deal more than was good for them.

Surrounded by these gloomy examples, my mother, young and energetic and still a comparatively new wife, embarked on raising poultry (or "keeping hens") and expanding my father's market-gardening efforts into the area of soft fruit.

The day-old chicks—the first step in poultry keeping—started their careers in the greenhouse. They would arrive, tightly packed together for security and warmth, a surprising amount of noise emanating from a container no larger, or, in fact, more substantial than a cake box. When unpacked there would be a hundred tiny chicks, for which Julia and I were responsible. Although the first impression was of fragility and sweetness, there was also a powerful sense of the will to live. A hundred tiny, one-day-old hearts were beating and a hundred tiny beaks were open, demanding food and warmth with a determination equal to that of any newborn human. The package in which they arrived was light enough for Julia or me to pick up in one hand, and yet there was no doubt that, on some basic level, it contained life.

We fed them mashed hard-boiled eggs and gave them water. We cooed over them, still in awe of their resilient little spirits as they fell over one another and into their water trough. Gradually, as they became scrawny and unattractive, the novelty value of the chore wore off. When they became older—gawky and adolescent— they were moved to an "ark," a large wooden henhouse comprised of an open run covered with chicken wire and a roofed area for shelter. The ark had no floor and was light enough for two people to move every few days, thus providing the chickens with a fresh scratching ground and precluding the necessity of cleaning the chicken house. Eventually the chickens would graduate to their final living quarters in the currant garden, where they would live in a larger house with a tarred roof, which contained nesting boxes to encourage them to lay eggs, and a big enclosed area outside. Those chickens which were not sold provided eggs for the house and eventually ended up, accompanied by lumpy white sauce dotted with parsley, on the dinner table. The natural surroundings in which hens were raised made them and their eggs better-tasting and probably more nutritious than the factorylike products we buy in the supermarket, but as a result eggs tended to be seasonal. To supplement the minimal winter production we used to preserve the surplus spring and summer eggs in a substance called water glass. We loved to watch, and begged to be allowed to help, as my mother lowered the eggs on a giant spoon, long-handled enough for supping with the devil, into the clear liquid in a large earthenware crock whose generous curves and graceful neck reminded us of Ali Baba and which today would probably fetch a couple of thousand bucks in an antique shop. The atmosphere of magic was not confined to the paraphernalia and the mysterious process of preservation; the necessary element of danger was also present—we were repeatedly warned against splashing ourselves with the chemical and there was always the risk of an egg slipping off the spoon and breaking not only itself but those beneath it.

The currant garden consisted mainly of blackcurrants, although we also grew some of both the red and white varieties. I have no idea why such quantities of an essentially not very interesting fruit should have been planted in the first place, but, by the time I was a child, they provided a small supplement to the household income.

But first they had to be picked. The fruit pickers were another source of employee drama to worry my mother. They were casual labour recruited from the city, usually teenagers but sometimes tinkerlike women of dubious character. They were paid by the weight of what they brought to the kitchen door at the end of the day. Occasionally they would increase the weight by pouring water over the fruit, and it was rumoured (hinted to us children by the maids and never mentioned to my mother) that some of them urinated over what they had picked. If true, the symbolic act of hostility was not only unhygienic but unwarranted. The fruit pickers were not exploited by my mother, who was a fair, if sometimes inept, employer: the profit margin was slim and she suffered a certain amount of emotional wear and tear, judging quarrels, providing lunch for the odd woman who claimed that hers had been stolen and who was quite sure, without any evidence, just who had stolen it.

My mother was considered a soft touch by the maids, and rather left-wing by my father's contemporaries, because she had a reasonable imagination about the lives of those less fortunate than herself. I never saw a beggar turned away without money, clothing or food. Down-at-heel travelling peddlers also found an easy mark in her. A governess objected that "they" told such awful lies and my mother gently asked what difference it made when the truth was so grim anyway.

And it was grim. There was no shortage of examples of those whose lives had fallen apart through no fault of their own. My fears were fed not only by the sight of the men from the asylum working in the frozen fields but by groups of shaven-headed orphans we would sometimes see out for walks.

I did not understand until much later that few of these children were literally orphans; nearly all of them were illegitimate. Ireland is, and was even more so then, a poor agricultural country. Families were large; the average family working a small farm lived very close to the poverty line. The farm would eventually be inherited by the eldest son. The younger ones had no prospects on which to marry and often the eldest son would wait for his parents to die before he himself married. Steady drinking and the ever-present shadow of the Roman Catholic Church repressed a certain amount of sexual passion, but the combination of human nature and the embargo on any form of contraception provided a high illegitimacy rate. These children might sometimes be farmed out, but more usually ended up in orphanages run by nuns.

I was not only sorry for these orphans but distressed by the implied suggestion of widespread parental mortality—a subject never far from my own morbid fantasies. I was a fearful child and the things I feared came in order. Death was the main fear. It was followed, a poor second, by poverty, with ghosts trailing some distance behind.

I was afraid that my parents would die. It is a fairly common childhood fear of abandonment and my feelings were unusual only in my complete inability to express them. I remember pedalling my tricycle furiously along the driveway with tears streaming down my face, my fear of loss triggered by a casual reference by my father to his old age. My fear, rage, confusion, insecurity were all impossible to communicate, even if I'd known what words to give these feelings. Even now I hesitate to say what it is that frightens me and I am angered when someone else names the forbidden thing that I fear, since I feel to do so is to play into the hands of the Fates, who might not have, until that moment, considered playing that particular card.

When I went to spend summers with my grandparents I extended my fears to include their demise as well. That fear was more reasonable since they were two generations ahead of me. I took some comfort from the rationalization that people died off in generational order and, since Granny and Grandpa were still alive, my parents were safe. For the time being.

At the same time that I used to indulge in these morbid daydreams, I had a glamorous godmother and occasionally would fantasize about how exciting my life as an orphan would be in her household. The future of my sisters in this scenario was never quite resolved.

During this period of fearful preoccupation with death, two members of my family did, in fact, die without my noticing it. My great-grandmother and my great-great-aunt Molly Carew were distinguished old ladies. I remember them sitting on either side of the fireplace at Ballydavid. (*Bal* is a Gaelic word for house, and the names of three of the four houses where I spent my childhood started with *Bal*. Ballycar, where my cousins lived, however, was apparently so named when someone lost his temper with an unsatisfactory early-model motorcar.) My great-grandmother and great-great-aunt wore long black or dark brown dresses and played patience in the afternoon. It took me a while to notice that they were no longer there. Some characteristic instinct told me not to ask an adult about their absence and I sought out Mary, the cook. Most of the maids were younger than my parents, but our assumption that they weren't fully fledged grown-ups was based more on their lack of power and status in the household and a recognition that their interests and attitudes were closer to ours. Mary looked me in the eye and, with no emotion, sensibly told me that they'd gone for a long walk over the fields. I accepted this painless and poetic explanation without question.

My inability to express fear about either death or financial problems was shared by the other members of my family. Since these matters were never discussed, I had no idea of what my worst fear could legitimately be. I had the feeling that we were all teetering on the brink of disaster, but since I had never seen anyone actually topple over the edge I had no idea of how far they could fall.

It was to a governess that I hesitantly admitted my fear of ghosts. Governesses could be confided in as easily as maids provided one was careful to avoid sensitive areas. These areas usually pertained to the status of the governess in our household. My governess told me in a commonsense way that there was no such thing as a ghost. I found this answer unsatisfactory and shyly went to my father. I was not tempted to consult the maids about this fear since they were more superstitious than I and would be only too happy to confirm my fears and to add a few details I hadn't yet thought of. Daddy said that there probably weren't any such things as ghosts, but if there were, they wouldn't hurt me. I was comforted by this answer, which validated my fear but, at the same time, mitigated it. I am now about the age that he was when he answered my question and understand the instinct that allows us to leave the door a little ajar for those we have loved and lost.

Life was so clearly full of dangers, fears and inadequately answered questions that I turned to, if not exactly literature, the written word. Unfortunately, most of the children's books available to me were Victorian sentimental rubbish left over from my father's childhood. He was born in 1903. Some of the books may have belonged to one of his brothers or to his sister, but that would still have placed them firmly before the First World War. My mother soon realized that these quickly reduced me to morbid tears and they were banned. Even quite harmless books such as *Orlando, the Marmalade Cat* had tragic undertones visible to no one but me. Gradually, standard fairy tales were included in the censorship list.

I can clearly remember sitting at the dining-room table at Glenville, finishing lunch on a bright summer's day. Outside the window stood the huge laburnum tree in full hanging yellow blossom. (Despite the pleasant memories of that tree, my mother makes gentle fun of the rather weaselly one I have in my garden in Connecticut, saying that it looks very suburban, "rather like something you'd see coming in from the airport." Certainly the only snobbish remark I have ever heard her make. The accuracy of her observation makes it hard to defend my poor tree, which doesn't much like the climate anyway.) My mother, Julia and I were quiet, each occupied with her own thoughts. Breaking the silence, I asked my mother, "Do you know the story of the babes in the wood?"

"Yes," she said.

"Tell me," I asked.

She considered for a moment, not long, and said, "No. It's a sad story and you'll cry."

"No, I won't."

"Yes, you will. You know you will."

I had heard of "Babes in the Wood" as a pantomime and my curiosity overcame my common sense.

"I won't. I promise I won't. Just tell me what it's about."

"All right." Definitely against her better judgment, my mother began: "There were these two babes and they were lost in the wood . . ."

She got no further. I had burst into noisy tears. It took some time to comfort me. To this day I don't know how the fairy tale ends.

But when I grew up a little—at least to the extent of private tears—I was left on my own as far as my choice of reading. I was not guided toward the elevating nor was I often forbidden the unsuitable. This was hardly rash of my parents since the government imposed censorship at an almost Victorian level of stringency. James Joyce was as firmly out of the question as was, at the other end of the spectrum, the popular lowbrow English Sunday newspaper *The News of the World*. Normal family magazines would be unavailable for weeks on end.

The only books which were taken away from me were *The Postman Always Rings Twice* (too late, I'd already read it) and *The Grey Man*, which contained passages about cannibalism in Scotland. My father, perhaps already bored with my herbivorous eating habits, was the confiscator of the latter.

These deprivations were more than made up for by the women's magazines and thin paperback romances I borrowed from the maids. They called them "books." Some of the magazine stories I can recall completely to this day, as well as the passion in the romantic stories, all of which were, of course, innocent of physical detail. But even then, although I yearned for more explicit sexual information, I realized that descriptions of longing were more effective in engaging my sympathy and identification.

Curiously enough, when it came time for me to steer my children toward the books that I hoped they'd enjoy, it was not on *The Grey Man* or James M. Cain we came unstuck. It was, instead, a childhood favourite, again passed down from a previous generation: Dr. Doolittle. I read the entire series at Glenville. The summer evenings in Ireland are long and the dark comes very gradually. I read until my eyes could no longer make out the words, long after I was supposed to be asleep. When I came to read these old books again, remembering Hugh Lofting's love for animals and high moral standards, I was astonished to find in them a series of extreme racial slurs. I am ashamed to admit that they had gone past unnoticed, as had an Agatha Christie novel, presumably also an early edition, in which the heroine and the man she finds attractive are drawn together by common dislikes—jazz and Negroes.

New books rarely came into the house. They were a luxury we could not afford and not one of my father's indulgences (the two not mutually exclusive), which is why my reading matter was out of sync by at least a full generation. Fortunately my parents belonged to the Royal Dublin Society library. They marked their choices in a catalogue and every so often two or three books would arrive by post in a large cardboard envelopelike box. When they had been read they were posted back in the same envelope and a new batch would arrive several days later. As soon as I had learned to read I was allowed to tick off a few books for myself from the children's section.

The importance of books in my life was connected to the absence of both radio or television. My father never owned a television or radio for his own use. My first memory of television is inextricably entwined with another milestone of the twentieth century—Coca-Cola.

My father sometimes used to take us for walks by the sea on Sunday afternoons. We would drive to Dunmore, a small harbour town where my father had spent his childhood summer holidays, and take a brisk after-lunch walk along the windswept pier. Afterward, we would go to an hotel called the Haven, where my father would order a real drink and we would occasionally have a Coca-Cola. It was a new drink and it was served unchilled. There was a certain amount of talk about its alleged secret ingredient. My father once gingerly tasted one of ours and said that he could solve the mystery.

"Cold tea and soap," he pronounced.

I don't remember actually seeing anything which we would now think of as a programme on the television at the Haven. The set was, of course, small and black and white. Usually it showed what appeared to be snowflakes, but occasionally a blurred image would appear on the only channel, transmitted from England. The content of the picture was, at that stage, secondary—our attitude not unlike Dr. Johnson's to a woman preaching. People might talk about having seen television but, with one exception, I never heard anyone talk about what they had seen on it. That one exception was the Coronation of the Queen. The Haven made an event of it, offering viewing to the public at a pound a head. We did not avail ourselves of the offer. I'm not quite sure why not. The pound a head would have been a factor, of course, as would have been the snowflakes—there was no guarantee that the historic event in question would actually be witnessed. But there was also another aspect to be considered. My father had been educated in England. He admired England, defended the Empire and colonialism, but he was not English. Although he would never have indulged in the faintly ridiculous behaviour of some of the English (never Anglo-Irish) who were so charmed by their first sight of the Irish that they tried to be "more Irish than the Irish themselves," he was equally uncomfortable with red-faced colonels toasting "the Queen, God bless her" with a glass of indifferent port. He never expressed himself on this subject but tended to end up a little to one side, just a bit separate. My father was quietly respectful of the British royal family, approved of their love of dogs and riding, admired their racehorses and thought Princess Alexandra the pinnacle of female beauty.

The Haven seemed an exciting and exotic place to Julia and me. Coca-Cola and television provided a link to a world of which we were gradually becoming aware, as did a record player which played a stack of current popular songs and dance music. Julia and I had, until then, only seen records played on a gramophone which had to be wound up before, and occasionally while, one played a record. At the Haven, we would stack a pile of records on the machine and run around the large room where dancing, to the same source of music, took place on Saturday nights. While we did so, my father would have another drink in the bar, making a move into the mid-twentieth century himself. The very name, the Haven, spoke of convivial English suburban comfort and values, to which my father may have felt both drawn and mildly disapproving. Even my mother, who did not join us for either the bracing walk or the treats at the Haven afterward, was also using the hotel to make a step into the future. She had framed some very pretty illustrations from an old and disintegrating book of orchids and they were for sale in a showcase in the foyer of the Haven. It was the first step toward a real career for her. Away from chickens and black currants and toward becoming an antique dealer and later an expert on paintings.

Apart from the insidious influence of the Haven, all other information from the outside came through *The Irish Times*. For my father it remained his primary source and became even a little less comprehensive toward the end of his life when he found a really minor economy which gave him some pleasure: he stopped buying a paper on Monday on the basis that Sunday is a slow news day.

The Irish Times is a very decent paper and it shows how superficial my tastes were that I can only remember three news stories: two murders (one a crime of passion, the other a botched abortion) and the Honor Tracy libel case. She was sued successfully by a priest in West Cork after she'd suggested the mild misuse of parish funds. Libel cases in Ireland used to be welcomed by the newspaper-reading public in those uneventful days. Irish laws allow plenty of redress for the sensitive and in this particular case the public felt that Miss Tracy had been game to the point of foolhardiness in taking on the Catholic Church.

The fact that I could read at all owes a lot to my mother's patience and leads me to reevaluate the series of governesses I had until I went to school. I started school a little later than my contemporaries and it took a long time for me to catch up academically. Socially, I never did catch up.

Apart from a short period when I insisted, at the age of four, on attending nursery school and shortly afterward insisted (maybe the last time in my whole life I insisted on anything) much more adamantly on no longer attending, I was educated, or at least supervised, by governesses.

There was evidently an organisation which sent foreign girls from good families to England or Ireland for a year to learn English. It was the naïve dream of my parents that Julia and I should learn to speak French. There was even an halfhearted attempt made to speak it at meals. We went through the stages of silence, one-word demands for edible nouns, and the attempt soon petered out, leaving only the ritual "prejermonally" on leaving the table. Both our early governesses, one Swiss and one French and both blended inextricably in my memory, learned to speak good English, albeit with an Irish accent. We never learned French.

Some years later, my father told me that when the second of these governesses had left, he'd been delegated by my mother, while he was in Dublin, to go to an agency—presumably not the one which had supplied the original two young women. He'd told the receptionist that he was looking for a French governess and asked if she had anyone suitable. She replied that she had several and offered to show him photographs. My father was nonplussed, not an usual state for him; he had tremendous composure in most situations. The combination of French governesses and photographs had set off an association with white slavery and suggestive advertisements in Soho tobacco-shop windows. He made an excuse and left.

This may have been why the next governess was Irish. She was a strange, neurotic woman who lived with us during the time my mother was giving birth to Alice, my younger sister. The first clue that she, the governess whose name I have forgotten, wouldn't do was when she mentioned, without a trace of humour, that she'd been so nervous while learning to drive that she'd been given lessons in a field.

Alice was born at home. I was unaware that her birth was imminent and any traumatic associations were avoided by my father's sending Julia and me for a long walk that afternoon, presumably with the nervous and unsatisfactory Irish governess. The excitement and attention caused by my mother's indisposition went to the unfortunate governess's head. She developed what would probably be called a sympathetic (but was, as is usually the case, more likely the opposite) hypochondriacal illness and took to her bed. The maids complained—two sets of trays to go upstairs each mealtime. My mother, from her bed in a spare room, assessed the symptoms and said that if our governess didn't feel well enough to discharge her duties she was welcome to stay in her room, but no further food would be delivered to her. The next day we had a functioning governess again. My mother descended soon behind her. She hadn't been starved out, but she had been unable to dissuade the cook, out of deference to her invalid status, from cutting up into tiny pieces the rapidly cooling meals sent upstairs to her.

The next governess, Miss Collins, looked after Alice as well as giving us lessons. She started out poorly with Julia and me by comparing us incessantly and unfavourably with her previous charge, a little boy named Jeremy. We hated him and all he stood for. She tended to compare Jeremy's household with ours, although not openly to our parents' detriment. I soon worked out that the other family had included her more, but this had not ameliorated her reservations about the mother. She told us once that Jeremy's mother didn't get up until twelve o'clock. I was astonished. Although Miss Collins was, on the face of it, discreet, it was clear that, in her eyes, her unfortunate former employer could do nothing right. For the first time I understood the strength of silent, powerless disapproval. Apparently also, when offering round a box of chocolates, the mistress of the house had been in the habit of saying, "Take two," a generous enough gesture, one would have thought. But her husband had undermined her by always saying, "Take a handful." Miss Collins had chosen to interpret "Take two" as "Don't take more than two." I inferred from this small anecdote a slight class difference between husband and wife. The wife trying with gracious charm to reach in vain across the gaping Protestant-Catholic, employer-employee abyss, and the husband, perhaps a country farmer, succeeding with one big, expansive, slightly vulgar gesture. No wonder the wretched woman stayed in bed until noon.

Miss Collins taught us reading, writing, arithmetic, history and, God help us, piano. We did "lessons" in what had originally been the billiard room. It was a large room with a parquet floor and an ugly modern table in the centre of the room where the billiard table had stood in the old days. There was a baby grand piano, which must once have been in the drawing room but because of our family's lack of musical talent had no place there. My mother was not the type to use a piano for interior decoration, with or without shawls or silver-framed photographs. I remember the piano lessons as half an hour of pointless obligatory boredom each day before lunch. They must have seemed even more depressing to my teacher. The arithmetic was painful also, but my laziness was at fault there, perhaps reinforced by the weight of Anglo-Irish gloom which hung over the entire household. There was an arrangement whereby I received sixpence from my father if I completed my "sums" correctly. Sixpence was a reward well worth striving for, and the task was not an insurmountable one. However, laziness and apathy prevailed, since I only once collected the bribe.

History, on the other hand, I remember clearly. My governess took a straightforward approach to it, although I don't know what her alternatives would have been. There was no suggestion that we should learn principles from history that would apply to the present. There was no questioning the bias of our only source, an illustrated book called *Our Island Story*. It wasn't, of course, our island's story. It was an English book and less a complete history than a series of dramatic incidents and portraits of colourful historical characters. Since Irish history is largely comprised of accounts of struggles against English oppressors, there is, not surprisingly, quite a difference between an English history book and an Irish one.

The full-page illustrations, in vivid colours, of heroic characters who usually met tragic ends made their mark on an impres-
sionable child. Mary, Queen of Scots, was a typical example and
I wept over her fate. There was an additional sentimental touch
concerning the luckless Queen's little dog, the memory of which
could invoke tears for years to come. Sir Walter Raleigh and the
cloak flung down to save Elizabeth's feet from the puddle was also
valuable grist to this kind of mill. I grew up believing him to be an
Errol Flynn character—adventurer, hero and eventually tragic
victim of the notorious fickleness of royalty. It was a very
Anglo-Irish view—ignoring not only his ruthless, bloodthirsty
behaviour toward the Irish but his poetry and other writings. It is,
of course, silly to expect him to have behaved in any other way,
but it seems sillier still to apply a coating of late Victorian
sentimentality to two colorful figures, both with an eye to the
main chance, who chose to live by the same rules by which they
eventually died.

It can't have been a comfortable life for our governesses. They
didn't mix socially with the maids, and although they ate lunch in
the dining room with the family, they weren't included in the
evening meal, which my parents ate alone. They were lonely,
awkward women, either silent and repressed or garrulous. Either
way, they irritated my father.

Nowadays, there is a small but steady stream of young
women who, for a few years, choose to live in comfortable
surroundings and earn a good living looking after children. (My
children have had a series of "keepers" with modified names: "my
Janie," "that Nancy" and "Joan here." We addressed ours
formally—Miss Collins presumably had a Christian name, but if
she did, we never knew it. Nor, it is possible, did my mother.) In
those days, such women didn't exist. Being a governess wasn't a
career, it was a sign that something had gone wrong. A governess
might, for instance, be the last unmarried daughter who'd stayed
home to look after ageing parents. After their deaths she had to
lead an uncomfortable existence in other people's homes, living

largely on memories inadequate to comfort her and of no interest to those now around her. The amount of money which could be earned in this way was unlikely to guarantee a comfortable retirement.

Miss Cullen, who became Cully to us, had a slightly better life than most. She came to us as a summer governess, since by then we were at day school and did not require full supervision. She lived at home with her mother, but during the school year she taught at a convent in Dublin, so she had a life of her own, however uneventful it might have been. She also had a home of her own, and this gave her an emotional security which most of the others lacked. I was shocked to find out that she was several years younger than my mother. It was the first inkling that privilege wasn't only apparent in birth, religion and material things. Ireland has a very moist climate and Irish women are known for their wonderful skin. But in those days a combination of inadequate diet and hard work, often outdoors, left most working-class Irish women old by thirty. The basic skin-care products which almost every woman I know uses were not widely available in those days. So my mother looked young and my governess looked old.

Cully used to tell us stories, and we loved them since they bore a marked resemblance to the ones in the weekly comic I read. Her familiarity with this genre is most telling. It was not possible to imagine her swapping paperback romances with the maids. Equally impossible to imagine her borrowing one of my father's biographies on loan from the Royal Dublin Society library. Where she belonged was with the children and even this was confusing. We knew that we would graduate from the schoolroom to the drawing room but that she would not. As though a caterpillar never turned into a butterfly but just grew into a larger and somewhat older caterpillar. Aware of this, on some level, we protected her.

I think that few of the children that governesses looked after provided them with much comfort. The bond between children and their nannies was closer, more physical, more emotional. A nanny took some of the child's love for its mother. A governess could rarely hope for more than the kind of affectionate tolerance the child might feel for an unusually friendly but inept school-teacher. For Julia and me they were not role models; nor did they contribute much toward our education. We didn't usually find them very interesting, but from their existence we learned something, never articulated, about caste and class, about power and pecking orders.

Moving freely between kitchen, nursery and dining room, as only children can, I became a diplomat, constantly on my guard to avoid betraying one group to another. In later life, these exercises in tact did not pay off. Instead of possessing social skills, I am left with a distaste for mediation, and privacy now seems to me to be one of the great luxuries of life.

THE DRIVE from what still remains of Glenville to the cathedral in Waterford takes only a few minutes. I have no memory of that drive, as I have no memory of the factory which now stands on the site of my former home. The changes which must have occurred along the way made no impression on the day of my father's funeral. They didn't even interfere with my childhood memories of the route. If I close my eyes and take it very slowly I can still walk it in my memory: top of the lane, where Kenneally's bus stopped; up the hill, you were likely to pass one of the two Miss McCoys walking a couple of greyhounds; past the nursery garden; Ballycar, where my cousins lived; down the hill, a laburnum and some fine horse chestnuts; the houses of a couple of schoolmates; Newtown, the grander Anglo-Irish school; two other schools, both Catholic; the park; over a bridge; along the Mall; and already the cathedral was visible.

During the early years of my childhood there were no private cars on the road. This was because petrol was still severely rationed and not for private use. It came in two colours. Farm machinery, when it was mechanized, ran on green. Dire penalties were meted out to those selfish enough to misuse green-tinted petrol and unlucky enough to be caught doing so.

Throughout this time there was a Ford Standard, on blocks, in the garage. We used to play in it. The best parts of the car, it seemed to me, were the little trays set into the backs of the front seats, which could be let down, as on an airplane. When petrol rationing ended, we used this car for a while, then replaced it with a Ford V-8.

It was a moment of extreme excitement when the V-8 arrived. I remember my father driving it up to the front door. It's possible that it was as much a surprise to my mother also. My father had a tendency to produce any large, expensive purchase as a fait accompli. Cars, a new horse box and at least one boat arrived this way.

But that was later. Before cars came back on the road, if we wanted to go into Waterford or to the beach, we set out in a pony and trap. The pony was cared for and harnessed by Rowe, the groom, who also looked after my parents' hunters.

I'm sure this means of transportation soon lost its charm for my parents. Weather aside, it took quite a long time to get anywhere. Nipping into Waterford for a forgotten item was not a viable option. Oddly enough, most of the things one is nowadays nipping out for didn't apply then. No one smoked, milk and bread were delivered, fruit and veg came from the garden. Snacks were almost unknown, as were carbonated soft drinks. I clearly remember, and only with pleasure, some of the outings which took place in the pony and trap.

The first was a trip to Waterford. It was my mother's turn to arrange the flowers in the cathedral. Glenville was covered with a large variety of unusual and exotic rhododendrons, but I think she'd chosen some of the run-of-the-mill purple ones. My mother was twenty-eight years old and very beautiful. She had no vanity at all and spent little time on her appearance. I don't think she had any conception of what she looked like. There used to be a photograph of her on the chest of drawers in my father's dressing room, taken when they were engaged, so my opinion of her looks was not mere childish adoration. It was a romantic moment, a beautiful young woman in a horse-drawn vehicle full of flowers, with two small blonde children beside her. (The chocolate-box picture did not quite hold up if one looked too closely; my sister was sickly as a child and had a somewhat wizened look, which I compensated for by having a fat little face, too heavy in the jaw, with a small, pouty mouth.) To complete the sentimental picture while we were driving down a poor street, my mother gave a branch of flowers to a slum boy who asked her for it.

Another pony-and-trap expedition which remains as a vivid memory involves a great-aunt. A great-aunt by marriage, not one of the two ghostlike old ladies from Ballydavid, but one who by a lopsided generational inequity had children who, though they were cousins of my mother, were not much older than Julia and I were. I set out from Waterford with her and her children. We drove to Ballinakill, one of the destinations of our longer afternoon walks. The weather vane on the church steeple and the old milestone, its legend largely obliterated by time and the elements, were objects of keen childhood interest.

My great-aunt had brought a large bundle of clothing which her family had outgrown. We stopped in front of a small group of cottages, which faced the ruined gates and destroyed driveway of what had been the approach to a large house. The cottages, which had once housed staff, were all that remained. My great-aunt exchanged the clothes for ration coupons. These coupons were for commodities such as butter which were very expensive and which would have been beyond the means of the large ragged family we saw clustered at the gate. (As, in fairness, would have been clothing of the quality being offered.) Butter, for instance, was one of the goods smuggled across the border from the North of Ireland, since it was more expensive in the South because of farm subsidies. Nevertheless, in our house, old clothes were given away to beggars who came to the door, not used for bargaining. The entire transaction took place out of doors, which added to the feeling that this was an exchange unsoftened by the usual Irish grace. Of course, we would hardly have all fitted into the cottage and the lack of light would have made the exchange even more complicated, but even so, I came away feeling that we had not distinguished ourselves.

I still remember with pleasure and nostalgia and a slight sense of loss a series of afternoons when my mother, my sister and I and, occasionally, my father set off to Woodstown beach for an afternoon of swimming, sand castles, sandy jam sandwiches and smoky-tasting tea from a thermos flask.

Woodstown was seven miles away. We would drive down the lane, along the main road, past Ballinakill church, past Ballydavid, past the stile into Ballydavid woods and the fox's walk, where we always carried a big stick in case we met the fox, past Woodstown House and to the beach.

Woodstown and Ballydavid are the scenes of my mother's most treasured memories. Maybe it would be more accurate to say that they are where my favourite of her memories are set. Woodstown beach is a mile long; the end where we picnicked was close to Ballyglan, home of Sir Robert Paul. When my mother was a girl she had had daily lessons with the Pauls' governess and Sir Robert had taught her semaphore and how to follow the different paces of a horse by the imprints in the sand. Sir Robert had, when a young officer, trained a camel to jump the steeplechase course in Cairo. He was not alone in this kind of eccentric behaviour. Other men of his generation, stationed overseas, felt the nostalgic desire to reconstruct, although often with major modifications, some of the pleasures of home. My mother's grandfather, on his way to India by boat, with a pack of hounds on board, unloaded them on Christmas Day in Egypt to hunt jackal. My pleasure in this great-grandfather is made greater by knowing that he was not some stereotyped bloodlusting Indian Army officer. He was also a code breaker and, as a hobby, would decode and respond to advertisements in the agony column of *The Times*.

If this were a weekday expedition my father would not be with us. He would have been at his office, having travelled there by bicycle.

We didn't use the word "beach." We called it the "strand." My father knew that "strand" is essentially Irish. He told me that when he'd inadvertently said "strand" at school in England, it had caused much laughter and elicited the then popular catchphrase "Have a banana."

At Woodstown the tide came in over several hundred yards of sun-warmed sand, so the temperature was pleasant and the water shallow enough for children to paddle. This was quite usual in that part of southern Ireland, and combined with the section of the Gulf Stream which hits the coast, serves to make the sea warmer than one would imagine possible in so northerly a latitude. Even so, my mother rarely swam. She looked very pretty in the brightly coloured floral-patterned bathing suits of the forties, the blues and reds a darker hue than one usually sees nowadays, but the only time I saw her swim was when she was pregnant. She was shy and carried a towel which concealed her condition until she reached the water. I was surprised that she could overcome her modesty to engage in an activity which I had never before seen her enjoy, and I didn't understand until years later, while heavily pregnant myself, I found temporary comfort in the weightless feeling one has while swimming.

At the end of these glorious afternoons we would pile back into the pony and trap with our picnic basket, in it the empty thermos and crumpled jammy pieces of waxed paper. On the floor were wet bathing suits, shells and some wildflowers. With damp hair and slightly sunburned faces and shoulders, we would drive home.

The early evening light would have grown soft by the time we, a little sleepy, would pass Ballybrickan, the birthplace of Freebooter, the brave racehorse who had won the Grand National and enriched Madigan.

The pony would be going a little slower by the time we passed Ballinakill church, with its familiar battered weathercock. In its largely overgrown graveyard, my father is now buried.

WATERFORD

WHEN I was a child there were three doctors in Waterford. The Catholic Doctor, the Protestant Doctor and the Black Doctor. The Catholics went to the Catholic Doctor; Protestants usually went to the Protestant Doctor. My family didn't, although my parents knew him socially, which may have been the reason. I still don't know who the Black Doctor's patients were. He was, in fact, Indian and he and my father used to play cricket on a team very loosely organized under the banner of the YMCA.

Two of these three men represented groups of people, divided by racial and religious differences, living in peaceful but careful coexistence. The third, the so-called Black Doctor, representing a minority so small that he may have been its only member, was not one of them. Colour was not what divided them. It was religion, history and a no longer valid social structure.

Waterford was our closest city, about a mile up the river. It is of Norse foundation and the second most important town in southeastern Ireland. It was where my father worked, where we went to school, where we shopped and where we went to church.

It is also where I first began to understand that being a Protestant was different from being a Catholic. Up to then I had understood it in a kind of maids versus management way, but when I became old enough to go to school I began to learn that I was Anglo-Irish and that we as a group were neither English nor Irish, neither accepted nor discriminated against, powerless though treated with respect. I also noticed that this respect often had a suspicion of hidden laughter in it. (The Irish are great ones for vendettas; there is no statute of limitations on revenge when it involves honour or betrayal. But they choose their victims very carefully. It is not by chance that the Reverend Ian Paisley has not been the target of an assassin's bullet. The Irish understand that while alive he will always appear ridiculous; dead, he might become a martyr.)

Unlike the original Irish, a race ancient enough for their beginnings to be lost in the murk of prehistory and sentimental inaccuracy, the origins of the Anglo-Irish are easy to trace. Anyone who came from England after the Reformation is Anglo-Irish. The Anglo-Irish were the most recent wave of conquerors and the only ones who did not assimilate. But they did not remain English either, and there were times when their interests and those of the English government were opposed. Those who arrived before the Reformation—starting with mythical heroes and their followers, through the characters of legend based on a thin historical thread, to the Formorians, Firbolgs, Danaans, Milesians, Gaels, Vikings and Danes, right up to and including the Normans—followed a time-honoured pattern. They arrived, looted and slaughtered, took possession, intermarried, assimilated and became "more Irish than the Irish themselves." This phrase is heavily featured in every history book but, tellingly, it is never enlarged upon. More Irish in what way exactly? However much one loves the Irish and is enchanted by their Irishness one can only be dismayed by the thought of a new wave of immigrants displaying exaggerated forms of already fairly extreme behaviour. Even the more attractive characteristics, such as the legendary Irish charm, could be exhausting if amplified even marginally. Of course, it is just possible that the original Irish were a mousey lot with barely distinguishable national traits and it took layers of conquerors throwing themselves enthusiastically into being more Irish than the Irish themselves to have produced the extreme national characteristics we know and love today.

The first Anglo-Irish were those who were given Irish land by Elizabeth I (Elizabeth's colonizations were called plantations, and the Ulster plantation led to the two-nation, two-religion impasse from which we still suffer) and the most recent were income-tax refugees from the postwar Labour government. They were all Protestant settlers in a Catholic country where religion kept them separate.

Both Catholics and Protestants were violently opposed to what we called "mixed marriages." A mixed marriage was, by definition, one between a Roman Catholic and a member of the Church of Ireland. It was, regardless of any money or social standing involved, considered a disaster by both sides. For the Catholics immortal souls were in danger, and for the Protestants there was the crossing of social and cultural barriers and the further erosion of the shaky rock on which they had built. The actual wedding ceremony of a mixed marriage would take place in a Catholic church, but the priest would not perform it at the altar. In order to obtain even this second-best ceremony, the Protestant involved would have to sign a paper guaranteeing a Catholic upbringing for any children who might result.

My father, whose keen perception and wide range of friends had made him aware of the many pitfalls of a mixed marriage, took a more philosophical view of the possibility of such a marriage occurring in his own family.

"I have four children," he said to me once. "The odds are that at least one of you will marry a Catholic."

(I have to qualify this unusually enlightened attitude by adding that he and I were having dinner together in his club in London long after we had both left rigid Waterford society. I suspect, although he was too kind to mention it, that he was also beginning to wonder if any of his daughters were ever going to marry anyone of any religion.)

Nevertheless we went to a Protestant school.

The national schools were government-run and free. They were, of course, Catholic and the Irish language played a large part in the curriculum. A higher standard of Catholic education, though sometimes fairly brutally taught, was provided by the Christian Brothers. Protestant children went to Newtown or Bishop Foy's. Newtown had been founded by the Quakers and the fees were slightly higher since Irish was not taught and the school, therefore, was not eligible for the government subsidy. Newtown was considered the better of the two schools and I never forgave a distant relative who commented scathingly on the strong accent my sister and I had picked up at Bishop Foy's. Her own little pets had, of course, gone to Newtown.

Bishop Foy's had been founded in 1707, but should not be thought of as Ivy League. It catered to day students from Waterford and the surrounding countryside, but the bulk of the students were boarders. One tends to think of a boarding school in terms of privilege. This was not the case with Bishop Foy's— Newtown was where those who could afford to usually sent their children. Those who could not—Protestant farmers in outlying areas and those who lived in towns too small to support a Protestant day school—scraped together the fees and sent their children to Bishop Foy's.

My father used to drop me off at school on his way to the office. His chosen time to commence business was half an hour later than the beginning of the school day. For the entire time I attended Bishop Foy's I was always half an hour late for Scripture, the first class of the day. At the time it seemed no great loss. My lateness dramatically reduced the odds of being tested on my homework and left me the only child in the class who, at the end of the school year, could not recite the Collect of the week. My father had announced to the headmaster that I would come to school late, and I was never penalized, but I think it did something to foster the feeling among my teachers that I was a special case. Not a good thing to be at eight years of age. On a broader scale, it was another instance of my father suggesting that the normal rules did not apply to us. It was an unfounded assumption with which I've had to battle all my life and, I think, a prevalent attitude among the Anglo-Irish when I was growing up.

Because I had difficulty communicating with my parents and, indeed, everyone, I frequently turned up either out of uniform or inadequately uniformed when this was clearly unacceptable. The school-uniform misery was more than partly of my own making. I was a depressed and apathetic child. Either I didn't take in that a uniform would be required for some special occasion or if I did I left it too late and stated my needs in so tentative a voice that my parents didn't take them seriously.

After two or three of these ordeals, my mother overcompensated by allowing my sister and me to be the only children to turn up, perfectly uniformed, on Speech Day. All the other children were wearing party dresses or suits. I don't think I felt as much discomfort on this occasion as I might have since I was gloomily sure that my party dress would have been wrong in some completely different but equally unacceptable manner.

In the same way, I was always in trouble for not having the right equipment in art, and in other classes not even the day-to-day stuff like erasers and rulers. I seemed to be unable to go home, look my mother in the eye and say, "I need a new ruler, a compass and some jars of paint for school." If I had done it after art when it was still fresh in my mind, there would have been a week to get organized. But I procrastinated and my father had a tendency to wave away as nonsense any inconvenient request not stated in bold enough tones. My parents were always a little vague about my day-to-day problems and it never occurred to them, for instance, to check whether I had any homework and, if so, whether I had done it.

Art and uniformed events were not the only aspects of school which I dreaded. In the lower grades, or forms, as we called them, singing was a regular part of the curriculum. No attempt was made to teach us anything—we would stand in a semicircle around an old piano and sing our way through as many songs as it took to fill the allotted time. Nearly all of the songs had a doleful theme, though probably not as a result of conscious policy; I suspect that our programme was formulated either by the limited abilities of our instructors or by the songbooks available. Certainly nothing new was attempted and the songs we sang came under the heading of traditional. Strangely enough, many of them were from the southern states of America.

Sometimes I would start to cry during the first few minutes, sometimes I would last until the period was almost over, but sooner or later and always before the bell rang, I would weep. I no longer remember most of the songs which made me cry, although I know that all of them dealt with loss. These tears were not quite the same ones as those, mainly caused by fear, which had been so bitterly and copiously wept in anticipation of the loss of my parents. They, at least, had been specific. This was loss in general. I don't know why, out of a class of thirty children, I should have been the only one to experience this grief, but I do know that, to this day, I have rarely dreamed of anyone I love without my losing the object of my love in a crowd.

The other children remained unmoved; after all, it was only "singing"—another half hour or forty-five minutes to be endured. I was not of a superior or more sensitive calibre than my phlegmatic schoolmates. Far from it—one of the songs which I never got past dry-eyed was "My Old Kentucky Home." The second line—" 'Tis summer, the darkies are gay"—might nowadays evoke a wide range of emotions, but I doubt that sentimental tears would be one of them.

Tears seemed utterly shameful. Today I could cry in public with a mere fraction of the embarrassment I felt as a child. Every now and then another child would ask me why I cried in singing. The question would be posed with the unspoken implication that if I could come up with a relatively acceptable explanation, I might not be considered quite such a pariah. It never once occurred to me to tell the truth—that I found the songs heartbreakingly sad—although I could never produce a convincing alternative. Nor did I ever tell my parents about my problem. My own children come home from school able to recount the mortification and humour of the thousand and one traps and pitfalls inherent in every school day. They have no idea how much I envy and admire their ability to talk about and laugh at the things that made them cringe only that morning.

We were taught Irish at Bishop Foy's, although parents who wished could make up the difference in fees (to compensate for the lost subsidy) and have their children excused. Few did this, and I envied two quite rich English children whose mother felt no need to put them through this rigorous course. Irish is an insanely hard language to learn. It does not have a Latin base and when I was a child it was still taught with its original alphabet. My parents occasionally used to discuss the possibility of Julia and me being exempted. It was my worst subject, it was of no practical use, and I didn't do well in school anyway. On the other side, I think my father thought that paying for the exemption would be slightly "bad form"; that being exempted would further distance me from my schoolmates; and there was, of course, the expense to be considered.

The unfortunate men and women whose responsibility it was to teach me Irish gave up the unequal task fairly early on, contenting themselves with an occasional almost rhetorical ques tion in my direction. I bitterly regret my attitude now, but then I spent most of my time keeping a low profile, with one eye on the clock.

This policy I extended toward school lunches, another deeply threatening area. My greatest fear was that I might be forced to eat the food that was put in front of me. Fortunately, I never had to, although I lived in daily dread and employed quite a lot of ingenuity avoiding a confrontation. Each day I would take the unsavoury knife and fork at my place setting and peel a boiled potato. Then I would mash it, the fork making sinister black marks, and push it around my plate until the meal was over. Grace, in Latin, would be said before and after lunch. Underwashed and overcooked cabbage, poorly drained, played a large part in the menu. The kitchen was run by a Protestant woman, referred to at governors' meetings as "the lady cook." My father later told me that he made a point of referring to her firmly as "the cook" almost immediately after she was so named. He didn't realize that, to me, the second word was the more inaccurate one.

Since present-day education demands that children go to school at a younger age than ever before while steadfastly refusing to teach them to read or add until a much later age than seems reasonable to me, much of the time in between is spent on what my children's New York school called "field trips" and I called "skites." To the best of my reckoning, my daughter, while in "the Fours," visited a fire station once every two weeks and was equally delighted with each identical Dalmatian named Sparky. We didn't have field trips at Bishop Foy's, but once we were paired off to walk to the Infirmary. The resulting line of children, two by two, a lumpish, navy-blue invertebrate, was known as a crocodile. Some of us bore modest gifts for the patients (wilted Michaelmas daisies are part of the memory).

The trip started badly. I was the only child not in complete uniform. Since I was a day student I rarely had the need for a school beret and my parents weren't aware that I was meant to have one. Then I didn't have a close friend to pair up with and, on these occasions, I inevitably ended up with a teacher or some other social outcast, sometimes even, horror of horrors, a boy. When we arrived at the Infirmary we broke ranks and waited for the lift. Something which I had never seen before. It was a lift I would approach with a qualm even today, but that wasn't the reason I dissolved into shameful tears. As the lift descended, the first aspect of it which became visible to us was two long black rubber loops and other apparatus of sinister appearance. It wheezed and clanged its way down through a metal cage with all its workings visible. We were in a hospital where any kind of horrible thing was possible and I assumed that we were to be hoisted, one by one, on the rubber straps. A teacher noticed my tears and, when I admitted that I was afraid of the lift, sportingly said that she would walk upstairs with me. As we set out, the lift came to a rest and I realized that my fears were based on a ridiculous misapprehension. But by then I was ashamed to admit my mistake and we walked up, thereby missing the high point of the whole outing.

On the wall outside the Infirmary there was a worn sign which read: "The Leper Hospital." In the old days, when Waterford had been a busier port, sailors had come off ships infected with the dreaded disease.

My father was on the board of the Infirmary. It was a responsibility he had inherited, one of many which were time-consuming and bore minimal prestige and little power. His place on the board of governors of my school was a privilege which condemned my sister and me to a third-rate education at the second-best school in the city. I remember my father coming home discouraged but amused from one hospital meeting. There'd been the usual discussion of how to cut expenses and some ancient, distant, female cousin had suggested, quite seriously, that bandages be thoroughly washed and used again.

Bishop Foy's School consisted of two separate buildings. The one where I showed up each morning, half an hour late, was the more modern building. It was reasonably light, with large windows, and in winter there was additional lighting from sputtering overhead gas lamps. The whole school smelled of an evocative mixture of gas, disinfectant, pencil shavings and ink. The lavatories were separate and outdoors and had a clammy, damp, mossy atmosphere all their own. As constant as the ever-present smell of the classrooms was the accompanying rendering of "Jesu, Joy of Man's Desiring" coming from the music room. Although the smell of a school or the sight of certain thick off-white crockery still causes a pang of distress, the equally evocative sound of schoolgirl piano practice has inexplicably pleasant associations.

To get to the second school building, accurately but inappropriately called the Palace, one had to cross the Mall, a fine wide street which swept down to the river and the Quay. One went up a narrow and slightly sinister lane between the theatre and the Palace garden, passing the Protestant cathedral, into the part of the school where the boarders slept, where the kindergarten was quartered and where we ate lunch. I have smelled pig swill sweeter than the stench that used to greet my nostrils before I even unlatched the door with the peeling, institutional dark green paint and entered the Palace yard.

The Protestant cathedral overlooked not only Bishop Foy's but the older and most interesting part of Waterford. Its site, above the city, had been chosen for its dominant and aloof position. But the oldest building in Waterford is situated beside the river. It is a Danish fort, Reginald's Tower, and it stands on the Quay overlooking the Suir. Waterford was a Danish seaport and, like many Irish ports, still bears its Danish name. It was in this fort that Strongbow, Earl of Pembroke, married Eva, daughter of Diarmid, the treacherous king of Leinster, after he had successfully invaded Ireland in 1170.

The Quay, with Reginald's Tower and a row of shops on one side and the river and docks on the other, was the real centre of the city. It was where we went shopping with my mother. If we parked on the river side of the street my mother would warn us away from the edge.

"If you fall in I won't jump in after you."

We knew she didn't really mean it, but I also knew that she looked at the cold, deep, thick, brown water with a special kind of fear.

Sometimes she would leave me in the car while she went to collect a package. Often she left her handbag in my care. As soon as she had gone I would open it, not to pry, but to feel the soft leather which lined it and to smell the mixture of face powder, leather and scent which was uniquely my mother's.

A variety of ships docked at the Quay, the most regular being the mail boat, which arrived every second morning. It came up the river past our house carrying not only the mail but passengers from England. My father prided himself on meeting the mail boat with scientifically timed, split-second precision. He saw the boat pass the house, leisurely drank a cup of tea, got into the car, drove to Waterford and met the mail boat as it completed its turn and docked. The boat moved at a slow, uniform pace and I am sure my father never cheated by hurrying, even when he was out of sight of the house. He took a certain pleasure from this minor ritual, similar to the one I feel in never filling my car's tank until I'm down to the last teaspoon of gas but never running out on the highway. A gambler's way of putting a little excitement into daily dull routine.

In those days there were two ways of getting back to Waterford from England—either on the mail boat or by the route my family usually took, from Fishguard to Rosslare. Coming back from England, when I was older, I used to take an afternoon train from Paddington to Fishguard, cross the Irish Sea overnight and then take a train from Rosslare to Waterford. It was a long, grim, dirty and tiring journey. The Irish Sea, at the best of times, is fairly choppy and I'm not a good sailor. Nor, unfortunately, were many of the drunken Irish labourers coming home on holiday. The best part of the trip was the substantial reviving breakfast served on the Irish train while travelling through the early morning countryside between Rosslare and Waterford.

Apart from the mail boat, there was also a regular, although less frequent, cargo boat, which struck horror in us. Horses were bought in the South of Ireland and exported, live, to Belgium, where they were slaughtered for meat. On the day they left, one would see them driven through the streets, old, uncared for, bones jutting out, sometimes lame. We knew that the conditions on the boats were barbaric and some of the horses would not survive the journey. For those that did, only the abattoirs of Antwerp lay ahead. We had been brought up with the unsentimental if somewhat privileged tradition that a horse at the end of its life would be shot and its carcass sent to the kennels to feed the hounds.

On the lighter side of dockyard activity, there was for a time a factory in Waterford devoted to the recycling of paper. This was more than thirty years ago, so there were no environmental, ethical connotations to this enterprise. Someone had figured out that scrap paper bought in Ireland and pulped could show a profit if made into cardboard or whatever by cheap Irish labour. There was some minor advertising or promotion connected with this, and my family saved old copies of *The Irish Times*, binding them up neatly and delivering them to the factory. (This kind of activity was very attractive to the Anglo-Irish, whose tiny moneymaking schemes usually involved trying to sell far from cost-effective products to people who neither wanted them nor could afford them. Here they were solicited to sell something to which they had previously given no value.) For some reason, cash was not paid on delivery. Several days later a postal order for some absurdly small sum like four shillings arrived in the post. My mother, who had done most of the work involved, was so disillusioned by the futility of this whole enterprise that she gave the postal order to Julia and me. To us, of course, it seemed like riches.

Other equally naïve and sometimes eccentric attempts at economy were made by some of my parents' contemporaries. An honorary uncle and aunt boasted that they'd saved five shillings in postage stamps by driving around and hand-delivering that week's mail. My mother was kind enough to wait until they'd left to point out that their expenditure on petrol would certainly have equaled if not exceeded the saving.

Perhaps because of the low prices paid for scrap paper, the Waterford Paper Company found that they were not getting enough raw material in Ireland and bundles of old newspapers had to be imported from England. To the delight of the dockworkers, and later the local youths, these bundles of paper were found to contain treasure in the form of old comics, *The News of the World* (the low English Sunday paper banned in Ireland) and other (by late forties and early fifties Irish standards) racy publications.

Also on the Quay, just by Reginald's Tower, was O'Grady's, the barbershop where we would go for a haircut on the rare occasions when one was due. We all had long hair, mine worn in plaits—my father disapproved of short hair on women and fought, with some success, any attempt we made to conform with the fashions of the fifties. Long hair was a mixed blessing. Hair washing, especially in the winter, was torture. My mother would wash my hair in the bathroom basin, then I would dash along the icy corridor, down the stairs and across the hall to the library, where my father would briskly towel me dry in front of the blazing log or glowing turf fire. Combing out the tangles afterward always led to tears. To this day I am impressed by houses which have modern plumbing and bathroom arrangements and never quite take for granted the luxury of washing my hair under a hot shower with full water pressure, then drying it with an electric dryer in a warm bathroom. Bathrooms were low on the list of priorities for the investment of the very rare windfall—far below horses, whiskey, horse trailers and hunt subscriptions—but this did not prevent them from having some fairly rigid taboos attached. On the ground floor of each house we lived in there was a cloakroom. But in Ireland cloakrooms were for men only. That in our family, at least until Robert was born, my father was the only male and my mother, I and my two sisters outnumbered him four to one, made no difference to the rule. In addition to a lavatory and washbasin, they provided storage for gum boots and, if large enough, guns and fishing rods. The Glenville cloakroom was large and the walls were hung with photographs of horses and the finishing lines of races and with a large mounted salmon. The masculine atmosphere was confirmed by the not unpleasant smell of the oil my father used to clean his gun. The ban on the use of cloakrooms by women and children was often flouted by those who would first calculate the odds of getting caught in order to avoid the trip upstairs to some outlying, chilly bathroom.

Even in the grander houses in Ireland there was rarely a bedroom with its own bathroom. I don't remember ever having the pleasure of a long soak in a hot deep bath. Perhaps because it was an experience so devoid of sensuality, my brother, thirteen years younger than I, showed a reluctance to bathe. When my sisters remonstrated with him, my father made a joke of it. "He's got the Goff clean skin," he would say. "A bath once a week and a light dusting in between is all that is necessary."

Further along the Quay were two department stores—Hearne's and Shaw's. We would watch with delight when my mother paid for our purchases. The money, along with the bill, would be placed in a small cylinder which looked like a metal tennis ball, put in a chute and projected up to an overhead set of tracks running around the store and ending up with an unseen cashier upstairs. A few moments later the cylinder would return with the receipt and change inside.

Also on the Quay were the bookshop we used and a sporting-goods store where my mother bought me a hockey stick so that I could join in the afternoon games on the Bishop Foy's playing fields at Ballinakill. Things went well enough on the first day of hockey. Although I was clearly lacking in coordination, I was not lacking in enthusiasm. I suspect I was the first member of my family willingly to join a team. While leadership may not have been a dominant characteristic among the Anglo-Irish, the tradition of being a follower was even less developed. For my enthusiasm I had the written, or more accurately, the illustrated word to thank. The English schoolgirl comic *Girl's Crystal*, to which I was addicted, was very clear about the importance of being in the first eleven. (*Girl's Crystal* consisted of several serialized stories, each illustrated and recounted in cartoon form and each ending with a cliff-hanger. The cover story—my favourite—was called "The Silent Three." It was about three girls at a rather grand boarding school who, in times of emergency or injustice—i.e., every week—donned a uniform which looked like a green version of that worn by the Ku Klux Klan, and righted wrongs. My father referred to them as "the silent flea.") A proficiency in hockey was as essential a quality in a heroine as honour, straight teeth, truthfulness and a clear skin. Looking at my schoolmates, I felt that I, unfairly, had more to put up with than had my role models. On a weekly basis, they battled injustice, false accusations (often from those naïve enough to have forgotten how embarrassed they had been only the week before when the tall blonde girl from the upper sixth had been vindicated) and mysterious criminals who had for some reason elected to carry on business from a girls' boarding school, but they never seemed to have to operate in an atmosphere of acne, running noses, chapped lips, body odour, talebearing, lack of team spirit—how could I score the crucial winning goal if no one ever passed me the ball? I was discouraged, muddy and a little bruised about the shins. But game.

At the end of the practice I left my hockey stick with those of my schoolmates in the sports pavilion—a shabby wooden building with the usual peeling dark green paint, completely unlike the structure where my fictional heroines changed their spotless tennis whites for equally becoming and well-cut school uniforms.

The following week when I returned, my hockey stick was missing. For a week or two I showed up and searched for it. I was sometimes able to borrow a spare, but soon I became discouraged. Eventually I stopped going to hockey altogether and my interest in any team sport on which I don't have a small bet has never revived.

My memories of the bookshop are happier. I often used to be given book tokens for birthday and Christmas presents. Although I did not consider books tokens to be very exciting gifts I remember with pleasure the visits my mother and I would make to the bookshop where she would help me choose from among the more entertaining classics. The major works of Dumas, father and son, were purchased this way, as was *Evelina*, even now one of my favourite antidotes to depression. I started off predisposed toward Fanny Burney when my mother told me—her interest in gossip being firmly and exclusively entrenched in the eighteenth century—that she, Fanny Burney, had been chased around the palace gardens by the intermittently insane George III.

At the end of the Quay, not quite the real end but the end defined by memory and habit, was the Waterford bridge. It spanned the river Suir and was a source of fascination. Whenever a boat of any size needed to go up the river, a barrier would descend and the huge and solid bridge would divide and slowly raise itself to allow the boat to pass through. The opportunity of witnessing such a phenomenon, usually from one of the waiting cars, was always an attractive one. Since the railway station was on the other side, as was the main road to Kilkenny and Wexford, my parents were understandably less enthusiastic. It was the same pleasure we felt when we arrived at a level crossing as the gates went down. The five to ten minutes my parents or grandparents spent drumming their fingers, we spent in eager anticipation of the train's whistle, followed by the excitement of the train itself, after which the crossing keeper or his wife would come out of their hutchlike house and raise the barriers. I even managed to extend this enthusiasm to the first traffic lights—on the outskirts of Dublin—that I ever saw. A relatively short-lived enthusiasm.

Beside the bridge stood the main hotel. There was no real restaurant in Waterford, although the hotel and a few other places provided meals on the order of a commercial traveller's lunch. Nor were there any shops in which ready-made food could be purchased, except for the cake shop on the Mall. In my family, the words "shop cake" were terms of disparagement—at least when spoken by adults. The everyday alternatives were a homemade sponge cake with a jam layer, and a jam roll (same thing, different shape). These cakes had only the virtue of being made with fresh eggs, butter and homemade jam. Not qualities likely to cut any ice with me as a child. What I craved were the sickly pink meringues with brightly colored "sprinkles" from the cake shop. When I was indulged I was aware that they tasted of absolutely nothing, which in no way swayed my belief in their superiority. There was, however, one cake that both grown-ups and children agreed on. This was a fine, dark fruitcake with marzipan and a pink-on-white icing which was made at Christmas and usually lasted well into January. We would meet it each afternoon at tea and I would occasionally find my father, when I came to kiss him good night, sitting reading with a whiskey and water and a small sliver of Christmas cake on the table beside him.

Apart from the cake shop, Bishop Foy's and the newsagent's where I bought my weekly comic, there was another centre of culture on the Mall—the Royal, Waterford's theatre. On my eighth birthday, a small group of my friends and I were taken by my father to a matinee of what was supposed to be *Treasure Island*. The curtain had not yet risen and I was unaware of the stage behind it. I assumed, with rising anxiety, that the action would take place on the foot or so of stage protruding in front of the curtain, or that the performers would give us the play, like tightrope walkers, balanced on the fat, brass guardrail. Before the curtain went up, it was announced that the actor who was to have played Long John Silver had broken a leg—a curiously appropriate accident, though method acting was not prevalent in Ireland—and that a performance of *Arms and the Man* would be substituted for the advertised play. The curtain went up and I lasted, clammily clutching my father's hand, for all of five minutes. Then Bluntschli broke in through the window and I whispered in my father's ear, "I don't think I'm going to like this," and I was taken home, where later my more resilient guests joined me for birthday cake. It was years before I was to make another visit to the theatre.

The plays which came to Waterford were repertory productions and from two touring companies, those of Anew McMaster and Lord Longford, uncle of the present Labour peer. These plays were always established classics. There was little audience for experimental theatre, and those who, a little later, tried it did so in Dublin and at their own risk. The attitude of the Church, the police, the press and the audience tended to be anything but apathetic when an innovative production was tried. I remember an abortive attempt to produce *The Rose Tattoo*, which ended in arrests. A friend, in later life, told me about working on a production of *The Ginger Man*, which resulted in not only the police arresting the cast and part of the production staff but a bishop turning up to ban it formally. According to my friend, a hitherto reliable but unconfirmed witness, the bishop was accompanied by priests on motorbikes, which gives a pleasing image of an emergency morality patrol. Both these instances follow in the tradition of the reception with which *The Playboy of the Western World* was greeted when it first opened at the Abbey Theatre in 1907, when the audience reaction was such that the police had to be called and few of the words spoken onstage were audible after the opening night. The play was savagely attacked for suggesting immorality among Irish peasant women and for the use of the word "shift."

As an adolescent, I would occasionally see American films which had been censored for an Irish audience. They seemed strangely short and the missing pieces made the plots almost meaningless. But as a smaller child in Waterford, I hardly ever saw a film.

I earned my living, when I was younger, in or around the movie industry, starting in England during the boom years of the Eady subsidy and later working in Hollywood. Much of that time was spent keeping my mouth shut, not through modesty, but through an unusual ignorance of the end product. I had hardly ever been to "the fillums," as they were called in Ireland. There were cinemas in Waterford and the gardener's children were regular patrons of the penny matinees at the least reputable fleapit, where they saw Cowboy-and-Indian movies. We were not allowed to go because of germs. When I grew up and went to live in London the germ line was usually good for a laugh. Now I realize it wasn't as neurotic as it sounds. Each summer in Waterford there would be outbreaks of typhoid and polio, and tuberculosis was an ever-present threat.

The only two films I remember having seen with the

permission of my parents were *Little Women* and later *Hans Christian Andersen.* The latter expedition was an error in judgment on the part of my grandmother, who thought it would be set among the Danish forests she remembered nostalgically from when her father had been the British Ambassador in Copenhagen. It never occurred to her that the Danny Kaye musical could have been shot entirely in a Hollywood studio.

I have never caught up entirely with the films I failed to see in those days, although it seems to matter less now. When we lived in Waterford they were thought of as entertainment of a very unserious kind, but when I later lived in London my lack of knowledge was a source of shame. It was a time when no one expected me to have read *Madame Bovary* but not having seen *Bringing Up Baby* was a secret well worth keeping.

There was, for a time, a tiny film society in Waterford. My parents went to see *The Third Man* and my mother talked about it the next day with some excitement, articulate enough to describe the fingers on the grating, the shiny, wet, dark walls in such a way that when, as an adult I eventually saw the film, I remembered, rather than recognized, the sequences she had described. My father enjoyed it equally, liking its economy and wit. But there was another occasion, when my mother complained humorously of my father's lack of sensitivity when he'd ineptly consoled her, during a sad movie, with the unimaginative words: "It's only a film."

The "It's only a film" moment—too slight to be called an incident—seems to me a metaphor for why my parents' marriage came unstuck. My father was neither stupid nor unobservant. He was, in fact, sensitive, although too inhibited to show any emotion. The real trouble was that he didn't pay attention. My mother's attempts to follow my father into his world were not always successful. My father's friends were non-intellectual, conventional, sporting—to the point where my mother's occasional accusation of "bloodlust" was not wholly unfounded. They represented one side of my father's world. The other side was

represented by my mother and his children. My mother, unfortunately, had no outside world with which to balance my father's
tweedy, muddy-gum-booted friends. I think that she could have
managed better without such a compensating world if the need for
one had been acknowledged. (My guess is that it is easier to return
empty-handed from a search for the Holy Grail if your mate does
not greet you on your return with a question about whether you
thought to pick up the dry cleaning while you were out.) The
validity of my mother's wish for something more should have
been acknowledged even if (perhaps particularly if) my father
knew how unlikely it was that she would attain it. "It's only a
film" snaps one back into reality; unfortunately the tears one is
shedding are usually not only for a fictional character.

It's just a matter of paying attention. A good deal of childhood
misery and fear could be eliminated if the grown-ups concerned
only thought to tell their children what was going on at any given
moment. In my childhood there was a certain amount of *pas
devant*, but only about interesting, scandalous subjects. Subjects
which caused worry or anxiety, such as the free-floating financial
crisis which hovered over most Anglo-Irish establishments, were
generally assumed to be something children didn't understand. I
understood, all right, and worried right along with my parents.
Given a chance, I would be just as guilty of evasion as they were.
The difference is that my children have the sense to ask direct
questions whereas I used to spend hours in fruitless speculation
and projection.

The brewery where my father worked, and of which he was a
director, is inextricably associated in my mind with financial
anxiety. The emotion that I would apply to financial matters is
anxiety approaching fear—the feeling so strong that simple ones
like avarice and greed seem pale and meaningless beside it. The
brewery was situated a little way above the Quay and docks. It
didn't do well. My father had spent some time studying brewing
in England and told amusing stories about his student life in
Stratford-upon-Avon. Although he knew quite a lot about how to

brew beer, he had no head for business. His nature was not designed for the tedium of day-to-day office work. After the war, small breweries found it hard to compete against the larger companies such as Guinness, and many of them were squeezed out. I don't know if it was later suggested to me or if I thought it up myself, but for some time I had the impression that being a small Protestant brewery had made it harder. It certainly can't have helped that my father's company was a Protestant one, although there is a flourishing Protestant brewery called Beamish. My father told me that when "Guinness Is Good for You" became the slogan under which our most popular national drink was sold, Beamish had started to launch a campaign with the words "Beamish Is Better." According to my father, they were persuaded to modify it to the less aggressive "Beamish Is a Better Drink." My father's brewery didn't have a slogan or an advertising campaign. He had been brought up to hunt twice a week during the winter months and never lost his interest in racing, so I can't imagine he put the necessary amount of time into streamlining the old-fashioned brewery to keep up with changing times. Eventually it went under.

We rarely went to the brewery. It was a large stone building with a pleasant smell of yeast. There were old-fashioned offices and a large, unkempt yard, with a Dickensian look to it, where the barrels, handmade by coopers, were loaded.

The man who drove the brewery van used to drive us home from school sometimes when my father was at a race meeting. He had a terminal illness, never named, at least to us. It was the first time I had ever met anyone who knew he was dying, whom those around him knew was dying and whom nobody could help. Apart from the pity and helplessness that I felt, I was shocked that my father could do nothing to change such a clear injustice. It forced me to admit to myself that my parents weren't invulnerable or omnipotent.

Because tuberculosis was common in Ireland in those days, maids would disappear from our household and there were panics about milk since many cows suffered from the disease. Then a cure was found and a nationwide campaign to stamp out the disease was launched. At school we were all X-rayed. Many of our schoolmates were found to be infected. At the same time, Ardkeen, the house next to ours, was bought and became the site of one of the new sanitariums.

Part of the old order changing. Ardkeen had belonged to the de Bromheads, a Catholic family of Norman descent. Mr. de Bromhead was a hunting and racing friend of my father's and he owned Ardkeen and most of the land on the other side of the lane. His mother, known as Old Mrs. de Bromhead, lived in a house overlooking the river on our side of the lane; her front gates marked where our afternoon walks ended. We would pause outside and then stroll down to the edge of the water—lush green grass up to the edge of the thick, rich, dark brown, muddy silt which lay on both sides of the river. Across from us was the Island, home of Freddy the Prince, one of our parents' most colourful friends, and his family. On occasions such as birthday parties we would be taken to the Island, the excitement of the occasion heightened by the heady atmosphere of a household where Irish blood had been diluted, or perhaps more accurately, enriched, by a Latin transfusion. The only access to the Island was an old wooden rowing boat. We would sit, our feet in party shoes raised above the puddles at the bottom of the boat, our party dresses gathered up around us. The delight was always more acute since there was a thin undercurrent of fear. The boat creaked, the ferryman had a withdrawn and doomed look, the water in the bottom of the boat suggested a leak, the small brown waves on the river made the boat seem insubstantial. I was never quite sure if my father's apparent lack of alarm came from his knowledge that we were secure or if it was just a manifestation of the stiff upper lip.

It was for a birthday party that I gained access to Old Mrs. de Bromhead's house. The driveway from the gates, at which we paused with governesses, led through a large field, filled with cowslips, and up to the house. I had been that far with my father, who occasionally took us for walks and assumed that a closed gate did not apply to him. We had picked the cowslips, which are my favourite flower, and had hidden behind my father when he stopped to pay his respects to the old lady, but neither Julia nor I had ever infiltrated the house before. This time we were part of the main event. The birthday party was given for Johnny de Bromhead, one of the younger children of my father's friend (there were seven or eight) and the doted-on grandson of Old Mrs. de Bromhead. Johnny was both a contemporary of mine and geographically desirable, so it is unlikely that this was my first meeting with him. But one tiny incident took place that afternoon which established him as an early member of my hall of heroes. He may even, it now occurs to me, have started me in a lifelong, misguided, deferential attitude toward the male sex. My memories of him are affectionate and inextricably connected with chocolate biscuits—the kind that have oatmeal on one side and chocolate on the other. I watched, spellbound, as he, to use my father's words, "put away" an entire plate of them. My admiration knew no bounds as I saw him suffer none of the ill effects so cheerfully predicted by adults on these occasions.

The second occasion on which I watched him pack away an entire plate of chocolate biscuits was even more impressive. This time he did it at *my* mother's table and almost under her eye. I can't now imagine how this improbable tea party had occurred. The protagonists were me, Johnny de Bromhead and a little boy called Jeremy, whose parents were also friends of my parents'. A cast of three suggests that it wasn't a birthday or other festival, but why my mother should have arranged a full-scale tea for me and two other children, complete with chocolate biscuits, I can't imagine. I could have told her it wouldn't work. Johnny had only come from across the lane, easy walking distance particularly if you climbed a stone wall, but the other child had been driven out from Waterford to be part of this debacle. Early on in the meal Jeremy took offence and retired under the table—I had a feeling then, which time has done nothing to dispel, that this was a standard retreat of his when life became too much for him. Johnny and I were, of course, thrilled by this drama. I had never witnessed this kind of carry-on before. Johnny, I suspect, frequently had, usually while playing the part of the villain himself. My mother, unstrategically, elected to match Jeremy's dramatic interpretation of the event instead of that of the two more phlegmatic and cynical children still seated and stuffing their faces, and got down on her hands and knees to reason with him and try to lure him out. She might have succeeded if it were not for a well-timed kick from Johnny which kept his rival below table level for the remainder of the meal. Two of us at least considered it to have been a thoroughly satisfactory social event.

Ardkeen, like Glenville, had a second-floor gallery but, unlike at Glenville, a safety net, often containing a ball or some stray article of clothing, hung over the hall. The safety net symbolized an attitude which I think admirable. It accepts the immediate physical dangers of life and also acknowledges that one's own children are not immune to them. Had I lived in that house I am sure I would have extracted, probably through moral blackmail, a promise from each child that he would not attempt a feat of daring on the gallery banisters or, no matter how provoked, push his or her brother or sister over them. The de Bromheads had more sense and put up a net. And they knew that the net was only one protection in a life fraught with physical dangers. Most of the family rode, one daughter on an Olympic level, and Mr. de Bromhead had been an amateur steeplechase jockey with my father. I have always noticed a kind of independent strength among boys who have been brought up that way.

Another family, who lived on the other side of Glenville, thereby providing a second geographically desirable possibility of companionship, was comprised of three boys. They were Protestant and we went to the same school. The second son, Owen, was in the same class as I was. He was small, wiry, and very athletic. Independent and energetic, he was often in trouble with our teachers, but I noticed that he was not compromised by it. He accepted punishment because he had no choice, but with the air of someone waiting for something unpleasant but unconnected with him to be over, an attitude I think he may have learned from the animals with which he and his brothers were surrounded. When the boys played in the woods their pet jackdaws perched on their shoulders or flapped above them. Julia and I once stood appalled by the door and watched the three brothers bouncing, out of control, on their parents' bed. I waited aghast for the inevitable moment when their yells brought their mother into the room and we were all, Julia and I unjustly but understandably included, thrown out of the house.

After Ardkeen was sold and construction of the sanitarium began, Julia and I used to play there, running along the deep trenches which covered what used to be lawns and fields. My father would stroll around, watching us as well as the crumbling of yet another of his landmarks. Within a few years tuberculosis was virtually wiped out. The sanitariums built to combat the disease have now been converted into hospitals and old-age homes.

The de Bromheads moved to a house on the other side of Waterford. In that house there was no balcony with a need for a safety net, but, as always, other possibilities presented themselves. One of the children came back from England with a large quantity of fireworks, not commercially available in Ireland, to be used to celebrate Guy Fawkes Day. As a safety precaution, these fireworks were stored under the bed in a spare room in the naïve belief that they would go unnoticed by the younger members of the family. Apparently two of them, one of whom I like to imagine being my hero and former playmate Johnny, discovered the cache and decided that they would try one small sample, sure that it would never be missed. They elected to light a small rocket in the room in which they had discovered it. Not surprisingly, it got away from them, ricocheted off the walls, ignited another firework and set off a chain reaction. I remember my mother asking my father what had happened then. "Oh," he said casually, "they closed the doors and waited until it was all over."

The presence of the fireworks in the house suggests that in happy families we define the acceptable areas of unacceptable behaviour. I cannot conceive of a household in which it is possible for a room to be completely stripped of its wallpaper by Catherine wheels and Roman candles, but I have seen other parents shocked by my children. One Sunday afternoon, my husband, I and a couple of friends were sitting on the lawn, under an old maple tree, finishing a leisurely lunch. Close by and indoors, many children—theirs, ours and a horde of visiting friends—were playing. As we drank our coffee, a ten-year-old emissary from my son approached me and whispered, "Max wants to see you. Inside."

I got up, already bored by the role of referee about to be handed to me, and went indoors. In the kitchen, what seemed like twenty or thirty children stopped talking when I came in. "He's in his room," one of them said. I went up the back stairs, aware of forty or sixty silent eyes following my progress. On the dark landing, a small group of children waited. Seeing their expressions in the shadows, I revised the referee assumption. It seemed to me now quite possible that blood had been spilled, or perhaps a bone broken. One child gestured dramatically to the closed door of Max's room. I knocked. A small voice bid me enter. I revised my fears upward. Could one of them be dead? I reassured myself that the most likely candidate had been among the group below in the kitchen and gingerly opened the door, aware of the eyes and breath of hundreds behind me. My son stood there, sheepish and proud, displaying a new haircut, the main feature of which was that he had shaved the sides of his head to the skin. I was appalled, amused, a little proud of him. Our guests were outraged by his action, even more by my lack of outrage. But I was thinking of the de Bromheads and about knowing what is important and what is not.

Each Sunday, Julia and I went to Sunday School in Waterford

while our parents went to one of the three underheated, quarter-full Protestant churches. Our youngest sister, Alice, went to Mass with the Catholic nanny. (The strict religious segregation which defined our lives did not come into play until about the age of six.) Each Sunday, Julia and I would be given a penny to put in the missionary collection box. After several months, Julia proudly announced to our parents that we were sending money to the Mission to Leopards.

I wonder who taught us Sunday School or, for that matter, what they taught us. Memories of both teacher and subject matter have disappeared into the atmosphere of dusty, mildly depressed boredom which covered most church-related events, although there was a brief period after Sunday School and before our parents came to take us home when we ran wild. For fifteen minutes each week, we would divide up into two gangs and fight, young, animal, high spirits rebelling against the boredom of the preceding hour. No one ever got hurt, although Julia and I would occasionally arrive at Sunday School "armed." This meant that small homemade wooden swords would be concealed on the floor of my father's car and carefully dropped into the gutter, for retrieving later, when we were dropped off at the church hall.

One character from those tedious mornings remains clear. The Dean. He was big and bluff and when he came to visit Sunday School he told a joke, thereby undermining our regular teacher and establishing himself as a good guy. Having gained our confidence, he shifted effortlessly into a muscular Christian approach to the Gospel of the day and offered a prize to anyone who could learn the names of the books of the Bible by heart. This prize was never won, or even seriously attempted—possibly because it was a churchy sort of prize and partly because those of the group capable of mastering the task must have been aware of how pointless it was.

Apart from deans, the Church of Ireland clergy were a depressed lot. They were badly paid and expected to have families. Unlike their Roman Catholic counterparts, who were, of course, celibate, they couldn't hang around racetracks or drink whiskey. In fairness, though, I never saw a Church of Ireland curate who looked as though he hankered after either of those forms of recreation.

The clergy's role in society was an uncomfortable one. In Jane Austen's and Trollope's novels, a country parson was often the recipient of a benign despotism which involved hearty meals and comfortable teas in front of blazing fires, but in Ireland he was more usually considered an unavoidable social obligation. The Anglo-Irish attitude toward religion was devoid of emotion. It was joyless, and I don't remember ever hearing a hymn played at anything approaching full speed. The churches were cold and almost empty, the organs infirm. The clergy were expected to visit parishioners, but did not expect an enthusiastic welcome. The Dean came to lunch, the Rector to tea, but my mother once greeted a new young curate who had bicycled out from Waterford by politely but firmly telling him she was busy. She sent him on his way with a bunch of freshly cut grapes nestling in his bicycle basket. Although he had made a two-mile round trip, he must have felt, as did my mother, that the visit had worked out as well as it possibly could have.

Innovation was not encouraged, nor would it have served a useful purpose. There were no straying, apathetic Protestants waiting to be lured back into the Church of Ireland by a curate with jeans and a guitar. If you were Church of Ireland you went to church. The empty pews reflected lack of population, not lack of enthusiasm—that was taken for granted and not considered an excuse to stay home.

The Church of Ireland was hidebound because of fear. Anything that even hinted of High Church was suspect. Crosses and real music were too similar to Catholic ceremonies. Incense and genuflecting were definitely Papist.

If we didn't meet our spiritual leaders at the racetrack, that is where we saw most of our friends. Race meetings were a large part of our lives. My grandmother Woodhouse told me that my mother had never quite forgiven my father for going to a race meeting instead of the hospital waiting room when I, their first child, was born.

From the time when Julia and I were quite small children we would be set free at a racecourse with a small but adequate sum for betting. Neither of us received regular allowances and it is telling that my father accepted the necessity of money to back horses but not to spend on candy or plastic junk. We would watch the horses parade in the ring, study the form on the race cards and make our bets. We did slightly better than one might have expected, thanks in part to tips from my father and his friends.

We wore our best clothes to go racing, and the four-day summer meeting at Tramore, which always coincided with my sister's birthday (maybe my grandmother was exaggerating when she said Daddy had skipped the birth of his firstborn), was a wonderful sight. Tramore was Waterford's main resort town and the holiday crowd was a sprinkling of tourists mixed with hard-core regulars. It was pleasantly sunny and warm with bright colours and the sound of bookmakers calling the odds.

Summer race meetings smelled of horses, tobacco and orange peel. In the winter we would go to point-to-points, amateur race meetings organized by the local hunts. They smelled of mud and crushed grass.

Again we would bet, but we were wrapped up in our warmest coats and wore gum boots. Hot soups in thermos flasks would revive us at lunchtime and there would always be something stronger for the grown-ups, either from a bottle in the back of the car or at the warm, noisy, cheerful, squalid pub tent smelling of stout and tobacco, where the glasses were rinsed perfunctorily in water which was a rich brown cocktail and, but for the minimal detergent, probably quite tasty itself.

I woke one morning before one of these long-anticipated treats and realized that I was ill. I secretly took my temperature and found that I was running a relatively high fever. I knew that in the excitement of the outing, the preparation of a picnic, the shouts from the hall to encourage us to leave on time, no one would notice my flushed face and listless manner. I said nothing and went to the point-to-point. It was a day devoid of pleasure in a way I didn't at first understand. Every promised aspect of the point-to-point was available to me, but I felt nothing. The run down the hill, from where we had a good view of the course to the finishing post, was almost as draining as the climb back afterward. The parade of horses in the paddock, after I had squeezed under the elbows of grown-ups to see them, meant nothing to me. Bets won and lost did not affect me either. The only bright moment was my share of the flask of hot tomato soup. I was bewildered by these feelings, confused because events which I had thought guaranteed to bring pleasure had become meaningless. I was older and less happy when I next felt like that. Childhood flu had given me a foretaste of what depression and unacceptable losses feel like.

The casualty rate among horses and riders was higher at point-to-points than it was at race meetings. The riders, all amateur, would occasionally break a leg or collarbone, but a horse who broke a leg had to be shot. This was traumatic for us. Sentimentality about animals seems to be more a characteristic of the Anglo-Irish than of the purebred Irish. At my boarding school we used to collect money and sell Christmas cards to benefit the Royal Society for the Prevention of Cruelty to Animals, and we agonized over the cruel ends to which so many animals would come. We, of course, were not encouraged to express such dramatic emotions. When some unfortunate horse came to an untimely end, we stayed very close to my mother and averted our eyes. These equine executions drew quite a large crowd. Moments later the carcass would disappear, to be used as meat for the hounds, and the next race would take place. These events would cast a pall over the journey home. Often, by the time we left, the mud in the field where we were parked would have become so churned up that we would be unable to drive out. My father would lose his temper and curse and wait his turn to tip a local farm boy to tow us out with a tractor.

This performance was repeated at least once a summer when my father would believe, despite past experience, that he could drive the car closer to the beach than my mother advised. The beaches we used were isolated and beautiful. The sandy and marshy land beside the beach provided a wonderful variety of wildflowers, sometimes even orchids. Very occasionally we would go to Tramore, and, to our disappointment, take a brisk walk to the distant sand dunes instead of loitering in the fairlike atmosphere of merry-go-rounds and ice cream. But once, accompanied by an indulgent uncle who probably shared our lack of enthusiasm for exercise after lunch, we were allowed to go on the merry-go-round. I lost my nerve at the last moment and jumped off before it started. My sister, a year and a half younger than I, stayed on for the ride. Afterward I was ashamed and ready to try again, but the moment of indulgence had passed. It was years before I got a second chance.

On a summer evening at Glenville, if the wind were from a certain direction, we would sometimes hear the distant sound of a fair in Waterford. Barely audible English and American popular songs evoked vague and only half-recognized longings. They spoke of fun and possibilities of romance and the big city. Somewhere in the back of my mind, by the time I was eleven or twelve, I realized that I wasn't going to stay in Waterford. The moment I was old enough, I would be moving on. "Destiny," "ambition," "fate" were not descriptions which I would have felt applicable to this feeling of sureness, although I was even then capable of attaching such labels to myself. Nor was there any self-congratulatory feeling that I was too good for all this. I just knew that when I grew up I would no longer belong there, and I had a childish confidence that there was a place where I would belong. Later, of course, this feeling was reinforced by the beginning of sexual awareness. It was clear to me that no one was going to get laid in the Republic of Ireland; not if she were Anglo-Irish, at least.

The summer evenings at Glenville were sensuous. The light was soft and sometimes we would lie in the grass overlooking the river. We chewed wild sorrel and watched the activity on the river. Sometimes the mail boat steamed by. We followed it with our eyes until it reached the bend in the river. Soon it would pass the Island, home of Freddy the Prince, then two other rivers would join the Suir and the boat would soon enter the Irish Sea. The next morning it would dock at Fishguard, halfway to London. City of glitter and infinite possibilities.

BALLINACOURTY

Each summer Julia and I would go to stay with our grandparents. My mother's parents. My father and mother would drive us, accompanied by a governess or temporary keeper, the thirty miles of winding, dusty roads, stopping at regular intervals to allow carsick children "to disgorge," as my father put it.

My grandparents lived in Ballinacourty. Ballinacourty could not accurately be described as even a small village. It consisted of one shop—half pub, half grocery store, the latter section about the size of a walk-in closet, its stock limited to a few basic items and sweets. Opposite the pub was the Dungarvan Golf Club, Ballinacourty's link with the twentieth century.

Even the fields seemed old. They were divided by banks, walls and fences that had been overgrown with moss and grass, and they were full of ridges suggesting the remains of ancient walls and burial places beneath. These narrow banks were common all over County Waterford and were the frequent cause of hunting accidents among those not accustomed to them.

Ballinacourty House was three-storied, the only habitation for miles around which was more than a cottage. My grandparents had bought it when my grandfather retired. It was a plain white house, not old by Irish standards, with a pretty veranda at one end. The driveway led through a field, and two gates had to be opened and then closed each time a car drove up to the house. My grandfather imagined it was funny to pretend to drive off after one of us had opened the gate for him. There was no statute of limitations on this or any other of his jokes. We exercised a similar policy toward his tendency to execute a couple of "bunny hops" after changing gears. It never failed to delight us and we never failed to show our appreciation noisily.

When we first started visiting Ballinacourty these gates were kept closed for privacy and neatness, and to keep out the moth-eaten donkeys who grazed on the roadsides, their wretched little legs hobbled to prevent them from straying. Later there was a pony to keep inside the field. My grandparents had neither the need nor the desire to own a pony, but my grandmother had inadvertently won her in a church raffle. When she was delivered she was turned out to pasture, named Thisby and never broken or used in any way. We used to feed apples to her and to the other horses we would find gazing out over the gates along the road. When my father discovered these treats, he made us ration the apples for fear of bringing the entire equine population down with colic.

Ballinacourty faced the sea, sheltered very slightly by some sparse trees which had managed to survive the salt air and winter storms. Rooks built their nests in these trees, at the same height as the third floor, where my sister and I slept. The noise level was rather higher than that of any New York or London street on which I subsequently lived.

Like many Anglo-Irish houses, Ballinacourty was a combination of beauty, taste, squalor and discomfort. The best things about it were the garden, the setting and my grandmother's drawing room.

Like Glenville, Ballinacourty had a wonderful walled garden. On entering through the latched wooden door, one found oneself in my grandmother's flower garden. It consisted of some semi-formal flower beds, in the centre of which lay a small lawn, slightly sunken and with a sprinkling of daisies and a slatted wooden garden bench. A well-placed apple tree or two helped separate this little garden from the larger one and made it a separate entity.

The garden was not completely symmetrical since at one time there had been a house or possibly a barn attached to it. The opening to this ruin remained, as did the outer walls of the building, and the area was used as a subsidiary vegetable garden. I still dream of this smaller garden, regularly and undramatically, but vividly enough not to be sure whether what I remember is an accurate picture of a past reality or a gradually developed illusion. The memories of the small garden with the lawn in the centre and of the second flower section, a herbaceous border facing a strip of lawn which led up to a large black fig tree in the corner, are warm and golden with a sense of well-being and sunshine. It was not only the delphiniums, dahlias, daisies and lupines which created this glow; it was physically warmer in the garden. The brick held the heat of the summer sun and the walls were high enough to keep out the wind and the sound of the wind. The garden was the quietest place in Ballinacourty.

Both the house and Ballinacourty village looked out over a long inlet with Dungarvan far to the right at the innermost point of the bay and the open sea to the left, a lighthouse marking the headland. The view offered an extreme contrast to the garden. Here the light was cold, not golden. It was bright and nearly always windy—to the extent that we very rarely used the formal, fanlighted front door and, instead, came in through a side entrance with a gum boot and potting shed atmosphere. The wind, the rooks, the sea all combined to suggest something beautiful but hard and unsheltered.

The drawing room was the best indoor place, and like the

garden, it seemed an Anglo-Irish pool of calm close to the menace of the Atlantic with its ceaseless erosion and threat of death by drowning. My grandmother kept the room full of unassuming cut flowers, snapdragons and sweet Williams, and the sofas and chairs were covered with old-fashioned chintz—large cabbage roses, pink and pale green and creamy glazed whites. The room itself was light, the windows faced the sea and there was a small french door onto the veranda. It had the charming atmosphere of a room for which nothing has been bought.

The worst places in the house were the bathrooms and the kitchen. If the elegance and the lines of the walled garden contributed to my love of the seventeenth century, the bathrooms of my childhood have left me with an aversion to Victorian plumbing (with the single exception of the heated towel rails in Glenville—often the only warm spot on the entire second floor) and twentieth-century linoleum and skimpy porcelain fittings. The main bathroom at Ballinacourty was cold and meagre in comparison with the rest of the house, which had character and warmth and generous proportions. It had been made over by my grandparents when they moved in, so I dread to think what it had been like before. The second-best bathroom was a dark attic, full of storeroom junk and boxes, at the far end of which a lavatory and washbasin had been installed. No other modification had taken place and it was a room which occasionally featured in my nightmares.

Ever since I learned to read I have mentally set scenes from my favourite books in familiar and sometimes wildly inappropriate settings. The kitchen in *Wuthering Heights* will always be for me the one at Ballinacourty. It wasn't all threatening—the window looked out toward the garden, and the sill held, alongside two or three stained and dog-eared cookbooks, a jug of flowers. There was a large wooden kitchen table—as with the one at Glenville, years of scrubbing had worn away the softer part of the wood and left deep ridges which made the scrubbing even more necessary. The bad areas for a small child were the deep, stained sink, in which there was often soaking a saucepan encrusted with burnt porridge; the cats' dish under the sink, sometimes containing a partially eaten fish or milk which had acquired a skin, partly of its own formation but with a layer of coal dust and the occasional cat's hair. I remember in that kitchen the cook good-naturedly suggesting that Julia and I be allowed to help in the preparation of some non-threatening food. Our governess told us to go and wash our hands, saying that all good cooks washed their hands before starting work. The cook, naïvely and half intending to set her right, said that she didn't, falling straight into the trap. My governess smirked, I kept my head down, but the cook, I think, missed the gibe. The floor of the kitchen was flagstone which always looked, and probably was, slightly dirty. The kitchen underscored the real and most extreme drawback of Ballinacourty. Food.

Meals were a constant source of anxiety for me in that house. The standard of cuisine was amateur at best—each cook would be a local girl employed in her first "position." She would be completely inexperienced and would need to be instructed in the simplest procedures. For this she would receive little more than a token wage, and as soon as she had acquired minimal skills she would leave for a better-paying job. It was a situation which didn't make anyone really happy and led to some ghastly lunchtime confrontations, usually between my grandfather and me. Often dishes in keeping with my grandfather's economical nature would appear at the table. Beef hearts was one ("Bee farts?" my son asked incredulously the first time I told him of it). I was terrified of being caught between my grandfather and the physical impossibility of swallowing the horror on my plate.

For breakfast there was porridge which had been slowly cooked overnight, on a stove which also provided all the hot water for the house. There was a similar stove or range at Glenville, and each was always referred to by its trade name, Aga or Esse. (One never spoke of vacuuming a carpet either; it was always Hoovering.) The fire in these ranges was guarded like an eternal flame, for if it went out it was a major task to cool down the range, rake it out, clean it, reset it and get it going again. During one of these calamities there could be no cooking or hot water.

Lunch was the main meal of the day and the one which I most dreaded. There was a late tea which included cheese or a salad. This held no fear for me and provided the main part of my diet. The day ended with Horlicks or Ovaltine and a digestive biscuit before bed. Despite the unappetizing aspects of two of the three daily meals, I don't remember ever feeling hungry. It was summer and the garden was full of wonderful fruit and vegetables. Apples, mostly the small sweet pink and gold Beauty of Bath, black figs and wineberries. Also peas, carrots and baby onions, which we would eat straight from the earth.

At the end of summer, apples were laid on racks covered with straw and carrots were buried in sand for consumption during the winter. In both cases time produced a softening and wrinkling effect. I suppose that more than half of what we ate varied with the seasons. Frozen food was unknown to us for two reasons: we thought of fruit and vegetables as free, and few houses had an icebox. Canned fruit was a disappointing luxury, special only because of its rarity.

Neither my sister nor I had particularly foul table manners—I was about to say "by modern American standards" (my father used to say when we were noisy or spoiled, "Don't behave like an American child." It was a bewildering prejudice since his acquaintanceship with underage United States citizens was limited)—but if we didn't come up to scratch, my grandfather would take his handkerchief out of his pocket and tie it, like a bandage, over one eye to shield himself from the sight of us.

I thought this heavy-handed behaviour unfair, partly because it wasn't really deserved and partly because I thought his own manners were far from polished and bore more than a trace of his colonial past. My grandfather had been born in New Zealand in 1881 and spent his childhood there. His descriptions of a tough, masculine and happy childhood sometimes sounded like an excerpt

from *Boy's Own*, but I imagine they were not far from the reality.
He told of robbing orchards (for me a charming and old-fashioned
crime since I have to coax my children to eat an apple), playing
truant, climbing mountains accompanied by a pet goat. He rode
bareback and lost his teeth in a fall while galloping over treacherous sands. His mother was highly religious and given to texts.
"Be sure your sin will find you out," she would say, and years
later my grandfather would quote her with a grin. As a child he
had been mortified by seeing her on the street singing hymns with
the Salvation Army. Not surprisingly, my grandfather attended
church only under extreme pressure.

When he was old enough he took off for Australia looking for
better prospects. For a time he drove a truck, but lost that job after
an accident. He swam well and held the local record for underwater
swimming. His leisure time was spent on the beach at Sydney
shooting breakers; his nights spent playing poker. After he was
initially stung, a friend, in the time-honoured way, taught him to
compute basic odds and he eventually became a successful gambler. From the time I was five he would give me simple and at that
time useless advice such as "Never stay in with less than a pair of
sevens."

At his first boardinghouse he asked the landlord where the
bath was and was told: "What do you want a bath for? I'm
seventy years old and I've never had a bath in my life." At the
same boardinghouse there was a row about bedbugs, won hands
down by my grandfather, who, perhaps still smarting from the
bath incident, came armed with a matchbox containing live
examples of his complaint. These stories, as may be imagined,
went down better with Julia and me than with his own generation.

When the First World War broke out Grandpa and his friends
enlisted. They were sent first to Egypt for training and then to
Gallipoli, where he fought with the machine-gun section of the
18th Battalion. His thirty-fourth birthday was spent in battle, his
section attached to the Gurkhas defending Kaiajik Aghala. He also
saw action in the second assault. Though never shy of an anecdote

depicting himself in a heroic role, my grandfather never spoke of Gallipoli. He saw his best friend's head blown off and this may have been the reason for his silence.

Then Grandpa caught pneumonia and was sent to a hospital in Alexandria and later to London General, where he met my grandmother, a VAD (a member of the Voluntary Aid Detachment), before he returned to active service in France.

His next misadventure was a happier one. My grandfather, veteran of Gallipoli, dislocated his arm in a boyish snowball battle. He and his Australian friends had never seen snow, or robins, before and were fascinated by both. Books and Christmas cards of English origin had not prepared them for how slowly and how silently snow drifts down. His dislocated arm took him back to London General and, in 1916, he married my grandmother in a registry office. Despite the intense disapproval of her family—he was not only a colonial but a noncommissioned officer and my grandmother's father was a brigadier general—a second wedding took place in a church with her family present. My code-breaking, jackal-hunting great-grandfather had been amused and eventually won over by Grandpa's disrespectful attitude. My grandfather was completely unawed by generals and British Army protocol and was equally at ease and friendly with all ranks. He took the view that he had suffered hardship and danger on England's behalf and that England should be grateful.

It was easy to see how my grandmother had been swept off her feet. He was strong and confident with crisp golden hair and very blue eyes. That I should be given, so many years later, a physical description of him was unusual enough for me to realize that he once had made a strong impression. This impression was due to his determined nature and literal-minded virility, as well as his undoubted handsomeness.

My grandfather had had a hard war, but he came through alive and, except for his unspoken memories of Gallipoli, unscathed. Few of the men on my grandmother's side did as well. Her brother Sainthill was killed in action at the end of August

1918, at the age of twenty-three. Just before his death, Saint, as the family called him, wrote to his mother: ". . . The war goes on monotonously, and everything that happens is just rather less than an event, and forgotten very soon." He was awarded the Military Cross and seventy years later my grandmother still mourns him.

His loss, among others not quite so immediate, gave my grandmother a lifelong interest, though mild by the time I knew her, in spiritualism. She'd been to more than her share of séances and would talk with enthusiasm, though not in front of my grandfather, about automatic writing and prophetic dreams. There were also bookshelves of what might be loosely described as case histories of messages and appearances from the other side. These books were not frightening and I read them for a time, but the unimaginative repetition soon bored me, even though they were based on loss, a theme never far, either then or now, from my thoughts.

Most families had suffered the cruel loss of at least one young man and I didn't need to be overloaded with imagination or compassion to see that any book or medium who claimed that this loss was not absolute would have a wide market among the bereaved. I once asked my father some childish question about "class" and he answered dismissively and with an uncharacteristic note of bitterness: "The entire English upper class was killed in the First World War."

My grandfather's stories always started: "In my young days in New Zealand . . . " and ended with an allusion to how soft our lives were in comparison. He used to tell us how the doctor came once a year. Teeth and tonsils were removed on the kitchen table. I do a modified version of the same thing with my own children, with tales of the dark ages when Coca-Cola and television didn't exist. (To their credit, both children greet these sanctimonious stories with hoots of derision and can do a very credible parody if the occasion warrants it.)

These stories were sometimes self-serving but never sentimental and there was no suggestion of any hankering after a family reunion. On the contrary. My grandmother lived in fear of New Zealand relatives inviting themselves for open-ended periods of time. The only sign that my grandfather had any interest in New Zealand was his subscription to *The Auckland Times*, which came by mail, somewhat out of date. It ended up, along with *The Financial Times*, cut into pink squares beside the lavatory in the second-best bathroom.

Each morning, Grandpa would wake us with a quotation from Longfellow, which ended with: "Still achieving, still pursuing, learn to labour and to wait." He followed this up with some lines from a music hall comic he'd admired, which included a reference to drinking his own bath water.

He habitually addressed us, not without affection, as "you little ticks," although if one were in particular favour one might be called "Blossom." He used to ask for the yellow, lumpy Bird's custard which accompanied pudding with the words "Pass the ointment, please." My grandmother would sigh. Later, I heard one of my great-aunts on my father's side refer to him as "that dreadful common man that Babbty married," but we found him interesting and entertaining if sometimes alarming. Of course, we were interested and entertained by moments which horrified my great-aunts. They probably had been present when he'd tried to liven things up with a touch of coarse humour. I can't imagine that "Every drop counts, as the monkey said when he peed into the ocean," did much to defrost a sticky social occasion. Or: "You need it up here," tapping our heads, "not down here," patting our bottoms. His habit of asking a Roman Catholic father who had had yet another addition to an already large family, "Did your mother never tell you anything?" was also sometimes received with poor grace.

He was fond or, at least, tolerant of me since I showed more interest in his stories of three-day poker games and stock-market coups than did any grown-up. Certainly no adult listened with as much wide-eyed avarice as I did to his calculations of just how much money he would make if the Russian government felt, for some reason not yet apparent to us, moved to pay off the bonds floated by the Czarist regime. His purchase of and enthusiasm for these seemingly worthless pieces of paper may have been one of the first reasons his family later had him declared legally incompetent. (Of course, now that some Russian bonds are being redeemed for a small percentage of their face value, he has been, in a sense, vindicated. There must be a moral in this somewhere, but I can't find it, unless it is to show just how worthless the phrase "I told you so" really is.) But in those days he still played the market a little and I, while still quite a small child, used to take messages when he was having his nap if his stockbroker, Mr. Cakebread (his Dickensian name shortened to Cakey by my grandfather), called. I proved quite efficient in dealing with messages and could tell my grandfather, when he woke up, just how many Gussies he'd bought or sold and for how much.

I was also my grandfather's willing accomplice in the baiting of the clergy. Our family attended church on Sunday mornings, with no great show of enthusiasm but as a matter of course. The females, even Julia and I, wore hats. My grandfather was the only one who ever abstained from attendance or whom I ever heard complain when a major church festival, such as Harvest Thanksgiving, made it necessary for him to show up. I was aware even then that, unlikely though it seemed, he was not a believer. Perhaps once a summer, the Rector and his family were asked to lunch. Apart from my grandfather's lunchtime bottle of stout, alcohol was never served at family meals by either my parents or my grandparents, but my grandfather, well aware that the Rector didn't drink, would always open a bottle of wine. He would offer some to the Rector and, when he refused, pour some for himself and half a glass for me. Then, going through his usual noisy performance of knife sharpening prior to carving the overdone roast, he would pleasantly inquire: "Do you eat meat?"

Apart from the seasonal teasing of the Rector, when my grandparents entertained they would ask people for drinks. The distances their guests would travel now seems quite extreme in light of the entertainment provided. My grandfather would mix his special cocktails beforehand and children would pick wineberries from the garden to float on top of them. These cocktails were generally considered fairly disgusting, and knowing my grandfather's commitment to economy, I'm sure they were. They had an unpleasant rich brown colour and contained quite a lot of vermouth. Perhaps because of this, there was always plenty left over and we would be given a glass, diluted by water, with lunch the following day. My grandfather, who was by no stretch of the imagination a heavy drinker (an opinion I can hold with confidence, as there were plenty among his family and friends with whom to compare him), had a kind of respect for alcohol. He thought the feeding of leftover cocktails was good for us, not just a way of avoiding waste. He taught us to pour his lunchtime stout into a glass without turning it to foam, and if we failed, he would tell us we'd never make good barmaids.

Once, when I'd been left alone with my grandfather, I felt sick and as though I were about to vomit. I told my grandfather. He looked at me thoughtfully and, knowing nothing of child care, gave me a small glass of sweet sherry. It did the trick.

I don't think that economy at Ballinacourty was a sign of eccentricity. My grandfather was a self-made man. By the time my mother was ten he'd provided his family with a good house in Kensington, a staff of three, and a decent education for his children. Then he lost all his money when the stock-market plummetted in 1929. My grandmother, whose background had left her totally unprepared for such a life, found herself running a household in rooms above a greengrocer's shop in Bayswater. My grandfather took a deep breath and started all over again. He played golf and kept company with people my grandmother considered "very common." Gradually their standard of living improved. They moved into a little house in Putney beside the railroad tracks and by the time he retired he was more than comfortably off. But the memory of the struggle had left its mark. Beef hearts and homemade lavatory paper might be more visible than the petty economies others practice, but I don't remember any simultaneous extravagances which would make these economies ridiculous.

To get to the rocky beach in front of the house, we went down a short gravel path and across a field where my grandparents kept a cow, which provided milk for the house. None of my family had any interest in the cinema, but the first cow, a pretty wide-eyed Jersey, was called Greta Garbo. We pronounced it "Greeta." A later cow of a darker-complexioned breed was named Jane Russell. It was not until I came to America more than twenty years later that I saw my first Garbo movie. But once, when my grandfather had been left in charge of me (perhaps the same visit during which he had successfully dosed me with sherry), he had to go to Cork for the day. Rather than leave me with the cook—a perfectly decent girl named Dolores—he decided to take us both with him. It was not a logical decision. There was a limit to how much trouble I could have got into at home, and he must have known that Dolores would have been responsible enough not to abandon me in the event the house caught fire. She was not the type to take advantage of his absence with raids on the sherry, entertaining stray males or child abuse. Having got us as far as Cork, my grandfather either had a lunch engagement or, it now occurs to me, decided he couldn't face eating with Dolores and me. There would have been a certain amount of awkwardness on all our parts if the three of us had shared a meal. So he gave her some money and told her to take me to lunch and a movie. To this day I am astonished by the complete reversal of all established rules. Dolores was seventeen, but I doubt she'd ever been to Cork before or seen a traffic light or, possibly, eaten a meal in a restaurant, and, if she had, certainly not as the one in charge. She was both shortsighted and overweight, which made her painfully shy, unsure of herself and unobservant. Nevertheless, she steered us both into a nasty little café and after nervous deliberation we both ordered sausages and mash. When our meals arrived they were covered with a grey-brown gravy I hadn't bargained for. I left mine but Dolores methodically and solemnly cleared her plate. Fortunately, there was a cinema a block away which involved crossing only one street. The film was *The Young Widow*, and the star was Jane Russell. For the first time I realized that for everyone except me (and possibly Dolores) the name Jane Russell suggested a human being. I had seen only three or four films in my life but I knew that this wasn't one of the all-time greats. Even so, the entire incident left a very deep impression. It was the first time I had ever benefited from someone's desire to shirk responsibility. It was a heady feeling. The casual, almost irresponsible attitude of my grandfather, and the way accepted rules had been waved aside when they became inconvenient, gave me an optimistic view of the future. I felt the same sensation again a few years later when my other grandmother, deciding one cold December afternoon that she didn't feel up to going to a church Christmas Sale of Work and spending an afternoon in a drafty hall, salved her conscience by giving Julia and me five shillings to spend on her behalf—more money than would normally pass through our hands in a couple of months. And in both cases the benefit so casually conferred. (My own children when granted too many requests in a row will ask: "Is anything the matter?")

The cows were not the only objects of interest in the field. Among the purple-headed thistles around which the cows carefully grazed there were wildflowers and sometimes a rabbit could be seen hopping away as we approached. Later, when Myxomatosis spread to that part of the country the rabbits disappeared, except for the occasional sight of one horribly dead. Hedgehogs, too, were usually only seen under sad conditions—a drowned one would sometimes be found in the morning, having perished while drinking out of the cows' water trough.

Grass grew right up to the edge where the field abruptly ended. There was a three- or four-foot drop, which we scrambled down to a pebble and seashell beach. Gradually the Atlantic storms were eroding the land as, in time, they would turn the pebbles and sharp seashells beneath our feet into sand. Where the pebbles ended the rocks began, covered with seaweed, crustaceans and other primitive forms of life. To swim, one had to clamber over the rocks, stubbing toes, slipping on the slimy green long-furred mossy growths, always a little nervous of crabs and scared of the worse unknown, out to where there was a glorious stretch of clear clean sand. The tide never went out far enough to transform this horseshoe-shaped haven into a beach, but it was a tiny, perfect harbor, created fortuitously below Ballinacourty House by a freak in the currents and tide.

This was where my grandfather taught me to swim. I was his eldest grandchild and I now realize that he was quite fond of me in an exasperated way. It would have been easier for him to deal with a boy, but I was happy for him to have to modify a certain roughness in his nature. It would be hard to say which of us was the more afraid of his provoking me to tears. He met me on any grounds he was able to and was always generous with his attention. This attention was not always welcome since I was a little afraid of him, of failure and of his attempts to teach me to swim. His impatience at my cowardice would be shown first at the moment I displayed it and would come up for review again during the next meal. Eventually I learned to swim, but the dominant emotion for both of us was relief rather than a sense of achievement.

Since there was no physical danger involved, I did a little better on the golf course than in the water. Grandpa liked to play golf, a leftover from his days as a stockbroker in London. He did not have golfing partners, probably because the golf course was almost exclusively patronized by the new Catholic professional class from Dungarvan. In lieu of a more suitable companion, I was often sent to accompany him. He gave me one of his old putters, repaired with sticking plaster, and there was talk of lessons and some miniature clubs, but they never materialized. I didn't then consider, nor do I now, that these were broken promises. Later he had me try to write my signature in an adult manner in order to own some shares in my own name and he talked about the possibility of my going with him on holiday to Knokke in Belgium. I was grateful for these attempts to build a relationship with me. He wasn't good with children and had been an indifferent father. Since he couldn't enter my world he was trying to draw me into his. It was not his fault that, by the time any of these plans might have been practical it was no longer possible for us to undertake them. He had become prematurely senile, probably suffering from what would now be diagnosed as Alzheimer's disease.

My grandfather had no interest in the arts and considered reading during the day a sign of laziness. He would drag me away from my books and set me to work outside. After an initial moment of confusion and mild resentment, I enjoyed the chores he set me. I never rake leaves or weed the raspberry patch or dig potatoes or undertake any other strangely satisfying, simple, repetitive task without thinking of hot summer afternoons at Ballinacourty turning hay. The tall grass would be cut with a scythe and left to dry where it fell. Later it would be turned by pitchfork, and the other side of the thin swatches of green hay exposed to the air and, with luck, the sun. When it was dry it was stacked into haycocks and then taken into the barn to feed the cows during the winter.

I remember turning hay one afternoon with a boy who worked for my grandparents. Most of my grandparents' employees came from the same labour pool, a large Catholic family who lived in a small cottage just down the road. A shiny new golf ball came over the bank which separated the field from the golf course. Tom quickly picked up the ball and stuffed it into a hole in the hedge. A moment later, he was looking the owner in the eye and denying ever having seen it. I watched, silent and phlegmatic. I think that used balls could be sold at the golf club for a few pence.

We used to walk over the golf course looking for balls although there would have been no question of either Julia or me cashing them in. It was more like searching for treasure. In the same spirit we would look for mushrooms that grew wild in the fields and take them home, where we would later fry them in butter and eat them on toast for tea. That children should be able, unsupervised, to pick and eat wild mushrooms is a metaphor for the benevolence of nature in Ireland. There is very little there to sting or bite or poison. Toadstools were, of course, poisonous but their shape and color advertised their danger clearly.

The golf course was also where we played with the local children. Some sheep and two or three donkeys lived there, grazing on the rough grass which grew on either side of the course. The boys would carefully approach the donkeys, which weren't broken for riding, although they would undoubtedly pull a cart before their shabby lives were through, and leap onto their backs. The donkeys invariably bucked them off, sometimes kicked them, and then clumsily dashed away.

Julia and I were as tight-lipped as secret agents about these games with the donkeys, even though neither ever played a part more demanding than that of an admiring spectator. I am not so sure now that our instinctive caution was warranted. Both my grandmother and my mother used to refer, with amusement, to a game which Aunt Anne, my mother's younger sister, used to play with the donkeys at Ballydavid. She would get under a rug which she had spread out on the lawn, at the far end of which the donkeys were grazing. (One should not infer from this that the lawn had been allowed to deteriorate to a point where a couple of donkeys could find a square meal on it. The lawn at Ballydavid, after an almost invisible boundary, joined one of a series of fields on a mild slope in front of the house, creating a pleasant open view of tall grass and trees. Gradually, when they had become used to the bulge under the tartan, she would creep a little closer, moving so slowly that they either did not notice or paid no attention. Eventually a moment would arrive, although not instigated by any sudden movement from the child under the rug, when the donkeys would register that the seemingly inanimate large colourful blob on the lawn was creeping up on them, and react with dramatic alarm, kicking and bucking before fleeing the monster.

Each year we returned we would find that one of our playmates, little older than I was, had joined the adult labour force and was no longer available for these amateur rodeos.

One of these boys took me fishing. One evening the sprats came in close to shore, followed by a shoal of mackerel which preyed on them. We stood on the rocks which jutted out into the sea, with spinners attached to our homemade rods. I caught my first and only fish. I was much too afraid to take the wretched thing off the line, let alone kill it. One of the boys did this for me and I took it home, where it was cooked and served to the cats on the chipped enamel dish. My father was allergic to fish and this exempted the whole family from eating it. I imagine my grand-parents didn't much like it either, since, although it was an inexpensive nutritious food, I don't remember anyone ever forcing me to eat it. Occasionally a van would come around and fish would be bought from it, but only for the cats.

The thrill of my first fishing evening lingered on for some time. The excitement of the boys seemed to have been a reflection of the frenzy in the water below. Despite my squeamish unwill-ingness to touch the fish, kill it or even eat it, I felt part of the event. One afternoon soon afterward, I was on the beach with my governess and Julia when the sprats, followed again by the predatory and convulsive mackerel, came in close to shore. I ran up the road to try to enlist some of the local boys. But it was daytime and, as the first mother I met—a beshawled and prema-turely lined widow—told me, they had to work.

From my grandparents' house, unless the weather was very rough, you could usually see small fishing boats in the bay. None of these fishermen knew how to swim. One of them told me that if he were going to drown he wanted it to be quick. That answer, though dramatically satisfying, particularly to a small child who was at the time reading *David Copperfield* (also containing some good donkey scenes), did not tell the whole story. The beaches were always deserted at Ballinacourty. Even allowing for the sparse population and the chilly summer days, there should have been other children swimming or paddling or playing on the sand since there were few alternative choices of free recreation. I think they all, fisherman and farmer alike, feared or at least respected the sea and did not regard it as a plaything. I had a glimpse of the menace which lay beneath the water when I saw a fisherman on the little pier near the one small shop in Ballinacourty catch a conger eel. It was huge and evil-looking and dangerous, and it took forever to die. I imagine it must have been caught by mistake, though perhaps for sport. It is unlikely that anyone would have eaten it, or even known how to prepare it as food. Fish was eaten on Fridays by the Catholic majority but was not otherwise popular.

Our exposure to the animal kingdom was not limited to fish and wild donkeys. It was at Ballinacourty that we first encountered pets. My father hated cats, and even dogs, which he liked in an unsentimental way, were never allowed indoors. He kept a Labrador or two but we weren't encouraged to play with them or show them too much affection. They accompanied my father when he went shooting and retrieved the birds he shot. If we were seen making a fuss over one of them he would say, "Stop making a fool of that animal." My grandparents, on the other hand, owned several cats. The cats lived indoors and slept on my grandparents' bed if they weren't out on a nocturnal feline errand. The window of my grandparents' room was left slightly open so that a cat could climb up the veranda, cross the roof and squeeze home when he pleased. The main cat was an extremely battered old tom called Atom.

Each summer a little bit more of Atom would be missing. First an eye, then chunks of both ears and eventually one foot, which he must have lost in a rabbit trap. The cats were loved by both my grandparents, and my grandmother, in particular, was grief-stricken when one came to an untimely end or died of old age. It

was never tactful to refer to the deceased. There was often a litter
of kittens in the house. One cat, I remember, chose my grandmother's underwear drawer for her confinement, and I saw
another litter born in my grandfather's study.

The constant presence of cats, and the place of honour they
held, was, if not exactly painful, certainly distasteful to my father.
One Sunday, when he and my mother had come to visit us, they
were sitting in the drawing room. My father was doing his best to
ignore a mother cat and kittens which Julia and I were cooing over.
One kitten, with the unfailing instinct felines have for a cat
loather in the room, ran up the leg of my father's trousers. It took
some time and the combined efforts of all the adults to dislodge
the fugitive since it had panicked halfway up and sought to secure
its position by digging its tiny but sharp claws into my father's
flesh.

I read my first full-length grown-up book during one of these
summer visits. Before, my mother had read out loud to me, trying
to whet my appetite for reading. She read *Lorna Doone* and then
Ivanhoe, skipping the descriptions of torture. Eschewing the fine
tradition she'd initiated, I started with a Bulldog Drummond
adventure story called *The Black Hand*. It took me some time;
many of the words were unfamiliar and most of the places and
people mentioned were far outside my range of experience. The
dialogue, even then, was more than slightly dated. After that I
read my way through a whole bookshelf of detective stories,
mainly Agatha Christie.

The next summer I tried to write one of these stories, but here
the limit of my experience in the world of butlers, diamond
necklaces and Rolls-Royces proved an insurmountable obstacle. I
asked my grandmother for information with which to fill these
gaps. She advised me to stick to subjects with which I was more
familiar. My life and surroundings seemed so dreary and banal
that I disregarded this advice as hopelessly naïve. I would have
disdained equally the suggestion that the day would come when I
would be slightly acquainted with the world in which these novels

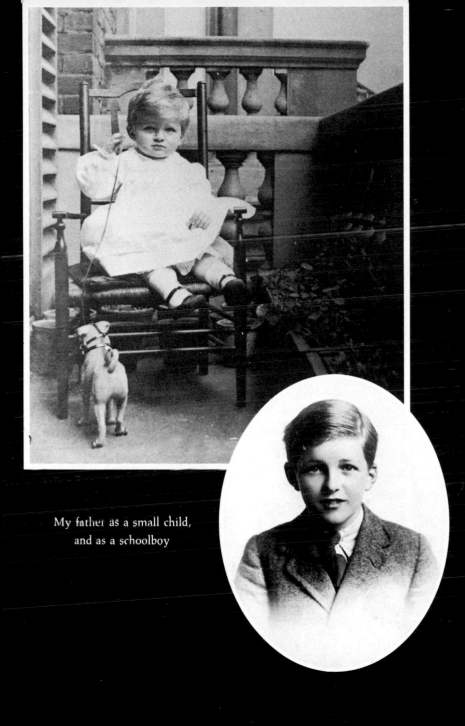

My father as a small child,
and as a schoolboy

My father as a young man

My mother as a girl

In the library at Glenville

The hall at Glenville in my grandmother's time

Above, one of the oval ponds at Glenville; left, my sisters in front of the greenhouse; below, inside the greenhouse

My father, before a steeplechase

My mother, photographed by my stepfather

My father late in life

Above, my grandmother Woodhouse as a
V.A.D. with her brother, shortly before he
was killed in action; left, my grandfather
Robert Woodhouse, a portrait taken for
his mother before he went off to war

My grandmother with my mother

Above, my grandmother Goff with her brother Charles; right, a drawing from the diary my grandmother kept as a girl

, "gellinot". We had'nt to much
nch, before we had to troupe into the

roff's

sin

way

but

nised   "Die Schauspielers"
Wirballen.

is in the train. She was very
played "patience" to-gether.
at Petersburg at about 8 in the

My grandmother Goff with my father (standing), his brother
Charles and his sister Dodo, on her lap

Colonel   Goffe –
A Drawing by W. N. Gardiner, from the Devon-
shire Clarendon Picture at Dr. Brooke's,
in Leaden Hall Street –

were very loosely set and that the day-to-day life and people of Ballinacourty would seem infinitely more remote, of greater interest and value.

Two or three years later this total immersion in faded, worn paperbacks was rewarded. I earned, or rather won, my first writing money and found myself printed in *Collins' Magazine* for children. I had won first prize in a competition for an essay about one's favourite fictional detective. I wrote about Hercule Poirot, Agatha Christie's Belgian detective, a character about whom by then I should have been comfortably able to write a thesis.

Soon afterward *Collins' Magazine* ran a competition for a full-length novel written by a child. Part of the prize was full-scale publication. I knew my limits and I never even contemplated this one. The winning entry, which was serialized in the magazine, was of a remarkably high standard. I used to enter competitions from time to time and occasionally won something. One time I narrowly missed a prize (characteristically I'd forgotten to mention my age) for a poem modeled after *Hiawatha*. Those early morning recitals of my grandfather's had left their mark.

My parents were pleased by these modest successes, in part because I did poorly at school. I was pleased by the attention I got from them and my other relatives but I wasn't particularly excited, since I suspected that the number of entries wasn't huge. Also I knew that two of my schoolmates, following my assurance that this was easy money (or in this case book tokens), had submitted their own efforts. One, a stiff, conventional romantic story, was accepted. The other, a Western, was not. The Western was the occasion of my first clumsy attempt at literary criticism. I told my friend, Alma, that she couldn't use the phrase "he laughed harshly." This advice was as gratefully received as unsolicited criticism usually is.

Most of my reading took place during the day. In the evenings we would listen to the wireless. My grandparents liked to listen to middlebrow concerts, but could sometimes be persuaded to tune in to a variety show. Julia and I had a passion for them, especially for the comics. I suspect that they also seemed funny to my grandfather, who had a fairly unsophisticated sense of humour, so we often had some uncharacteristic indulgence from him when we made these requests. While we listened my grandmother used to play patience, and taught me one or two simple games. She played the type which more often than not "comes out." My grandfather, who regarded this kind of thing as an unproductive waste of time, would occasionally play a variation of a patience, but his version had more stringent rules and could rarely be successfully solved. Even then I realized that each had chosen the game more suited to his nature.

One evening I sat alone with my grandmother while she sorted through a drawerful of old letters and photographs. As I watched her, fascinated, she would read a letter, pause, then throw it in the fire. Photographs she would linger on for a moment or two longer, sometimes with a trace of sadness. Once or twice I would ask to see one of the photographs which seemed to move her more than the others. Each time she refused, saying it wasn't a good likeness. I asked why she was burning them and she told me that when she was gone there would be no one left to whom they would mean anything. I accepted this, since both my grandparents seemed immeasurably old to me. Another time, reinforcing this impression, she said to me, "When I look back it seems to me that just yesterday I was your age." She would say this perhaps twice a summer, getting my attention by addressing the subject of mortality, about which I had so much unspoken fear. Other adults used to offer such platitudes as "Don't wish your life away" or "You'll be old soon enough" in response to our quite reasonable impatience to arrive at a point where we would no longer be controlled by arbitrary and seemingly pointless rules. Their clichés I quite rightly disregarded, but my grandmother made it personal by both speaking of her life passing and allowing me to see, for the first time, that the fears I held about the mortality of others also applied to me.

Circuses were the high point of our summers. Soon after we

arrived in Ballinacourty we would start to see small posters stuck
on telegraph poles on the Dungarvan road. Slightly larger ones
would appear on the walls of the town itself. There were two
travelling circuses which would come through Dungarvan each
summer. One of them was called Duffy's. Soon after the first
poster had been spotted, the process of working on my grandmother would begin. The possibility of appealing to my grandfather did not occur to us. The circuses would be some weeks ahead
and Granny would rarely give us an unqualified promise. Usually
it was "Let's see closer to the time." There always seemed to be
a real possibility that we wouldn't go, but I don't remember ever
being disappointed when the day arrived.

No entertainment I have seen since, however magnificent or
original or artistically valuable, has ever produced emotions to
equal the anticipation and delight evoked by those visits to the
circus. We would arrive in the late afternoon and enter the tent,
which had been erected that afternoon. There would be the
exciting smell of damp canvas, bruised grass, tobacco, animals and
the crowd; the uncirculated air tinged with a little breath of the
warm summer's day outside. The music was thin, cheap and tinny
and heightened the excitement we felt as we took our seats, crude
wooden bleachers, a few feet away from the edge of the ring. I
have no memory of any refreshments or souvenirs being sold, but
if they were, I know that we neither expected nor received them.
Few of the audience had money to spare, and the circus proprietors
understood what the market, one evening's worth, in these poor
and sparsely populated areas would support. Few had the means,
or indeed the tradition, of impulse buying or instant gratification,
and the lack of demand limited the supply. The actual level of the
circus was of no higher quality than one would expect, but we gave
it our entire concentration, watching each act with wide-eyed
fascination. Our favourites were the clowns, but we were equally
entranced by the fat ponies and bareback riders, the trapeze artists
and tightrope walkers, slightly less so by the shabby lions,
although we did not allow our sympathy for them to detract from

the extreme pleasure of the outing. I can't imagine where these performers came from; it seems unlikely that all of them were Irish. Perhaps the Irish circuses were the ones where performers ended up if they didn't make it to the big time. But we loved it all in a way that seems impossible to feel about the three-ring extravaganzas to which I used to take my children.

After the circus, for sixpence, one could tour the caged animals. There weren't any sideshows, and the tour served only as a gentle letdown after the excitement of the circus itself. Next day the tent would be pulled down, and the circus would move on to the next small town, leaving nothing behind except crumpled candy wrappers and frayed posters and inspiration for a new set of games and make-believe.

Before familiarity breeds contempt it encourages a jaded tendency to take achievement for granted. We were dazzled by the circus performers but only respectfully impressed by the standard of horsemanship at the Dungarvan Show. An Irish circus was by definition limited, but a show jumping event in a small town in Ireland might include some of the competitors at the Dublin Horse Show, an international event in which Irish horses and riders competed on equal terms with those of any country in the world.

The Dungarvan Agricultural Show would be held on the same site where the circus had taken place. The neatly printed catalogue would arrive by mail some time before and contrasted with the orange and red on the circus posters in a way which reflected our attitude toward the two events. My grandmother would enter fruit and vegetables from her garden. We would compete in two flower classes: one for the best flower arrangement, one for the largest variety of wildflowers. I was always beaten in the flower-arrangement class, once by a collection of marigolds in an earthenware jug. It had a Van Gogh look and was quite effective, but I thought the judges' decision was unfair. "I didn't know you were allowed to do that," I complained in the time-honoured way, like a representational painter whining about the first successful abstract artist. For the largest-variety class, we worked hard, scouring the hedgerows and fields we passed on our afternoon walks. There were an enormous number of wildflowers, most of which I have never encountered in America. Of course, the same opportunities were available to the other competitors, and although each year I felt confident I would win, I never did.

Walks were a daily afternoon practice. I cannot imagine today's children embarking on them with the same monotonous regularity. I'm not quite sure what function they were meant to serve. Probably to structure the day and to get us out of the house while adults napped. It can't have been for the exercise. Our afternoon walk would have followed a morning on the beach running about and swimming. We would already often have walked what my children would consider a tremendous distance to the beach since we didn't only patronize the one in front of our grandparents' house. Walks were basically boring but had occasional redeeming features. Stories from our governess if she could be persuaded, dogs and horses to pet, pleasant fears of geese and turkeys. And, of course, collecting the wildflowers which were to make our fortunes at the Dungarvan Show.

Even without a circus or agricultural show Dungarvan was an exciting place to visit. It was a small market town, and my grandparents would drive in to shop once or twice a week. These outings were the high points of our week and, I now suspect, were also welcomed by my grandmother and grandfather as small breaks in the monotony of uneventful retirement. Julia and I would accompany my grandmother on her errands. We would start at Fleming's in the main square. It was an old-fashioned grocery shop which also stocked wines and spirits and had a small bar in the back. It was like visiting a scene from Dickens. The polished floors, the painted canisters, the side of bacon sliced to order into streaky rashers, the bottles of wine and sherry, the freshly baked bread, the cheeses and baskets of fresh tomatoes all suggested a cheerful maintenance of standards. Something solid and durable, redolent of a time summed up in a phrase, never long absent from Anglo-Irish conversation: "the Good Old Days."

There was one other commodity, Lyle's Golden Syrup, which, with its bright yellow-and-green tins, not only was an integral part of the atmosphere but had some special properties of interest to children. First there was, on the front, a picture of a lion and the legend "Out of the strong came forth sweetness." I spent a good deal of time contemplating the illustration and inscription—even when it was explained that it was a biblical reference (Judges 14) and referred to a swarm of bees and honey in a lion's carcass. The contents of the tin, the bright thick golden syrup, would be used to enhance a plain milk pudding or a slice of bread and butter. A child, helping herself to a spoonful, could trace her initial on the pudding or bread with a thick satisfying stream. As the syrup ran from the spoon to the plate below it became thinner, but it was a long time before the thread broke. The child, half mesmerized, would have long since run out of space or inspiration before the source was exhausted.

After Fleming's we would go to the department store. It was a complete contrast, selling thin scratchy woollen sweaters guaranteed to attract lint, nylon blouses and a not very wide selection of other perfectly respectable but depressing clothing. These were the days before soft Irish tweeds, vegetable-dyed fabrics and hand-knitted sweaters gave Irish clothing and Irish designers a valid place in contemporary fashion. The store was owned by a Church of Ireland firm and employed Protestant girls and women, also providing them with lodgings. These girls were expected to attend church and we would see a pewful of them each Sunday. It is true that they were independent and employed, and that there was a certain security in their positions, but one had the impression that no one had considered liberty or the pursuit of happiness to be their unalienable rights. It must have been a lonely and depressing existence for these girls, with few prospects of advancement or marriage—the older women providing the younger ones with constant examples of what their lives would, in time, become. There seems to be something inherently dishonest in an arrangement in which two parties agree that one of them, in return for some basic human need such as food, shelter and little security, will give up certain hopes, deny certain instincts, forgo certain rights.

If my grandmother stopped at the butcher's shop, I would wait outside, holding my breath for as long as possible. Always suspicious of meat, even when cooked and seasoned, I was repelled by the smell and not at all reassured by the sight of the carcasses hanging in the open air, vulnerable to flies, dust and even the occasional brave street mongrel.

Once a month, there would be a cattle fair. We would avoid these days if possible, since the streets would be covered with manure and the smell would be extreme. We were also uncomfortably and helplessly aware that the bullocks and calves we saw penned in the noisy, crowded, dirty square would end up as carcasses in a butcher's shop. Later in the day the pubs would be full of drunken farmers and dealers recirculating their money in the traditional Irish way.

When we had learned to swim we would often, instead of shopping with my grandmother, be left for a morning at the Dungarvan public swimming pool. It was cold, somewhat slimy and smelled of chlorine. By that time I was keen to learn to swim well and there was an instructor who gave lessons. I mentioned these lessons with rather more than usual courage, but my grandfather sourly asked who I thought would pay for them, and the subject was never brought up again.

At the end of the morning we would collect my grandfather, whom we had left at Fleming's for a drink and some chat, from a bar where he had had a second drink and, I imagine, a variation on the first chat. More often than not, on the drive home, we were allowed to stop for a twopenny ice cream at a little shop by the railway tracks on the way out of Dungarvan, where we would watch the shopkeeper cut a slice of ice cream off a large block and place a wafer on each side. The trick was to lick the cold, delicious but swiftly melting, vanilla-flavored delicacy the whole way around. Otherwise there would be drips on our clothes or the car seats and recriminations would follow. We used to call the process "getting your ice cream under control." Then we would drive the four miles of coast road back to Ballinacourty, the dramatic possibilities of the outing not quite exhausted, since there were two level crossings where we might be lucky enough to get stuck waiting for a train to pass.

When Julia and I were older and my family had moved away from Glenville to a house called Ballinaparka in West Waterford, we found ourselves closer to Dungarvan. For a brief time my parents were part of a genteel amateur moneymaking scheme which not only was a more sophisticated idea than usual but had some chance of working on a modest scale. The idea was a Saturday market where Protestants could sell vegetables, flowers, fresh eggs, bread, jams, honey, fruit and other home-raised produce. (It wasn't Protestant in the sense that Catholics weren't allowed to join—although I don't remember any doing so—but Protestant in its doomed, halfhearted lack of realism.) This kind of enterprise often makes money, for a time at least, in big cities or in the kind of community which caters to rich weekenders. The quality of the goods was, by and large, high and there was even a simple but practical form of accounting which involved each partner keeping a small account book with a list of his goods and sales. Julia and I joined enthusiastically and made two pots of blackberry and apple jam. One of them sold; the other didn't. Neither was as firm as we might have wished. I suspect now that our enterprise, viewed with tolerant amusement by the adults, was a metaphor for what was wrong with the whole undertaking. Julia and I had made the jam and considered its selling price to be clear profit. We were somewhat taken aback when the second pot didn't sell. And we failed to compute what it cost. The blackberries were free; they grew on the roadside. The apples were almost the same; they dropped from the old trees in the garden. We discounted the cost of labour in the same way; neither we nor our adult colleagues had ever had any basis for considering our time worth anything much. The same with energy; the old range would have been hot whether we used it or not. And yet there was overhead. The sugar, the petrol for the trip there and back, the percentage subtracted by the management for the rent of the space—a kind of mews yard off Dungarvan's main street. So Julia and I were mildly disappointed that our sloppy second jar of jam didn't sell no matter how often we took it to market, and some of our elders were outraged that the bunches of Michaelmas daisies cut from their own gardens were ignored by the impoverished Dungarvan women, who had neither the means nor the acquired tastes necessary for some of the goods offered them. My father, who had joined in as enthusiastically and probably more efficiently than most, treated the whole venture with a great deal of humour and used to refer to it as "the very common market."

M O R N I N G S on the beach at Ballinacourty were interesting. The stony, gritty sand offered up minor treasures such as shells and sea glass, which we collected and took home, and the rock pools had a fantastic collection of life. There were sea anemones, which would suck one's finger in an interesting and slightly frightening way, and some small fish, trapped by the tide, which were ugly and fast and looked as though they might have sharp teeth. Various small shellfish clung to the rocks, and one of our governesses (needless to say, not an Irish one) used to prize them off the rocks and eat them raw. Sometimes we would catch shrimp and carry them home. Unfortunately, our catch would not always receive the attention it deserved and all too often we would find, days later, jam jars containing tepid seawater and motionless unnaturally pink shrimp.

One summer I was moved to collect a very large quantity of orange-and-black-striped caterpillars, perhaps fifty or sixty in all. I don't now remember what my objective might have been. Perhaps I was planning to observe the process of metamorphosis on a large scale. I took them up to my bedroom in a jam jar and left them, uncovered, on a large window ledge where I read and kept my treasures. Since this was an attic room, the ledge was above and behind my bed. Soon afterward I went downstairs to face another lunchtime ordeal. When lunch was over I was distracted by some other activity and it was late afternoon before I went upstairs again. To my disappointment—not a severe one, since there were plenty more caterpillars where those had come from—most of my captives were gone. A few remained close to their jar or on a nearby wall and were easily recaptured. The remainder I wrote off to poor planning and forgot about. Fortunately, I did not find this setback worth mentioning to anyone, since a day or two later my grandfather announced, with some surprise and not much pleasure, that he'd found an orange-and-black caterpillar in his bed. I appeared as amazed as everyone else. Several others were observed on the lower floors of the house during the next few days. A few may, perhaps, have even made it down all three floors and back to the outside world.

The room that my sister and I shared that summer was one in which my grandmother stored the remainders of fabric used for covering the sofas of her sitting room. There were so many patterns that I think she must have also saved pieces of fabric from slipcovers or even sofas she no longer owned, thinking, as I now would, that they were too large to throw away and might someday come in useful. Julia and I used to wrap ourselves up in them and use them as costumes in various games. The only game of our own invention that I can clearly remember was called Drug Addicts. There were no rules and it was not competitive. The game consisted in its entirety of jumping up and down on the beds shouting loudly. We never had time to get bored with it or develop it any further (perhaps fortunately, since our knowledge was limited entirely to what I had gleaned from the works of Sir Arthur Conan Doyle) because someone would always come in and tell us to stop bouncing on the bed, we would break the springs.

It was in this room also that I decided to make my fortune in the mother-of-pearl racket. I had read that it was valuable, and having been told that the pretty pale multicoloured lining of some of the seashells we collected was mother-of-pearl, I put two and two together and decided I was on to a good thing. The first problem I encountered was how to extract it from the shells. After a little thought the obvious and, indeed, only solution seemed to be to crush the shells and collect the fragments. The most practical way seemed to be to put the shells between the pages of a heavy book and hammer them to pieces. I did this for some time, but the quantity and quality of the fragments were not encouraging and I realized that, in the unlikely event that my grandfather ever referred to the books on the upper floor, I would be in serious trouble.

As we grew older we went to Ballinacourty less often. Once or twice I stayed with my other grandmother at Stradbally. We never questioned the change and it was only later that I connected the end of our summer-long visits with my grandfather's decline. He became increasingly vague and in time my family had to accept that, despite his remaining physically fit, he was suffering from rapidly progressing premature senility. At first my grandmother tried to continue their life together in the same pattern. She would drive to Dungarvan, drop him at Fleming's, where he would have a drink, then pick him up at Merry's. He could still make his way down the street to his old haunt. My mother once met him en route. He looked at her as though he knew her from somewhere, then the moment passed, the thought faded and he continued on his way. The last time I saw him was also on the street. He didn't recognize me at all. I hesitated, helpless in his non-recognition, then he passed by and I never saw him again.

After a time it became necessary for him to have a companion. This was more of an inconvenience to my grandmother than to my grandfather—an extra person in the house, particularly a companion or a governess, causes a series of small problems and not so small embarrassments of the jealousy-in-the-kitchen and small-talk-in-the-dining-room variety. For my grandfather it can have been no more than a mild irritation, probably offset by having someone with whom to play golf. But his surprisingly rapid deterioration as Alzheimer's disease took hold soon made a companion inadequate and a nurse took her place. My grandmother found herself living with a husband who barely recognized her and a stranger who, of necessity, treated this husband as a small child. Her life was composed of that soul-destroying mixture of irritation and pity we feel when we are forced, over a period of time, to watch a figure who has been one of authority and even mild tyranny become bewildered, fumbling and apologetic. In addition, there were, of course, the daily abrasions of ferrying, days off, meals on trays, bright and meaningless chatter.

In time my grandmother and a nurse could no longer adequately care for my grandfather and he was put into a nursing home. Soon afterward he died.

WHEN WE WERE little my grandmother kept hens. Most of them were confined in an halfhearted way to the farmyard, but one favourite called Salsify was allowed to accompany my grandmother around the garden and lend a claw or beak when she weeded her rockery.

The rockery was the scene of one of my clearest childhood memories. Few plants could survive the wind and salt air at Ballinacourty and the rockery was the one area outside the walled garden which my grandmother cultivated. Of necessity the flowering plants were hardy and low to the ground—grape hyacinths and little white creepers.

I stood beside the rockery one windy and cold summer day, looking out across the bay to Ring, one of the few surviving Gaelic-speaking communities in Ireland. The sea was whitecapped and white gulls were following the fishing boats back to harbour. I was about eight years old and I was wearing a faded blue cotton print dress. I thought: I shall remember this moment forever. There had been no event or remarkable change in my life to cause this decision, but I can still feel the bright sun and cold salty wind on my bare legs.

There is now a cement factory where Ballinacourty stood; its white dust covers the countryside that I remember so clearly. My grandmother, whom I thought of as an old lady, now is an old lady and lives in Tipperary. She remembers Ballinacourty. So, I expect, does Dolores, who may well be a grandmother herself by now. So does Julia. So do I, but when I am in my garden now I hear noon marked only by the siren at the fire station. When I was that skinny child in that washed-out cotton dress, I used, at noon, to hear the Angelus.

STRADBALLY

My GRANDMOTHER Goff was a small woman and, by the time I knew her, plump. She'd been christened Marguerite but nicknamed Daisy since early childhood—a good Victorian name now making the rounds again. My mother called her Aunt Daisy. She was an accomplished but not an educated woman, set in her ways and holding strong opinions about the correct way of doing almost anything.

My grandmother had long been widowed and lived in reduced circumstances. She spent some years being passed around among her children, which was not much fun for anyone and least so for her, since she did not have a friendly relationship with any of them. Eventually she settled in her own tiny, perfect little house in Stradbally. She was a cold woman (although later, when I read her account of her own childhood and description of her parents, I suspended judgment) and her children bore some scars from her lack of maternal warmth. I wonder if she had a sense of having reaped what she had sown when it became clear that she was not going to be able to live comfortably with any of her four children.

Before she came to live with us at Glenville, she had spent some time, about a year, in Kenya with my uncle Charles. It may not seem surprising that a grown man, hardworking and living in a pleasant climate and beautiful surroundings in the country of his choice, should be independent enough to have his mother to stay for a period of time, offering her, I have no reason to doubt, comfortable accommodation. "Country of his choice" is the key phrase in that sentence. My uncle Charles, an ex-commando, had voluntarily made his home and earned his living in Kenya. That it is necessary to pause and emphasize this point will be recognized by anyone familiar with the ground rules by which my family and many other families of that era, class, religious, socioeconomic background operated. Traditionally, unsatisfactory males were dumped in outlying areas of the Commonwealth (still thought of by those who consigned them as the Empire or, at least, the Colonies). I can safely say that for a long period of time the sun never set on the rejects of my family. My grandmother didn't disclose much about her experiences as a mother who had followed her son to the colonies, but she did have one comment on barely pre–Mau Mau Kenya: "The natives weren't grateful for anything you did for them." (My mother, of course, joyfully added this to her mother-in-law repertoire. Though often irritated by her, my mother got a certain amount of fairly innocent fun out of her, like the time my grandmother announced at lunch: "When I was in Waterford this morning I met several people who were *very* pleased to see me.")

For a short time, she lived in a small house on my aunt's estate in Kildare. This Jane Austen–like situation clearly did not work out, and my father was the sole remaining possibility, since her other son, Timmy, though not yet carrying the white man's burden, was fast qualifying for the traditional one-way ticket. No one seriously suggested that my grandmother should stay, or "stop," as she would have said, with Timmy. He himself was of no fixed abode and was travelling on the same circuit; competing, so to speak, for the same accommodation.

Apart from visits to her sisters in London, with whom she genteelly quarreled after a month or two, my grandmother lived with us for long periods of time. It was an arrangement which suited no one and must have been discomforting to my grandmother. I never heard her complain of the impermanence of her situation and it is only in adult life that I can see that she had a "side," too.

My grandmother's rooms were always at least ten degrees warmer than any other part of the house. It was also the first place that I had ever been to which the adjective "cosy" could be applied.

Grannie, as she liked her name spelled, had "her own things" in her quarters, which consisted of a bedroom and dressing room. By common consent she had the exclusive use of one of the two icy bathrooms, both of which were some distance away from her bedroom. The bedroom had an electric fire—which drew us mothlike to its anaemic yellow coiled-wire bar—and heavy curtains to keep out the drafts. The bed and chairs and the "pouf" were upholstered in a rich, generously pleated imperial purple fabric. These opulent traces of fin-de-siècle luxury were not an extravagance; all the work had been done by my grandmother herself. The small pieces of furniture and the array of tiny objects and silver-framed photographs which covered them were left over from "better times" (another name for the Good Old Days)—a period about which we children had heard a lot but had never actually seen.

Almost, but not quite, as attractive to visiting children as the fire was my grandmother's radio. The competition would have been a little closer if we had had any say in station selection. Although she never went to the theatre or cinema and had no interest whatever in the arts, before lunch on Sundays she used to listen to a programme called "The Critics." It can hardly have been as an aid to conversation, since she was unlikely to meet anyone better informed than herself in those areas. The programme's end and my grandmother's arrival in the library coincided with lunchtime and our immediate remove to the dining room gave the impression that we had all been waiting for her to finish a matter of importance before eating the ceremonial Sunday roast beef. That it was often a little overcooked may have added substance to that illusion.

Like most small children, we were delighted by small physical peculiarities. We were fascinated by her habit of twitching her nose like a rabbit when disapproving (most of the time) and by the occasional series of small, regal farts which often marred her otherwise stately progress toward the dining room.

Grannie Goff was a magnificent needlewoman and my father's chamois riding gloves were made by her, as were his sweaters (vee-necked and knitted on small needles for a tiny tight stitch) and socks. She used to knit herself pastel twin sets in extremely complicated designs, frequently of the kind which had little ornamental holes in them, giving us a good view of her equally expertly hand-sewn, pink satin camisoles. Over these garments she usually wore a string of large, fat pearls, left over from happier times.

Jewelry was not an area in which my grandmother distinguished herself. As a young bride, while my grandfather was still a rich man, she'd blithely handed her jewel case to a porter on Waterford station. He retired on the spot and was never seen again. Later, while living in moderate circumstances, she got into the habit of selling off jewels rather cheaply in order to take a trip or go on holiday. The pearls, I'm afraid, disappeared in this way. My father told me when I was older that these were not, strictly speaking, hers to hock. I have remained faithful to this family tradition. The Fabergé star sapphire brooch given to my grandmother by the Empress Marie, together with everything my father left me, was stolen in a burglary in New York.

My grandmother once opened a church bazaar with a speech which came out strongly, and I'm sure without premeditation, in favour of keeping the various denominations of the Protestant faith firmly apart. The view was, I suspect, motivated, though perhaps subconsciously, by a fear that the social boundaries might fall if they amalgamated. This speech must have gone down badly with the Dean, coming at a time when a little solidarity among the minority Church of Ireland (Protestant Low Church) factions might have seemed their only chance of survival. My grandmother's refusal to mix socially with any class other than her own would have been, if challenged, justified with the useful phrase "We wouldn't have anything in common." While not condoning the motive behind it, this statement was hard to argue with. Her firm stand on the future of the Church of Ireland did nothing to prevent, like Yeats, a brief flirtation with the Rosicrucians.

My sister and I did most of our Christmas shopping at these church bazaars. One of the booths was in aid of the Mission to the Jews, a touch of Protestant arrogance which did not sit well with my mother, although the chances of the few shillings the booth took in bringing even one wandering Jew into the Church of Ireland must have been extremely slim. I am reminded of Becky Sharp's attempts to reinstate herself in respectable society by painting hand screens for the conversion of the Pope and the Jews.

One summer, in the late forties, before she settled in Stradbally, my grandmother made an attempt at seaside living and took a small cottage in Annestown, a tiny village in County Waterford. I don't know if this had been intended as a temporary dwelling place or if it had originally been envisioned as a permanent solution.

In my adult life, when I was becoming interested in gardening as a pleasure suitable to middle age, I was taken to visit a garden on Cape Cod. I was amazed and moved by the beauty and simplicity of what I saw, and while I was wandering past a small bed of unassuming flowers a wave of largely forgotten memories swept over me. I turned and walked back the way I had come. The same feeling occurred. I stopped and looked for a clue among the flowers. I could see none. My companions went on to look at something else. I stayed and struggled with what felt like the frustrating attempt to remember a quickly fading dream which, on waking, had seemed to contain something of significance. The feeling was not quite so sharp and I feared that I would never make the association when I suddenly realized that it was the smell of sea pinks which had brought back memories of Annestown. They don't smell sweet, but they are distinct—it was a smell which pervaded that whole summer—the cliff at the end of the beach where the gulls nested was covered with them.

Julia and I went to stay with my grandmother that summer for three or four weeks. Although I was only a small child— maybe six years old—some memories of sunny, sandy days and a few small events remain.

From a child's point of view, events which to an adult would appear varied in importance often seem equally significant. From that summer in Annestown, I can remember the following occurrences equally well—an unexploded mine; being told not to swing on the garden gate (and continuing to do so at judiciously chosen moments); being encouraged to pick nasturtiums (another surprise); and a moment of social embarrassment. Slightly less clearly, I remember my grandmother cutting my sister's hair. Hardly at all, though not entirely from callousness or naïveté, since efforts were made to conceal it, can I remember my uncle's suicide attempt.

In order to give the appearance of having matured somewhat since I was six, I'll start with my unfortunate uncle. Most of the people in this and other mysteries of my childhood are now dead. Dead without satisfying my curiosity. I hope that if I live to a time when my children reach an appropriate age, say thirty-five, I will remember to tell them, not only that they may now see the forbidden R-rated movies of their childhoods, but the truth about any matter I may be currently concealing or about which I may even be lying to them.

What seems to have happened is that Uncle Timmy, a deeply disturbed (or, as they said at the time, "very difficult") man, had been staying (euphemism for living) with my parents at Glenville. He'd gone racing with some friends, disappeared, reappeared in

Annestown, taken a massive overdose of aspirin and then swum out to sea. There had been some real risk of death but, at the same time, the supposedly final swim had taken place in broad daylight with people he knew on the beach. Suicide was, at that time, against the law and anyone who failed in his attempt could find himself reflecting on his worsened situation from behind bars. Anyone who succeeded—unless he got a very humane coroner— was denied a Christian burial. Psychological insights were not rampant in County Waterford in those days and a suicide attempt was not seen as a "cry for help." Uncle Timmy was rescued, returned to Glenville and subsequently placed in a hospital by my mother. Public opinion, mainly from those who offered no constructive alternative, went against her. My mother called Uncle Michael, husband of my father's sister, and asked him to intervene. A meeting was called, which my mother did not attend. Uncle Michael defended her, extracted his brother-in-law from the bin and offered him an allowance as long as he went to . . . it's not impossible to guess . . . Australia. (This may be the moment to mention that my own prolonged stay on the North American continent has been largely voluntary.)

To this day I am impressed with the strong-mindedness of my grandmother's *pas devant* policy. It still amazes me that Julia and I should have had so little information about this family crisis. This was in part because my grandmother had no maid at Annestown. The combined presence of maids and children in the households of my childhood made secrecy an impossibility. By an unspoken but rarely breached agreement, children and maids pooled the information essential, although in different ways, to their well-being. Children, almost as quiet and invisible as the mice behind the skirting boards, scurried back and forth, catching tiny crumbs of news, interpreting a tense silence, overhearing a raised voice or a sigh; maids, who emptied wastebaskets, changed sheets, washed clothes, waited on table, could not, even if they had wished to, have remained ignorant of the secrets, however elevated or ignoble, inherent in every household.

A childhood like this made me realize the inefficiency of the posed question. Although it was telling that I was unable to ask questions, it did not limit the amount of information I received. Once one has taken away rhetorical questions, blatant cries for reassurance ("Was it good for you?" does not offer multiple-choice answers containing, as one option, "No, as a matter of fact, since you ask, only fair"), there are few, outside the "More mashed potatoes?" category, which elicit accurate and complete information. (I have a friend who claims that the most self-defeating question ever asked is "When are you going to leave your wife?" while my daughter adamantly insists that the most frequently asked question, possibly in the history of the world, and the most enraging, is "Are you Max's sister?")

It seems to me now that Julia and I may have been grateful to be excluded from something so clearly out of our depth and were, therefore, accomplices in the cover-up.

The mine incident, in contrast, is a moment of absolute clarity; like a photograph, but like a very old photograph. I remember it with faded colors and frozen time, but I have no record of what happened moments before or moments after the oddly satisfying event.

We were building a sand castle on the beach when a boy came out of the water holding something he'd found, his expression half triumphant and half curious. The adults reacted much faster and with much more attention (hence the satisfaction of the moment) than they usually did to an interesting shell or piece of decaying ocean life. He was carrying a mine, unexploded, left over from the war, rusty and encrusted with barnacles, and now washed up on what used to be a neutral beach. I wish my memory did not give out at that point. I would give a good deal to know the procedure for bomb disposal in Annestown in those days. It occurs to me now that the mine may just have been replaced in the ocean a little further out.

An early memory of social clumsiness is just as clear, my embarrassment caused by a combination of my natural awkwardness and a lack of adequate information. As a small child, I spent quite a lot of time observing the ground rules. I don't know if my sister did—maybe she looked to me to interpret the seemingly unfathomable ways of the adult world. We both knew that whatever deals we had going for us at home were subject to renegotiation in any household headed by my father's mother. In the adaptable way of children, we fell into the new routines and rules with very little discomfort; they were not entirely without benefits, since children are keener on structure and order than they often let on.

A friend of my grandmother's called Mrs. Heather came to visit her. There were two parts to the cottage. One was the little house where we ate and slept, and the other, a large studiolike room, was separated from it by a few feet of gravel and a narrow flower bed. Although my childhood was not a halcyon one, most of my memories are of days of golden sunshine. I clearly remember the large sunny room—its seaside-bleached wood so much paler than the interiors I was used to—and the small bunch of wildflowers I was arranging in a jam jar when my grandmother and Mrs. Heather joined me. Aware that we might be playing by rules with which I was not fully acquainted, I was particularly careful of my manners and greeted Mrs. Heather warmly enough. But I came unstuck when she offered me a small roll of individually wrapped, chocolate-covered toffees. It was a gesture totally outside my experience. I understood the annual ceremonial box of chocolates which arrived every Christmas from our doctor, also the occasional sweet distributed after lunch by my mother, but I didn't understand her gesture and was not sure whether she was giving me the whole thing or whether I was supposed to take one and hand the rest back. I looked at it. I looked at my grandmother and Mrs. Heather. No clue was forthcoming. Playing for time, I returned to my flowers and started fiddling with them. Both adults were clearly shocked by my lack of manners, but I was inarticulate and unable to explain my quandary.

The haircutting incident was in another league altogether.

Both Julia and I had long, pale blonde hair—misery to maintain but very pretty—which my parents liked and would never have considered cutting. Since that summer we spent our days on the beach, in and out of water, playing in the sand, our hair required more than usual in the way of washing and detangling and I suppose we complained about it. My grandmother may also have felt that Julia's long hair emphasized her waiflike appearance. She was a delicate child, tiny and thin. Unknown to us, she was allergic to gluten and every attempt to build her up with starch, and to reduce the fat which the doctors blamed, caused the opposite effect. So the idea of the haircut was perfectly sound; but it wasn't her child. It was an extraordinary coup to carry out, and the fact that she did it casts a little extra light on her relationship with my parents. It may also be significant that her action was condoned, since no attempt was made to regrow Julia's hair. If I had been in my mother's place, Julia's hair would have gone uncut until she married or my grandmother died. Not necessarily whichever came first.

Traditionally, irrevocable and destructive acts take place during the night hours. The ever-regretted emotional letter, the misguided telephone call, even suicide. They all seem nocturnal activities. A certain amount of energy, however, is needed to generate courage; to undertake a grand gesture; to suspend one's better judgment. Acts stemming from drunkenness and rage may take place after dinner, but anything which requires premeditation and a steady hand is unlikely to be perpetrated by me any later than teatime. Heavy demolition invariably takes place in the earlier part of the morning.

Sometime after the morning beach activities and before lunch was when it happened. I suppose my grandmother had just finished the midday combing-out of tangles and decided that she couldn't face repeating the process, accompanied by tears, on both children later that afternoon. I think it might not be going too far to suggest that she managed to invoke a small token of principle along with an appeal to common sense, practicality and humanity.

I once witnessed a comparable performance by a woman of my acquaintance who, while staying at a mutual friend's house, successfully ordered the execution of an ancient, crippled, unhappy and foul-smelling hound during its owner's absence.

Neither Julia nor I was in the habit of questioning decisions made by adults. Nor had it occurred to us that such decisions might not be unanimous, that what one adult might decree another might forbid. So when my grandmother announced that she was going to cut Julia's hair, although there was no evidence of recent communication from my parents (there was no telephone and the post had not included a letter from them), we assumed that Julia was to be shorn with their blessing. Less interesting to me than "Will she get away with it?" was the discovery that my grandmother possessed both the necessary tools and expertise. I was fascinated without experiencing any other emotions. I was neither worried nor frightened. I neither desired my sister to be transformed into a beauty nor wanted my grandmother to come unstuck with an incompetent haircut. I had no vested interest since it never occurred to me that my grandmother, flushed with the triumph of one successful haircut, might feel the desire to perform a second one on me.

The day before's edition of *The Irish Times*, which had been passed on by thoughtful neighbours, carefully read but in pristine condition, was spread on the kitchen floor. Julia was placed on a pile of books (not the telephone directory, since the entire Irish directory was then less than an inch thick) on a kitchen chair. A bathtowel was wrapped around her shoulders, covering her entire body, including hands and feet. Our grandmother produced a good sharp pair of scissors—every tool she possessed from buttonhook to professional upholstery equipment was old and perfectly maintained and kept in its own place—and set to work. I noticed with interest that she clearly knew what she was doing. With a moment's consideration, of course, one should have known that any woman who put her hair up each day, and kept it firmly and elegantly in place regardless of whether she was fox hunting or waltzing, would be more than qualified to give a four-year-old child a haircut.

It was the work of three or four minutes. Julia suddenly had a neat fringe over her eyes. Her hair fell to a straight line on a level with her chin. She was transformed, though neither prettier nor less so than before. The waiflike suggestion of the long wispy hair was replaced by something a little more knowing.

Each time Julia moved her head during lunch she looked surprised. I watched her experiment with quick darts from side to side, pausing to miss the experience of long hair flicking across her back and neck. By the end of the day she was used to it. By the end of the week we had almost forgotten than she had ever had long hair. I do not remember a moment of confrontation between either of my parents and my grandmother. I doubt one ever took place.

The house in Stradbally, in which my grandmother eventually settled and in which she lived for the rest of her life, was one of a row in the centre of the village and was owned by Lord William Beresford, uncle to the present Marquis of Waterford. The Beresfords lived in a beautiful house at the bottom of the hill, close to Stradbally beach. I don't know if it was by design or chance, but all their tenants would have fitted quite comfortably into Mrs. Gaskell's *Cranford*. (I'd read *Cranford* with pleasure when I was ten or eleven and no one had warned me that not all her books were in a similar vein. I spent a soggy summer morbidly weeping over them at my other grandmother's house.) The Beresfords were kind to my grandmother and their other tenants in a variety of small ways; dropping by with magazines, and vegetables from their garden. Later, when I was living in England, my grandmother's letter always contained some reference to the Beresfords and usually to the activities of their two daughters, with whom she used to compare Julia and me unfavourably. There was another family, again with two daughters who were also used as a yardstick against which we never measured up. I was young enough to be offended, instead of amused as I should have been, since I knew that both the girls in the second family, despite their jerseys and pearls and sensible shoes, led extremely racy lives while away from home.

It was perhaps my grandmother's comparing us with the Beresford girls which caused me not only a moment of interest and curiosity but also one of pleasure and vindication when I found a reference, many years later, to Lord Beresford's book *How to Really Beat the Bank at Monte Carlo*. Pleasure only slightly diluted by the awareness that the author's title is either incorrectly reported or that he was not of the immediate family. It's the word "really" that I particularly like.

My grandmother wrote in a childish, rounded hand and her spelling was, at best, uncertain. Each letter could have been a carbon copy of the one before. This used to make me laugh, but now I realize these letters were an accurate account of a life in which little changed from day to day, month to month, year to year. And my own letters in return contained a fairly guarded report of my own doings.

No one reading her letters (or, on reflection, mine) would have imagined the writer to have entertained literary ambitions, but my grandmother did attempt to write her memoirs. Not, I think, from vanity, but from a widely held misconception that, when all else fails, anyone can earn a quick buck by knocking off a book.

Simenon has shown us that there is no life which is not interesting enough to write about. But he has also shown that it requires skill, talent and a painstaking attention to detail. Unfortunately, this is not the approach my grandmother favoured. What she did, basically, was to copy out her diary.

I saw the diary once, and remember it being illustrated with small pale watercolours. I imagine it lay open with the paint drying, first on the schoolroom table, later somewhere more grown-up but no less public. Not surprisingly, it was not a private record of her thoughts and feelings. Nor, sadly, was it a writer's notebook.

My grandmother's book never found a publisher, and for

several good reasons. Even with the sort of padding which suggests help from a not very adept ghostwriter, it doesn't come to quite thirty thousand words and her reckless disregard for spelling and punctuation is balanced only by her carefulness not to betray any emotions, give any opinions or take a chance of any kind.

My great-grandfather had been a diplomat and my grandmother was born and had spent her early childhood in Germany. She was one of six children, five of them girls. They later lived in Berne, Copenhagen and, by the time my grandmother "came out," St. Petersburg. Her father was by then the British Ambassador. In those days an ambassador was expected to dip fairly heavily into his own pocket for the glory of his country (not in the American campaign-contribution sense, but in order to keep up appearances on an inadequate expense account), and it was a constant struggle to keep the side up. One of the sacrifices made for the British Empire had been the education of his daughters.

The opening pages of her memoirs include a description of her father which makes it very clear that no one should expect any startling revelations from her:

Father who became Sir Charles Scott was as I have said a Diplomat. His reminiscences went back very far. He could vividly recall his time as Charge d'Affair in Mexico and used to tell us many stories of the last days of Emperor Maximellian.

Perhaps he could, but the ability died with him. Either my grandmother didn't remember them or she chose not to share them with us. Making it clear she's not going to blow the whistle on her family, she passes on to her observations about the political situation (this is twenty years before the Russian Revolution):

When people talk of the down trodden peasants of the Emperors days, I picture to myself again those drives home

*from Mourina late in the evening. As we passed village
after village the peasants would be seen dancing out in the
open to the music of a few balalaikas, while their elders sat
round, laughing and clapping their hands in time to the
music.*

Now that we know what we're not going to get—a book,
among other things—it's worth looking at this manuscript as an
adaptation of her diary with some accurate, though never personal,
descriptions of her life up to the time she married in 1902.

Her descriptions of balls and state occasions are detailed and
quite interesting, but the pieces which really get my attention are
not intended to be dramatic. She casually mentions the circumstances surrounding her birth:

*I had actually been promised away before my arrival to
a childless Aunt and Uncle if I turned out to be another
girl. So it was trying of me to behave like this and many
times in those first months my parents must have regretted
their change of mind. Aunt Hatty and Uncle Henry O'Hare
—who later became Bishop of Cashel and Waterford, were
bitterly disappointed, everything was ready for me
even to a nurse being engaged. Years after we used to be
shown the Steeple on Colraine Church and told that was
built out of what should have been my dowry.*

In fairness to my great-grandparents, it should be mentioned
that two subsequent daughters were born and neither given away.
My grandmother does not describe her parents in a way which
would allow us to form any judgment of their characters, but she
often mentions her mother's beauty. All children think their
mothers beautiful, but my grandmother's loyalty was justified.
Although beauty and elegance are rarely considered anything but
an asset, my father once suggested that his grandmother's beauty
had proved a liability at one point in his grandfather Scott's career.

Apparently, the Prince of Wales, later Edward VII, a man by no means insensitive to female beauty, asked the Ambassadress for a photograph of herself. I never really understood why this was an improper request until I read about Proust hounding the Comtesse Greffulhe for a photograph and her refusal to give it to him. ("One didn't give them to outsiders.") The Comtesse Greffulhe gave a dinner party for Edward VII and Queen Alexandra in 1910—an evening referred to by Proust in *The Guermantes Way*, and the King, while still Prince of Wales, had been a friend of Charles Haas, the model for the more public aspects of the character of Swann. I choose to believe that the Prince of Wales was pressing my great-grandmother for a photograph at the same time that Proust was vainly attempting to obtain one from the Comtesse. The Prince of Wales was only marginally more successful. Great-grandmother Scott did the proper but perhaps unwise thing: she went to her husband and told him. He sent a suitably inscribed portrait (maybe even of both of them), making it clear that it was from him. The Prince of Wales might, had he lived to read it, have felt a flicker of recognition at Proust's sentence: "To obtain Gilberte's photograph I committed acts of baseness which did not get me what I wanted, but involved me for the rest of my life with some extremely boring people." The story is that he never quite forgave my great-grandfather, who, though by no means discriminated against, received no further promotions or plum assignments.

There is another fortuitous Proustian connection, which gives me great pleasure. Madame Straus, one of the other hostesses on whom the character of the Duchesse of Guermantes is based, used to entertain some of the English diplomatic corps at her salon. Among them was Sir Reginald Lister (his wife, Barbara, was also a close friend of Madame de Chevigné, another model for the same character). To my amazement, in my grandmother's slightly less guarded account of her childhood, there is a reference to the same man, when he was attached to the British Embassy in Berlin:

One of the Attaches we particularly disliked was Reggie Lister. He was large and fat and had a baby face. Periodically he suffered from a complaint he called "nursey" which he said was the result of his nurse letting him catch a chill when he was a baby. We thought it was when he wanted more attention, because every one fussed round him and we felt rather neglected.

"Nursey" indeed. And that's not all. There is another reference to Mr. Lister, as he then was, in a childhood story about my grandmother's sister Eileen.

She went up to him announcing "I loves you Mr. Lister because you squints and you turns in your toes just like me." Rather funny because Mr. Reggie Lister on talking about us children had once remarked about the youngest "a nice little thing a pity she dresses so badly" and no wonder her clothes having been handed down all along her row of sisters.

Unfortunately, there are no more surprises of a literary nature, but in the middle of some mild anecdotes about royalty and diplomatic life there is a reference to a guest at her parents' house who seemed particularly entertaining:

We were rather frightened of him too because he was vigorous in his games and idea of fun . . . Father was quite indignant when we came home one evening [from playing with him and his two small sons] delightedly announcing we had fought the English and beaten them.

A few pages later she says that when this guest came to dinner with her parents, a messenger would arrive in the morning with a case of special knives and forks joined together since the Prince had the use of only one arm. And there is a later reference which makes it clearer still: "trying Queen Victoria's patience, his devoted Grandmother, who generally made allowances for his erratic behaviour."

Although my grandmother wrote her memoirs in the late forties or early fifties and had been married to a man who fought in the First World War, she does not seem to make any connection between the Crown Prince and the man who was later to become the Kaiser.

It is not only history which gets short shrift—later she saw Pavlova make her debut and Nijinsky in *Le Spectre de la Rose* but tells us nothing except that she was impressed by him. But there are a few moments when the book comes to life. My favourite scene, so metaphoric that it is almost poetic, reads:

> *We used to play with the Edinburgh Princesses when they and their parents were on a visit to the Neuer Palace at Potsdam. My clearest recollection of them was at hay-making time. We used to play a most exciting game. The Princesses built large nests of hay and played at mother birds and their young. Princess Marie's nest was always well ordered and rather dull, those of us in it were fed regularly and put to sleep. Princess Victoria's was more exciting, hers and Princess Baby's were either fighting among themselves or being raided by their brother and his tutor. In the end, we the young birds were stolen or flung about like ammunition. If the fight reached Princess Marie's nest she generally dissolved in tears and that was the end of the game.*

An enchanting rural summer scene, a little heavy on the princesses, perhaps, but when one realizes just who these Edinburgh princesses were, it becomes something else. These children were the grandchildren of both Queen Victoria and the Czar of Russia. Their innocent but territorial games were childhood variations of what would come later. Albert, who would have become the Duke of Saxe-Coburg-Gotha, died of venereal disease when he was twenty-five, but the four princesses married into different European royal families. When the First World War broke out, Marie was about to become Queen of Rumania; Victoria was married to Grand Duke Kirill of Russia; Alexandra to Ernest, Prince of Hohenlohe-Langenburg; and she whom my grandmother called Princess Baby was married to Alfonso, Infante of Spain. Their mother was Russian by birth but by marriage first Duchess of Edinburgh and later Duchess of Coburg. My grandmother mentions a title or two but ignores the fact that her playmates would grow up to fight with more serious weapons than handsful of hay.

There is also a description of a court ball which gives a sense of the splendour and beauty and elegance of a kind which has never been attempted in my lifetime—starting with the men in uniform and the women in evening dresses being helped out of their fur-lined shubas, having arrived in horse-drawn vehicles over the snow; the marble; Princess Youssoupoff's famous string of black pearls; the dances; the seated dinner for four thousand; banks of flowers; mounds of asparagus on huge blocks of ice. At the last ball my great-grandmother attended, after my grandmother had left Russia, instead of asparagus they substituted mounds of black truffles. The gardenlike theme of the rooms was complemented by the paintings on loan from the Hermitage.

All this I should have liked to see, and there is a good deal more I should like to know. Where did the mounds of asparagus come from in midwinter? Where did the truffles come from? How did they eat them? Didn't the truffles, forgive me, smell a little? I want to hear more about another ball, also with a horticultural theme, at which the tables were fitted around giant palm trees. But most of all I would like to know what my grandmother felt. I know how splendid it all seemed since she tells us that, but did she have a sense of living in a moment of history? It was beautiful and magnificent, but what else? Did she feel her dress wasn't elegant enough? Did she long for the jewelry she saw? Was she shy, overwhelmed? Did she fall in love with the romantic young officers in their dramatic uniforms? Or did she see it all as a glimpse of something which could never be hers? Was there some kind of bitterness that someday, someday very soon, she'd better find as substantial a husband as an impoverished girl from a good, but not brilliant, background could, and settle down and forget all this?

In 1901, as though to underline this reality, she spent the winter in Waterford. Her parents quite reasonably felt that "so many grown up daughters was a mistake" and two of them were packed off to Ireland for the winter:

Alice and I took a little time to settle down in the [Bishop's] Palace in Waterford, a very different atmosphere to that of the Embassy in St. Petersburg. The Palace seemed cold and bare after the luxury to which we were accustomed.

This was the same building that I went to school in nearly fifty years later.

My grandmother met my grandfather, married him and lived in Waterford. There is no way of knowing whether she missed the beauty and sparkle of court life or whether she was glad to have a secure position in society, a title, plenty of money and a house of which she was the mistress. No longer a bystander or spectator, no longer taking turns and sharing with her sisters. Later her husband, who wasn't particularly nice to her, lost his money and died soon afterward, but by then nobody was waltzing in St. Petersburg either.

In addition to the five sisters, there had also been a brother, my great-uncle Charles. He was the fourth of the six children (my grandmother the third) and the eagerly awaited son. The two eldest girls, Vera and Alice, and the two youngest, Marie and Eileen, were paired off, certainly by age and circumstances and

probably by choice. I have to assume, then, that in early childhood
my grandmother and her brother were thrown together. I never
heard my grandmother or great-aunts mention his name, so I was
fascinated to find him referred to affectionately in Grannie's book.
The first time is during a summer holiday spent in Potsdam,
where the Scotts took a "cottage" for the summer. The cottage
had a thatched roof but, from accounts of weekend entertainment,
though informal it must have been quite large:

*Sometimes Sir Edward and Lady Ermyntrude Malet [he
was the British Ambassador to Berlin and since she had
a title in her own right she presumably had the blood to
carry off the name Ermyntrude] spent Sunday at the Cottage, and then we were on our best behaviour. Sir Edward
was especially fond of our brother, so Charles, or Pop as
he was called, had to curb his usually high spirits so as to
make a good impression. He used to have to sit on Sir
Edward's knee after lunch and once to our great delight Sir
Edward went to sleep and poor Pop had to sit bolt upright,
holding onto a lock of his hair to prevent himself from
falling back on Sir Edward and waking him up.*

You wonder a little why his parents didn't rescue him. I don't
think it was out of fear or undue respect for the Malets, since the
second passage, also an incident from a Potsdam holiday, shows
that they didn't have a great deal of imagination about or
consideration for their children's feelings:

*My brother and I were playing near the road when we
heard some one calling to us. Looking up we saw it was
Prince William on horseback. He asked us to give Father
and Mother a message that they were expected at the
Palace for dinner that night. We were so taken by surprise,
that it was not until the Prince told my brother to remove
his hat, that we remembered our manners; I had forgot-*

*ten to curtsey too. We were much upset and ran to give
Mother the message and tell her what we had done. We
wondered what would happen because we thought Prince
William looked very stern. Mother promptly said Pop's
head would be cut off. Though it sounded very harsh, we
quite believed it, it was always happening in fairy stories.
Marie who was always the gentlest of us, was in a terrible
state and asked Mother to beg for his life that night. She
promised to go down on her knees and ask pardon for "her
little brother because she loved him so" [she was younger
than he was]. Next day we were told he was pardoned. I
am sure this had been quite a joke among the grown-ups
but we children had spent a miserable day and night.*

Next heard of, only indirectly, Charles was at school in
England. He is never mentioned again. A classic black sheep, I
believe he'd been sent to Canada, following the tradition of
dumping unsatisfactory male members of the family in the
outlying regions of the British Empire.

Presumably my great-uncle died in Canada, though I never
heard of his death. It is possible that the family was never
informed. When I was a small child, my grandmother received a
letter or message from him, the contents of which were not
disclosed or had been forgotten by the time I heard about it. She
did not respond to it. Drink, my father hinted, had been the
problem. My great-uncle's family had cut him out of their lives
with ruthless Victorian tough-mindedness. My father's surviving
brother is called Charles, but named after his grandfather rather
than his uncle.

My mother also had an uncle who proved unsatisfactory. In
his case the situation was complicated by the fact that he already
lived in the colonies, so the classic formula did not apply. He left
of his own volition, running off with a woman who was not his
wife (there may have been some additional problem involving
money) to San Francisco, where he led a hand-to-mouth existence

as a small-time con man. At one point he had a job as a night clerk and so was awake to experience the earthquake. He survived the natural catastrophe but later, coming to the end of his resources, murdered his wife and killed himself.

The guideline for dealing with the unsatisfactory male, even when he was the only and longed-for son, seems to have been clearly laid out. But what on earth would they have done with a female who went bad? Even allowing for the fewer opportunities open to women in those days, one would have expected at least one Jean Rhys character for all the remittance men obligatory to each generation.

My generation should be grateful to my grandfather Woodhouse. Although his father had been a remittance man and gambler sent to New Zealand by his Northern Irish family, my grandfather had made the symbolic reverse journey from the colonies to the British Isles, and the transfusion of tough, literal-minded common sense may have been what my family needed. His son spent his working life in the Forestry Department in Kenya, but retired home to Ireland, and my brother lives a happy productive life with a job and family, which is a relief since he was, to some extent, bred to be a character in a Somerset Maugham short story.

The village of Stradbally was at the top of a steep hill, half a mile from the beach. Until the last few years of her life, during the summer months my grandmother would walk down the hill, swim and walk back for lunch. I have always been fascinated by her mixture of primness and physical toughness. It is the combination of any two extreme qualities or achievements that fascinates. I can imagine being a ballet dancer. I cannot imagine, however, being able to dance *and* keep my hair in place. My grandmother once told me that when living in the British Embassy in St. Petersburg, she had sometimes been awakened by a rat running across her bed. Her memoirs also give quite detailed accounts of long voyages (St. Petersburg to Waterford, for instance) taken by boat and train, with no allusion to the discomfort and exhaustion which must have been part of the journey. I can imagine doing it in jeans and sneakers, complaining all the way. I cannot imagine doing it graciously and looking elegant as I do it. Nothing was seen by my grandmother or her sisters as an excuse for a slackening of standards. If I am alone I eat dinner on a tray in bed, reading at the same time. When my grandmother was alone she ate at the dining-room table, with proper, though modest, courses and the correct place settings. I'm sure that she sat up straight as she did so. Her day had a structure, despite the lack of content. She arose at a certain time, ate her meals at set hours, gardened or did needle-work. Even the radio was turned on and off for specific but infrequent programmes.

Changing times and standards were ignored, as were small inconveniences and embarrassments. Her little house was cosy, with ornaments and photographs in silver frames on the mantel-piece and side tables. But there was nothing she could do about the bathroom, which was above the living room. If anyone had to use the lavatory, the sound was as audible as though that person were relieving himself in the same room. Those who were sitting below would raise their voices by a decibel or two and pretend that nothing embarrassing was happening.

When I went to visit my grandmother at Stradbally I went alone. Summers at Ballinacourty had always involved Julia and me and sometimes a governess. These holidays served the dual function of getting us to the seaside and our grandparents, while relieving our parents of two children essentially the same age. A visit to Grannie Goff lasted a week and was on quite a different basis.

Her house was much smaller than Ballinacourty and babysitting was not her function. If I went to stay with her, it was as an adult, or as close to adulthood as I could manage. Although she didn't adapt herself to me, it was a surprisingly pleasant place to stay: I got a great deal more attention (as opposed to affection) than I was used to and the food was less frightening than at Ballinacourty. In fact, the meals were good in a modest way. I don't remember quite how my grandmother managed and I do remember my mother tactfully, with artificial casualness, asking if I was getting properly fed. Most of the cooking was done by a local woman who came in several times a week and to whom my grandmother was uncharacteristically attached. There was no fridge in the house (nor was there one at either Glenville or Ballinacourty), and food was kept on a marble slab under a fly-deterring net in the pantry. The bedrooms were comfortable, with fat, dull purple satin eiderdowns, and although we knew that my grandmother was far from affluent there was more of a sense of luxury or, at least, comfort and cosiness there than I ever met elsewhere in my childhood. It was not achieved through expenditure of money, but by refusing to let slip her standards. Furniture and silver were kept polished, frayed armchairs were reupholstered by my grandmother herself and the tiny house was fairly easy to keep warm.

I was allowed a greater amount of freedom at Stradbally than I had been used to. This freedom was hardly licence. It consisted of permission to go to the store on the other side of the square by myself—the shilling of pocket money my grandmother gave me feeling like riches. She provided the stamps for my letters home, and the new feeling of grown-up status did not prevent me from accepting them gratefully and spending my shilling on ice cream.

When I first started to read the novels of Dumas, my keen enjoyment was slightly marred by having no idea at all what the crowns and louis d'or mentioned were worth in sterling, or what they represented in buying power. Later when I started to read the Russian classics I experienced the same frustration with roubles. So: when I was a child, there were twelve pence to a shilling, twenty shillings to a pound. In terms of buying power, a shilling bought six twopenny ice creams. The change to decimal currency has made many of the coins of my childhood obsolete. The large copper pennies, the smaller halfpennies, the silver sixpenny and threepenny pieces are gone, as is the ten shilling note.

Occasionally, this newfound and unearned assessment of myself as a responsible adult whose word could be taken at face value would backfire. On one visit, my grandmother arranged for me to ride a neighbour's hunter. My father would never have permitted such a thing. He would have looked at the horse, looked at its owner, looked at me, remembered how uncoordinated I was and refused. My grandmother, who had allowed her own children to ride the most dangerous brutes as a necessary part of their education, did not question my ability. I had been boasting about how well I could ride (breaking the rule that the top floor of a skyscraper or, better still, a ship at sea is the only safe place to claim that kind of skill) and had been believed. I didn't know how to say that I didn't want to, which would have been correctly interpreted as being afraid. It is hard to tell whether the badly trained animal or I had less enthusiasm for our tentative and increasingly brief outings.

By the time I was grown up (these visits had taken place when I was twelve and thirteen) and left home, my uncle Timmy came back from Australia. He was by then crippled with arthritis and dying of cancer. He lived the last few years of his life with his mother. It was not a happy time for either of them. She, as her sister Eileen had, outlived not only a husband but a son.

Self-sufficiency and inner resources were what I most admired in my grandmother, although I never then put those names to her qualities. Recently I've come to realize that most members of my family who survived to the extent of being allowed to live in the British Isles had these qualities to quite an advanced degree. In a society based on such depths of reserve, if you don't have one or the other, or both, you tend to perish.

As recently as a few years ago, my stepdaughter, fresh from a stint in Southern California and all that that implies, said that we should learn to express our emotions more. I said, briskly, in a manner my grandmother would have been proud of, that I thought, on the contrary, we should work hard at expressing them less. Then, as in childhood, I had an instinctive fear of the hell which would break loose if anyone started saying how he or she actually felt.

My grandmother Goff was protected by the rules and code of conventional behaviour instilled in her as a girl. She showed no outward resentment toward her vastly reduced circumstances. I remember her saying apropos of smoking, long before the lung-cancer reports, that she'd stopped smoking when the bad times had come, intending to start again when "the good times come again, but now I suppose they never will." It was said with no trace of self-pity or bitterness.

Good times didn't come but neither, I think, did bad times. My grandmother retained her health and a reasonable degree of mental alertness right up to her death. By then I was living in California. My father wrote, rather than telephoned, with news of her death. There had been no question of my returning for her funeral. The letter took some time to reach me, since I had just changed addresses. I'm afraid I left my inadequate letter to him for longer than I should. I didn't quite know what to write.

I would know now. I was too young and too thoughtless, and Southern California, that land of Rousseau-like vegetation and instant gratification, was not the place where I eventually came to understand a few basic unflashy principles about courage and strength.

Now my grandmother is dead and also her son, my father, to whom I should have written that letter. I understand that Hemingway's definition of guts—"grace under pressure"—becomes, if the behaviour continues for long enough, a definition of true courage. Especially when that behaviour extends, unacknowledged, to the end of a life essentially spent alone.

I would define courage as understanding that behaving well in adversity is its own reward, and that there is no viable alternative.

BALLINAPARKA

W H E·N I was thirteen years old I was sent away
to boarding school. Some years before, my parents had looked
through prospectuses for schools in England. I had done a far more
extensive study of these brochures than they had, having brought
to them the additional glow of fantasy and dubious information
gleaned from my weekly comics. Intrigue, glamour and above all
a code of honour seemed an everyday part of life in those exotic
surroundings. I remained fascinated by these prospectuses, with
their photographs of chapels and lavish lists of uniform require-
ments, long after my parents had realized that English school fees
and the expense of travel back and forth each term made an
English education impractical.

In the end I was sent to Hillcourt, a Protestant boarding school
just outside Dublin. It is a sign of the euphoria induced by *Girl's
Crystal* that on the first day of term I scanned the notice board to
see if my name was on the first eleven hockey team for the
following Saturday. Gradually I worked my way down through
the second eleven, the third and so on until I found my name listed

for beginners' practice. Nor did the idealized versions of boarding-school life, which I had so avidly read, mention school food or the disgusting smells it produces.

Within a few months I had decided that school would provide me with a yardstick against which to measure my later life. I thought that it was unlikely that I would ever be more miserable. So far I have found that this holds true.

While I was away at school having rather more edges knocked off than I had bargained for, my mother gave birth to another child and I came home that Christmas to a new brother and a new house.

My brother, Robert, was an enchanting baby, resilient and good-tempered; qualities he retained long after the emotional temperature of our new home had become bleak and frigid. He had, even as a small child, a dry humour. He was enthusiastic, energetic and not given to encouraging self-pity in others. He wore little long-sleeved nightshirts, and frequent laundering of a primitive kind soon turned them into a uniform tea-stained beige colour. Since they had a drawstring at the hem to keep his feet warm, he often looked like an unbearably sweet human tea bag. I was thirteen and home only during the school holidays and he was an infant who lived in the nursery, in winter at least, rarely visiting other parts of the drafty house. Despite the limited time he and I spent together, I formed a sentimental attachment to those worn nightshirts and saved them when he had grown out of them.

The house to which I returned that Christmas was called Ballinaparka and was an improvement on Glenville in every way. It was older and smaller, architecturally superior and easier to keep up. Instead of being on the outskirts of a city, it was a country house built on a small hill close to a tiny village in West Waterford called Aglish. One approached the house along an avenue of ilex and yew trees, in which lived some guinea hens; they had been left behind by the former owners. They added an exotic and oddly cheerful touch to the otherwise sombre ever-greens.

Like Glenville, Ballinaparka had a walled garden, but the rest of the grounds were smaller and more manageable. We filled the house and stables and the comfortable fit gave me a secure feeling. I had found the unused and, by Anglo-Irish definition, deterio-rating empty rooms at Glenville depressing and a little frighten-ing. I had been drawn, occasionally but intensely, toward those empty rooms, full of ghosts and treasures. The cellar contained elk horns and a ceremonial sword and had darker recesses I never, even with Julia as a companion, gained the courage to fully explore. In addition to the unnamed, formless horrors which lurked there, there were also dust and spiders and the guilty fear of being asked sharply what I was doing if a grown-up chanced by. Although technically guiltless, I could never explain my curiosity and was aware that these doors were intended to be kept closed. I knew that my mother, too, was demoralized by the stored junk, to which a smaller house would have ruthlessly denied space.

Ballinaparka was Georgian and had wonderful proportions. There was a fanlight over the front door and a generous hall. A staircase with a wide curve which started in the center of the hall led up to a huge window overlooking the stable yard, divided and swept on to a central landing, off which lay all the main bedrooms. Every room was light with large and beautiful windows. The front of the house looked over fields sloping down to a row of trees which marked the boundary of the property and hid the road which ran along two sides of our land. The drawing room and study, a shabbier and cosier place to sit than the more formal drawing room, looked out over a lawn where we played croquet. Rhododendrons and another field sloped down to a stream. The back of the house looked down on the stable yard and it was pleasant to lie awake in the morning and hear the sound of horses' hooves on the cobbles below.

The move to Ballinaparka should have been a step away from

the Anglo-Irish trap, not only because it was charming and light and graceful but because it was easier and more economical to run. Unfortunately, although my father had bought Ballinaparka after he had been led to believe Glenville had been sold, the sale fell through at the last moment and there was a period of intense financial anxiety as a result. Some time later Glenville caught fire and burned to the ground, apparently as a result of an electrical failure in the basement. The insurance company took a while before it reluctantly paid up, and my father was subjected to some heavy-handed banter on the subject of arson, although I don't think anyone seriously pictured him with a box of matches and a petrol-soaked rag. It occurs to me now that their confidence in his character was enhanced by their knowledge that though large houses had routinely been burned during "the troubles," they had traditionally been torched by what my parents' friends would have thought of as "the other side."

Furniture which had come from Glenville was rearranged. The huge library bookcases now stood in the hall. Two or three sofas were fitted with new slipcovers in light fabrics and placed on either side of the fireplace in the drawing room, but very few new things were bought. Apart from the obvious reasons—lack of money and the low quality of new furniture—there was very little emphasis on interior decoration among people we knew. Nor do I remember hearing a decorator (who would surely have been known by another title) mentioned as a luxury enjoyed in more affluent times. What our houses looked like inside was very much determined by finances, architecture and what our families had left us. Even the occasional new curtains or slipcovers would be much the same as their predecessors, since they were, to a large extent, determined by what had been there forever.

I had a large, light front bedroom, which had one severe disadvantage. Bats.

The house was surrounded by trees, which provided shelter not only against winter storms but for bats, who found their way into the house with ease but were not so adept at getting out again. I can remain calm in the face of mice and don't make too much of a fool of myself with snakes, providing I have adequate notice of their presence, but bats terrify me. They also frightened my mother, but I remember her valiantly swiping at them with a tennis racket while I lay cowering under the bedcovers.

At the back of the house there was stabling for four horses. My father gave me a beautiful chestnut hunter called Strancally. I was an indifferent horsewoman and the daily exercising sessions were initially more frightening than enjoyable. After I had managed to get myself thrown off my new horse approximately once a day and had shown less and less enthusiasm for remounting, my father took pity on me and swapped the horse for an older mare of his own. She was called Lil and I loved her. She was bay, small, narrow and light and a gentle contrast to her more flashy predecessor. Riding once more became a pleasure. My sisters and I spent happy summer afternoons taking our bored horses over jumps constructed of bales of straw and poles.

My sister had a small plump pony inappropriately named Patience, and each day of our school holidays we would ride over the hills or through the forestry preserves. Sometimes we would ride through part of an estate called Dromana.

Dromana was a beautiful Georgian house incorporating the remains of an older castle. The house had belonged to a friend of my father's and had once been the scene of hunt balls, house parties and lawn meets. Now it was empty, the rooms cold and the corridors murky, the curved ballroom overlooking the Blackwater lit only by soft summer sunshine or the cold grey light of winter. The driveway was full of holes and puddles, during the winter holidays frozen white or with broken ice revealing muddy dark brown water below. The land was farmed by the son of my father's friend. Their family name was Villiers-Stuart.

The rides through Dromana woods and along the ruined driveway evoke even more powerful memories than those of the heather-covered and fenceless hills. The empty house was the most dramatic metaphor for Anglo-Irish decline that I had yet seen. Some years after, when we no longer lived at Ballinaparka, I read a passage of Pepys's diary which recorded a moment in the origins of the Villiers-Stuart family. Pepys was visiting the Earl of Sandwich, his cousin and patron, at Sandwich's house in King Street, Westminster. The house was next door to one which had previously belonged to Whalley, one of our ancestors. In 1660, at the Restoration, Whalley and his son-in-law Goffe had fled to America and the house had been sold to Roger Palmer. Barbara Palmer was a daughter of Viscount Grandison and her maiden name was Villiers. The young Palmers were objects of curiosity in King Street, and Pepys describes why:

And great doings of Musique at the next house, which was Whallys; the King and Dukes there with Madam Palmer, a pretty woman that they have a fancy to make her husband a cuckold. Here, at the old door that did go into those lodgings, my Lord and I and W. Howe did stand listening a great while to the Musique.

Barbara Palmer was created Duchess of Cleveland in 1670 and the children she bore the king were named Villiers-Stuart. To complete a circle which has no significance but which gives me pleasure, just as Barbara Villiers moved into my ancestor's house in King Street, the present-day Villiers-Stuarts now live in Ballinaparka.

These daily rides were not only for our exercise; they were also to keep the horses fit. In the summer these horses lived out of doors, eating the rich grass and clover and lazily flicking away flies with their tails, but during the winter they lived in their stalls and were kept in peak condition so that my father could go hunting with the West Waterford hounds once or twice a week.

I remember a meet in Aglish which took place on Armistice Day. An Englishwoman, whom we knew slightly, approached my father and sold him an Earl Haig poppy. He reluctantly forked out a pound and said he would expect a pound from her for an Easter lily on the next Easter Monday. A noticeable chilliness ensued. Politically my father would have been more likely to wear a poppy for Britain's fallen than a lily to commemorate those who died for Ireland in the Easter Rising of 1916 (about which Yeats wrote: "A terrible beauty is born"), but I think he found it poor manners and worse taste for someone English to be hawking poppies in a Southern Irish village where many Catholics, joining their Protestant neighbours in one of the few social events where they mixed company, might still with some justification think of England as the enemy. The unexpected necessity of parting with a pound would not have thrilled my father either.

The village of Aglish did not have electricity at the time we went to live there. Ballinaparka had its own generator, which supplied electric light. Fires provided the heating, and cooking was done on a stove, which also heated the bath water.

The day came when the villagers had to vote on whether or not they wanted the Electricity Supply Board to extend its services to Aglish. They would be charged so much a mile to bring it from the nearest town already serviced. The initial poll returned a negative vote. That Sunday the parish priest took matters into his own hands, starting his sermon with the following words: "There are children of light and children of darkness and you lot are children of darkness." A few months later the village had electricity.

Communication, not only on a personal level, was a problem at Ballinaparka. Not only did Aglish not have electricity; it lacked a telephone exchange. If we wanted to make a telephone call we had to wind a little handle on the side of the phone and wait for Mrs. Crowe in the neighbouring village to pick up to give her the number we required. Sometimes she didn't pick up very quickly, and when she did she had to go through the same routine with another primitive exchange to complete the transaction. We had no area codes or even multiple-digit numbers, just the name of the exchange followed by a single number. My father often found it quicker to drive thirty miles over the mountain and speak to a business partner face to face than to get through on the telephone. One of our childhood heroines was a woman who had become so enraged by the service that she'd taken a pair of scissors, cut the receiver off her telephone, driven to the local post office and thrown it through the window.

Aglish was a tiny village consisting of a couple of rows of cottages, a few pubs and a post office which was also a tiny shop, if that's not too large a word for a wooden counter and a few shelves with cigarettes, sweets and some food items. We used to shop in Cappoquin, seven miles away, itself not a sparkling metropolis. Each time, about once a week, my mother went to Cappoquin to buy groceries we piled into the car as eagerly as though we expected something to happen there. What happened, in reality, was that my mother took her shopping list into the grocery store—wooden-floored and smelling deliciously of coffee—read off her list to the grocer, who wrote it down in her red account book, loaded the produce into the car, and we went home. The only additional excitement possible would have been stopping for petrol or exchanging a "good morning" with someone we knew bound on a similar errand. Each Sunday we would repeat the journey, dressed in our Sunday clothes, girls and my mother wearing hats, to the tiny Protestant church. Off we would drive after a last-minute panic about prayer books and gloves. By this time I no longer wore castoffs from my cousin, but could fit into discards of my mother's and even the occasional coat with a couture label from my rich aunt, who was approximately the same size as I was. However, she wasn't the same age, and though I tended to fancy myself, I probably looked like an adolescent dowager.

The Church of Ireland prayer books we used were old and contained, as part of the morning prayer service, a prayer for the King. We skirted around this one with a catchall alternative. Clearly we couldn't pray for "Dev," as we called De Valera.

After the service we would shyly exchange hellos with the sons of our parents' friends if any of them happened to be home from school or university. This was, at first, the extent of our social life. Eventually there would be hunt balls and even an occasional private party with dancing, but we knew we had to wait. No girl was allowed to grow up before she was seventeen. And then it was all at once. There was no gradual negotiable process—the concept of teenagers had not yet caught on in Ireland.

T H E   B I R T H of my brother took us back into the era of nannies just at a time when governesses had become a thing of the past. Julia had been weaned from the process gradually and, for a brief time, shared a governess with another girl with whose family she stayed. We were aware that the woman in whose house Julia was living was not only a hunting friend from my father's youth but a writer, who under the name of M. J. Farrell had had several plays performed in London, one of them very successfully. Years later we boasted of having known Molly Keane when we were children. Her tough, accurate descriptions of Anglo-Irish life can even now make me shiver with the recognition of long forgotten associations.

Robert's first nanny was a delightful young woman whom he called NeeNee, as gradually, one at a time, the rest of the family came to do also. After a while she became thin and ill. Tuberculosis was diagnosed. She was admitted to one of the new sanitariums, cured fairly quickly and shortly afterward married a doctor.

Her successor was also called NeeNee, but Julia and I called her NeeNee Witch, as did my parents in unguarded moments. She was a grey-faced older woman with an ungenerous spirit and a talent for making everyone feel uncomfortable. Everyone except Robert, he revealed years later. It was a combination of this unfortunate woman's nature, the onset of my adolescence and being away at school part of the time which pushed me out of the no-man's-land of childhood. The days of drifting, passportless, from nursery to kitchen to drawing room were over. I wasn't quite in the adult camp but there were an increasing number of doors closed, or closing, behind me.

I felt no loss at what I was leaving behind. I did not understand that I had reached the end of an era in which my most important memories had been formed.

Rather later than she should have, my mother fired NeeNee Witch. I sympathized with her then, and do so even more now. I have inherited her fear of confrontation and am just as paralysed by having to deal with domestic crises to this day. Twice in my adult life, finding myself with a nanny who had, to put it euphemistically, long overstayed her usefulness, I had to pack up, leave the house with the children and delegate the task of firing her to my husband. This cowardice is not a quality of which I am proud. The difference is that my husband and I saw it as a shared problem and occasionally swapped unpleasant tasks when it was clear that one of us was better able to deal with a specific problem. My father not only saw the firing of NeeNee Witch as woman's work, just as he had seen the dismissal of Nelly from the Little House at Glenville many years before; he also tended to leave to my mother problems that he should have handled. He didn't delegate them to her, he just left them, apparently unconcerned with consequences, until she could stand it no longer and did whatever was required.

The need to dismiss NeeNee Witch came at a very unfortunate moment for my mother. My parents' marriage was breaking up and work sometimes took my mother away from home for several days at a time. Work involved a partnership with the man who was later to become our stepfather. I can imagine now my mother's desperation. My father was cold, angry, ungenerous in his own misery, withdrawn. Robert, the angelic baby, in the care of a hard-faced nanny who, although it subsequently turned out she enjoyed a warm and loving relationship with him, refused to give my mother that reassurance. And Julia and I, no longer the arch-spies, silent and depressed, seeking reassurance and begging not to know what was going on.

I was later told that on her way back from Dublin my mother would stop halfway at an aunt's house for a drink, a weep and some moral support. But when she arrived home she was always perfectly composed. The strain on her must have been appalling. If she had lacked a support group in the form of family or female friends in the past, she was clearly even more on her own when she started breaking all kinds of previously unchallenged rules. It would be inaccurate and naïve to suggest that there were no failed marriages or separations among the Anglo-Irish, but those that did exist were presented to children (and not necessarily dramatically reworded for adults) in terms such as "she couldn't stand the country, so she spends most of her time in London." Even these cases, for financial reasons among others, were fairly rare. It didn't make it easier that my mother had chosen someone far outside Anglo-Irish society. If he had been hard-hunting and hard-drinking and had done his time in a good regiment, a splinter group of sympathetic public opinion might have been possible. My grandfather was worried, but only once referred to my future stepfather in my presence. "Feller wears scent," he said. The reality—after-shave or civilized soap—would not have been an adequate defence and there was no question of any further discussion. The sentence sticks in my mind not only because it sums up the unbridgeable gap between civilized Europeans and the Anglo-Irish but because it was one of the few remarks I actually heard spoken on a subject which must have had an important place in everyone's mind. My memories of that time are largely of silence, of short exchanges of words—the words themselves fairly innocuous but the tone one of barely restrained anger.

Since there was no way I could be unaware of the atmosphere and emotions which surrounded us, even though sometimes ignorant of specifics, the rare occasion when a whole pertinent sentence was uttered was an important one.

"He died of a broken heart," my father explained, speaking of a friend dead before I was born. I was impressed, shocked, curious but unable, through fear, to inquire further. The sentence, out of context, is inextricably connected in my memory with my father sitting alone, late in the evening, a whiskey and soda by his side, a book in his hand, looking out over it and his glasses at the slowly darkening summer fields outside. It was a sentence which, once heard, could never be forgotten. As remarkable and memorable as one in my first history book at Glenville: "He never smiled again," we read about Henry I, after his only legitimate son was drowned in the wreck of the White Ship.

I was already acquainted with the idea of passion as described in the maids' magazines and I was sure, to the extent that I recognized the yet unexperienced emotions, that what I read in books would apply to me. But I was shocked by the idea that these feelings and unsustainable losses could ruin the lives of people like my parents and their friends. I never doubted that my father's friend had died in the way my father told me. Nor do I now.

No one else's mother worked. This information should not be the occasion of feminist outrage; the employment rate among the fathers was pretty low also. By the time we moved to Ballinaparka my mother had a modest but expanding career as an art dealer. The remoteness of our new home and the expansion of her business necessitated the long trips which left her so dependent on Robert's unsatisfactory nanny.

She started her career quietly, when I was a child. The first money I remember ever earning came from sorting out a crateful of old papers she'd bought at auction. Most of it was without value, but a few pieces were interesting enough to be sold to collectors or museums. I also learned to clean old pewter, employing a lethal mixture of cigarette ash and vinegar. One time she bought, from a house about to be demolished, a roomful of antique wallpaper. (The workmen tearing down the house had found a silver spoon and a few old coins under the floorboards. I was pleased by the image of lost and hidden treasure lying silently and patiently in the dusty dark.) Using a watering can, my mother had removed the already damp and peeling wallpaper from the equally deteriorated walls and laid it over bamboo sticks (no shortage of those at Glenville). The paper, which was French, was spread flat on the floor of the large, disused, unfurnished room which had once been the drawing room. I have no memory of the representational aspects of the design—Captain Cook on a South Sea island was one image—but I have a clear memory of the large pieces of flaking green paint, almost separate from the paper, realizing but not quite able to imagine that it would all be restored, sold by a dealer in London and find itself once again on the walls of a fashionable house. Like the silver spoon, it would have a new and unexpected existence.

The first items my mother bought were less exciting than the wallpaper and of no great artistic value. Perhaps ironically, since my mother's career as an antique dealer was supposed to be a step away from market gardening and poultry keeping, she once again found herself buying and selling hens. This time they were antique china hens sitting on china nests. The hen could be lifted off the nest and I imagine that they had once been used as fancy serving dishes. There were two prices for these hens. One for the plain white hens with red beaks and a higher one for those more brightly painted. I think the prices were three and five pounds, respectively. My mother would pack them and mail them, by sea, to a woman in Maryland. The first one arrived broken, but after that she learned the art of packing them with lots of crumpled newspapers and, thanks to the cushioning qualities of the *Irish Times*, there were no further disasters. The other day, in an antique shop on Lexington Avenue, I saw one of these hens, admittedly the more expensive coloured version, for sale for a couple of hundred dollars.

Later my mother started to buy portraits, reselling them on

the same principle. For military subjects there was also, regardless of quality unless it was by a known artist, a set price. Ten pounds for a blue uniform, fifteen for a red. They, too, went to the United States, where their ultimate purchasers, we were told, often claimed them as ancestors.

We loved to accompany my mother when she went to view an auction, enjoying the new faces and change of scenery and the possibility of treasure being unearthed. Even more we enjoyed the uninterrupted time with her in the car. I once spent a week alone with her in Dublin. I was having braces put on my teeth and in between the dentist's appointments we walked around the city, going from antique shop to antique shop. My mother doing a little business, learning a little, noting prices and keeping up with what the other dealers had in stock. Occasionally I would give her hand a squeeze and she would return it. But neither of us thought, or possibly was capable, of accompanying it with any words of affection. And yet I loved, and still love, my parents. And the love was returned. When I went through the agonies of adolescence the growing pains I had were private; resentment toward the older generation was neither expressed nor, I think, felt.

We spent that week in a small residential hotel. The first morning when we came down to breakfast we found ourselves to be, apart from the landlady serving breakfast, the only white people there. My mother was slightly taken aback and the following morning we had breakfast in our room. This was more a symptom of shyness than racial prejudice. Very few blacks lived in Ireland and those who did were part of the professional class. Our fellow lodgers would have been educated and comparatively affluent young men who were studying at either Trinity College or University College Dublin, both of which maintained a very high standard of education.

Another tiny incident which I remember from this trip is also associated with race. I watched what seemed to me an exotic, almost Dickensian scene, although completely devoid of threatening overtones. My mother sold a couple of gold watches to an elderly Jew. (There is a small Jewish population in Ireland—two thousand when Joyce wrote *Ulysses*.) He weighed them on a jeweler's scale and paid her a price entirely calculated by the amount of gold they contained. These watches, however, were not the fruits of pickpocketing activities on the part of my mother, nor were they the last couple of trinkets left in the family. She'd bought them at auction in the country and was just going about a small sideline in her business.

My mother deserved a better education than she received. Her school days started off well, though unconventionally. When her father lost his money, my mother, the eldest child, was sent to live at Ballydavid. My great-grandmother and great-great-aunt offered to take a child in order to simplify my grandmother's life. My mother was a favourite of theirs since she reminded them of Saint, my mother's uncle who had been killed in the First World War.

My mother lived at Ballydavid, her mother and sister and brother joining the family for holidays. Each day she rode her pony to a neighbour's house where she shared a governess with the daughter of the family. She was left on her own a good deal, separated from her parents and without any close friends of her own age. My mother describes this in a way which makes me believe it was the happiest time in her life. She loved Ballydavid, a fine Regency house with beautiful grounds. She loved riding her pony through the woods and on the long smooth Woodstown beach. She also used this pony for expeditions searching for bird's nests, and kept a journal which described those she had found. No one else shared these interests, and I think that, at a very young age, my mother developed the inner resources and inquiring mind which made her into a self-sufficient and interesting woman.

When it came time for her to go to boarding school, her parents inadvertently sent her to a Christian Science school. The Christian Science part had not been heavily stressed in the sales pitch and had gone unnoticed by her parents for some time. (Her mother, actually, since there is no reason to suppose my grandfather would have despised the teachings of Mary Baker Eddy more than he did those of the run-of-the-mill denominations.) When my grandmother realized it, it was too late. Uniforms had been bought, fees paid, name tapes sewn in, so my mother was given a mildly Christian Science education. Curiously enough, the better non-Catholic school in Waterford (the one we didn't go to) was a Quaker school, but it was not aggressively denominational either. Soon after my mother left school, war broke out and she served as a Land Girl on a farm until she and my father married.

My father was fifteen years older than my mother. He was charming, witty, a brilliant horseman. Despite his lack of money, he was considered glamorous and sought-after.

I observed my parents' marriage carefully. My earliest memories are not so much of my father or my mother but of their marriage. I was keeping tabs on it, and them even then. And yet there was no room for the piece of information my mother casually dropped into a conversation long after I had left home. Long after I was married myself, and after my father's death. She mentioned, in passing, tennis parties at Ballydavid which my father had occasionally attended as a young man. I asked her, with astonishment, whether she had known him when she was still a child. Not well, she told me. A moment later she added something she'd just remembered. She had taken my father to see a butterfly which she had reared from a caterpillar. (There doesn't seem to be an appropriate verb to describe the keeping of a lepidopteran as a pet—"raised" suggests an involvement which is not earned; "supervised" sounds a little bossy and claims a degree of authority not necessarily recognized by the chrysalis or larva; "imprisoned" is not quite fair when the only motivation is scientific curiosity modified by a touch of affectionate excitement.)

I thought of the days I had spent eavesdropping when I was a child, the fears grounded and ungrounded about which I had worried obsessively and understood that this particular piece of information had always been available to me if I had asked the right question, or if the conversation had happened to wander in that direction.

Immediately I started to weave my mother's memory into the ragbag of information, belief, values, superstitions, habits and random debris which tend to guide most of my actions and which determine who I am, and even, to a tiny extent, who my children will be.

Those of us who are at least partially governed by our memories have to play by very careful rules. This account of a long-past incident has to be considered thoughtfully and built upon slowly. There is some information available—the age difference, for instance. If my mother was ten, my father must have been twenty-five. Too much younger and my father would not have been interested, too much older and my mother would have been shy. Then the location—the greenhouse was where I finally set the scene. It didn't seem likely that even domesticated insects would be welcomed in the reception rooms of her great-aunt's and grandmother's house or that my mother would have been likely to have expected anyone to accompany her to a distant indoor location such as an attic or nursery quarters. The kitchen or adjacent servants' quarters would hold the risk of someone "pitching out" a perfectly good dormant caterpillar. Red Admiral or Cabbage White, I wonder—or maybe a Tortoiseshell—even here there is available information since I remember my mother being interested in a Red Admiral I captured when quite a small child at Glenville. I like to think that it was a greenhouse where my mother brought my father to see her butterfly. I can imagine them, him in tennis whites, her in a light cotton dress with bare brown legs and long hair tied back, silhouetted against the glass as they lean toward each other to look at a perfect Red Admiral in a glass jar.

Memories are more delicate and fragile than dreams. I have observed my mother as she, expressionless, silent, watched me freeze a conversation in which an important memory was threatened by an alternative version of the same incident put forward by my sister. I could no more afford to argue the point with anyone who shared that memory than I could to question my mother about the butterfly, but whether it is to protect her or to protect me, I don't know.

That is all that I know or can deduce about the butterfly moment, but it makes all previous information either irrelevant or slightly inaccurate. It is the single most interesting thing that I know about my parents' marriage. And I can't understand, if he was the man who looked at that butterfly with that little girl and, later, when she grew up, married her, why he couldn't have made her happy.

At first, marriage must have seemed wonderful to my mother. But I imagine that the pressures of financial worries, my father's family (a semi-dependent mother and two brothers who never seemed to settle down satisfactorily), the keeping up appearances, the problems of dealing with difficult and untrained staff, stuffy Protestant Waterford society, my father's non-intellectual horsey friends, must have started to depress her. My father was not supportive or even particularly aware in some of these areas. I have noticed that those brought up with plenty of money do not panic about the lack of it in a way that those unused to it at all do. My father was hardworking, had a strong sense of honour, but was unfazed by the stack of unopened buff envelopes containing unpaid bills. They would lie first on the hall table and later would be stacked on my mother's desk. She would worry about them and not be reassured by my father's belief that a groom and two hunters in the stables were a basic necessity of existence.

Waterford society must have seemed dreary and unrewarding. My mother, by now with some amusement, tells how, as a young married woman, she took me to a tea party at the Bishop's Palace. I was very small and apparently less than completely housebroken. A puddle was noticed on the drawing-room carpet. My mother was mortified and her shame was not abated when the Bishop's wife called for a maid with a mop and *lots* of disinfectant.

There was not, in those days, a younger, less formal set where a humiliation of this kind could be turned into an asset in the form of an entertaining anecdote.

There is, however, a particularly Irish form of jeopardy for the proud or stuffy. A deflating remark or apposite nickname can outlive its victim. A man whose heavily insured property burns down may, for instance, find himself referred to, though never quite in his hearing, as "Matches" for the rest of his days. The Bishop's wife who had embarrassed my mother had been christened Isabel, but was privately referred to by curates who had suffered similarly at her hand as "Jezebel." Even as my mother endured the rest of the disastrous tea party, she could look back at the time she had been a teenage guest at a legendary Palace party. The Palace was large. With plenty of underutilized space, it was a natural setting for a game of Sardines. The Bishop, who was a distant relative of my father's, had not been present, since he was upstairs sick in bed. One of the smaller children, looking for the "sardine," had mistaken the slumbering Bishop for his quarry and had crawled in beside him. Soon they were joined by another child, and then another, and so on.

Although these memories and stories gave a lot of innocent pleasure, there is surely something very lacking in a social life which can only be enjoyed in retrospect.

When after eighteen years of marriage my parents started to separate, we were never, of course, told what was happening, but we were aware of an appalling tension. As in most families, meals were the fields on which these largely wordless battles were fought. Lunch, which was served in the dining room and usually consisted of something in the order of mince and Brussels sprouts followed by queen of puddings, would be conducted almost entirely in silence. My parents would occasionally speak to each other in tones of barely controlled bitterness and anger and we children would speak in inverse proportion to our age. I, the eldest, the most inhibited and the one with most information (or at least strongest suspicions), would remain almost completely silent. My sister Julia would have a little to say, and Alice would be quite chatty except that she would be answered, if at all, in monosyllables. Robert, when he was old enough to join us, would chatter about subjects which seemed extremely dangerous to me. The table at which we ate lunch was placed in the generous curve of the windows and outside it was often raining. Inside and out there was an atmosphere of extreme gloom. In the drawing room there was a cheerful turf fire and some possibility of curling up with a book, but the dining room was unmitigated, concentrated misery. The cold, the lack of cheerful light, the rain outside, the poor and repetitive food, the silence, the unhappiness, all fed the feeling that the explosion I feared above all else might erupt. After that explosion everything would be destroyed; nothing could be rebuilt. The concept of clearing the air with a good fight was alien to us. Of course, the explosion never took place. None of us was capable of that. If it had, it might not necessarily have been a bad thing.

Since there is no divorce in Ireland, when my mother left my father she lost all rights to her children. Though there was now one person less at those gloomy lunches the range of dangerous subjects expanded. We three girls never mentioned our mother's name. I don't think we ever commented on her absence. Certainly for some time it was never acknowledged out loud that she had left. I can still feel a tight knot in my stomach when I remember Robert, the baby of the family, innocently saying something about his mother. Worse still, he sometimes talked about her flat. Never mentioned, though this now became the greatest fear, was the man who, after interminable legalities, would become our stepfather.

The first Christmas was the worst. It always rained at Ballinaparka at Christmas. As a child I approached holidays with the same uneasy feelings I still experience during most festivals. I felt unequal to the occasion, unable to drum up, still less to express, the appropriate emotions. I was oppressed by the demands made on us by the holiday season. I feared my failure and had fears of everyone else failing also. These fears were to some extent realized every year. Of course, as a child I didn't know how to name these feelings, and it was only after I had come to live in the United States and first saw the work of Norman Rockwell that I understood the burden of expectations created by sentimental ideals. It was only as an adult, also, that I understood that I was not alone in this. Every year, people drawn together by unrealistic expectations and good intentions find themselves playing for higher emotional stakes than they can afford and for every Norman Rockwell golden-skinned turkey carved there are tears and hurt feelings and disappointments. As time goes by I have managed to spread this discomfort to include Thanksgiving, New Year's Eve, Easter and birthdays and can drum up a wealth of inadequacy and embarrassment to cover all these events.

So St. Stephen's Day is my kind of holiday. It is an exclusively Irish festival. St. Stephen was the first Christian martyr, but his name day, December 26, is, like Christmas, a Christian holiday superimposed on an ancient pagan celebration. St. Stephen's Day requires no human cheer, cooking or gift exchanges and is celebrated in an entirely pagan manner. Only a fragment of the pagan tradition is left and its origin is completely lost. Traditionally, on St. Stephen's Day boys go from house to house singing—they are called the Wren Boys and the song they sing is the Wren Song. They are rewarded with small sums of money. By the time I was a child, very often these boys turned up with an accordion and tried a rendering of some contemporary American popular song, but at our house we insisted on the original: "The wren, the wren, the king of all birds . . ." It was usually delivered in a low, fast, monotonous chant by a small boy resolutely refusing to meet one's eye, which served to make the rendering more mysterious, its significance more elusive, and enhanced the ritualistic aspect of the extremely brief performance.

Although I don't remember a Christmas at Ballinaparka without rain, I don't remember a St. Stephen's Day which was not mild and even sunny, with birdsong and a cheerful atmosphere of relief. There was the feeling, despite the odd hangover, emotional or otherwise, that another bridge had been safely crossed.

My father tried to make the first Christmas after the separation festive, but we couldn't do it. The following year we went to Switzerland for three weeks of skiing, and every year after that we went to one of the less well known ski resorts for the Christmas holidays. It was an extravagance, but a wise one. My father proved fairly adept at hotel life, some aspects of which provided him with an outlet for his dry sense of humour. The term "après-ski" seemed to him, as it does to me, quite funny. He would refer, straight-faced, to the Irish tweeds he changed into after skiing by that name. At one hotel he invited a lone English clergyman to sit at our table for dinner each evening. This man, not memorable in any other way, was referred to by my father as "my chaplain."

We all learned to ski, even my father, although he never acquired any great degree of skill. Since he was nearly sixty when he first took it up and was beginning to feel the legacy of past hunting and racing accidents, this was not surprising. Even so, he thought of skiing as an old man's sport.

My brother learned to ski immediately and very well. Julia and I would return from trips on the more advanced slopes and see Robert, like a tiny pilot fish, guiding my father down to safety and lunch.

One of the hotels we stayed at offered a kind of coupon, a French equivalent of the Luncheon Voucher, to those who didn't choose to lunch in the hotel dining room. These vouchers could, at a mountaintop café, be turned in for a sandwich and an amazing quantity of rough red Algerian wine, after which we would ski home like birds.

My father, perhaps by way of compensation for the unaccustomed financial splurge, or more likely taking the opportunity of being away from Celtic gloom, used to announce that he'd cut out drinking for the holiday. This excluded only whiskey or gin. Wine with meals clearly didn't count, since we were in France or

Switzerland or even Austria, where wine with meals was the same as water at home. Beer also didn't count, especially since he could put a couple of bottles out on his balcony and drink it at a welcome and unusually cold temperature. The quaint local after-dinner liqueurs didn't count either, as they fell into the category of liqueur chocolates, not booze.

I T W A S at Ballinaparka that I perfected two ways of withdrawing from life. Books and sleep. It was also here, not Switzerland, that I got drunk for the first time.

While my parents were going through the final stages of their marriage I was struggling with adolescence, although I didn't know enough to give it that name. I thought I was feeling an understandable need to leave school. I felt then, as keenly as I would now, the humiliation of being an uniformed schoolgirl, complete with gym slip, knee socks, lace-up shoes and hockey stick, while my body and mind were telling me that I was becoming a woman.

I understand now that many of the humiliations and discomforts of boarding school were caused by my own attitudes and actions. Clothes were always a difficult area. Although I complained as bitterly as the other girls about the school uniform, I suffered agonies when I didn't have the right non-uniform clothes or enough of them. This was a time of ugly adolescent fashion— felt skirts with poodles on them were one of the highlights and the more affluent girls would return to school each term with something new for me to envy. Then an aunt offered me and Julia a dress each. We went to the tweed mills and chose two lengths of beautiful pale purple and blue material. My sister had hers made into a human dress. I, missing the opportunity to improve my wardrobe by, say, eighty percent, elected to have mine made into a very fancy and rather low-cut dress. I never wore it with any confidence. Needless to say, I didn't have the right shoes or stockings. In order to compensate for this, when my father asked me what I wanted for Christmas I chose a pair of black Cuban-heeled shoes. Again all wrong and too much. By this time I was reading more than my contemporaries and came upon a phrase in a Graham Greene book: "standing on her dignity like a schoolgirl in her first pair of high heels." I was able to feel superior because of appreciating the simile while simultaneously feeling mortified.

I loathed my school, and the discomfort, boredom and physical hardship, not too strong a word, added to this feeling of revolt. I was also aware that none of the women who were in charge of us was qualified to guide us through the transitional stages of our adolescence. Like our governesses, they weren't there through conviction, but because something had gone wrong in their lives. We regarded them with the insensitive, intolerant and unearned superiority of confident youth. Although most of us wouldn't have had to look very far from home to perceive loneliness, insecurity, fear and frustration, we assumed that our lives would be different and that we would be immune to the random disasters—poverty, failure to marry, hormonal imbalances—which had brought these unfortunate women into the field of education. Their lot was clearly worse than ours, but we were too callous to see it, too unimaginative to understand that although the school food tasted just as awful to them, they were permitted to express themselves even less freely than we were. We unquestioningly and ignorantly believed improbable and often impossible things about them. I remember a perfectly respectable woman who taught us geography. She was good-natured and cleaner than most of our instructors. Her only peculiarity (and they all had something) was one which many of my former schoolmates, some of whom were going to run to fat in later life, might now envy—she was unusually slim-hipped, particularly when seen in profile. One of us decided and we accepted, with utter disregard for biology or logic, that this was the result of an illegal operation.

By the time I was finishing my second-to-last year I realized that the whole thing was fruitless. I would have been, if not happy, at least resigned to completing the final year if there had been the possibility of real education. In fact, the combination of a shaky home life and uncertainty about my future left me very suggestible and for the right teacher I might have become a devoted pupil. But there was no such person at Hillcourt. I flailed around for something solid to hang on to and found books. Unfortunately, they weren't easy to come by. I don't remember ever being taught about the wealth of literature which our country had produced. Predictably, "Innisfree" was the only Yeats poem included in our classroom anthologies. The school library boasted the entire works of Mazo de la Roche but had little else to offer. My parents didn't buy books, and time and geography did not allow me access during the school year to those they borrowed from the Royal Dublin Society library. The dearth of the romances and thrillers which I would have preferred forced me to explore the books in my parents' library. I started with what seemed the lightest and gradually worked my way up to the thicker volumes. One term I returned to school with *War and Peace*. It may have been an attempt to show off, but I don't think so, and I was depressed when a teacher, in a perfectly friendly way, asked if, when I'd finished it, I was next going to tackle the Bible. She'd seen it as an attempt to break some kind of record; I'd seen it as a temporary respite from hockey and watery cabbage.

What I lacked most at school was guidance and a kindred spirit; the specific advice a teacher could have given me about what next to read was secondary. That knowledge I later gradually acquired from friends and by chance, sometimes the source adding to the pleasure of the discovery. The two regrets that I have about my lack of instruction in English are that I did not learn any grammar until I was an adult and that, through blind ignorance, I did not read *Tristram Shandy* until I was forty.

Joyce had a higher recognition factor at Hillcourt than Tolstoy did, though even fewer of my teachers were likely to have read *Ulysses* than *War and Peace*. The former was, of course, banned in Ireland. Although our minds were protected from the corrupting influence of the writer they thought of as a notorious Irish pornographer, our bodies, exercised when possible as an alternative to cold showers, were sent on Sunday afternoons to, among other places, the Martello Tower at Sandycove—the setting of the opening scene of *Ulysses*.

The afternoon walks varied with privilege and seniority. Initially we paired up and walked in an unsightly crocodile through the streets of Dun Laoghaire; twice to church on Sundays and once for afternoon exercise. Dressed in lint-attracting navy blue coats and nasty little caps which wouldn't stay on, we were a sorry sight. As we grew older we were allowed to go for walks in smaller, unsupervised but carefully vetted groups. We were on our honour not to modify our uniforms (take off our caps) or to go into shops. While not breaking these rules, I once voiced the opinion that "honour" was a bigger word than was implied in this context and said that I wasn't sure that I felt bound by it when it was invoked only for the convenience of the management. This turned out to be a minority view, and I retreated from the argument aware that it was not only the school and its staff but also most of the pupils that I longed to leave behind me.

It was the term when I had smuggled in *The Cruel Sea* and *The Constant Nymph* (past the school censor, even more stringent than the one that De Valera and Maynooth had set up for the nation) and my ideas about sex, love, honour and loss were inextricably and emotionally entangled in my mind. To be seventeen years old and to feel honour-bound to wear a humiliating school uniform and to deny oneself a shop-bought snack to supplement an inadequate lunch seemed silly. The loneliness of school life and a sense of loss, anticipated rather than experienced since I had not yet had what I feared I must inevitably lose, made the wasting of time seem unforgivable and hardened my resolve to spring myself free. I wandered around with a sulky expression and red eyes (*The Constant Nymph*) for the rest of the term.

Not every girl in the school had to go on these Sunday walks. After church and choir practice, those who lived close enough were allowed to go home for lunch and to return in time for evening prayers and bed. My parents lived a hundred and fifty miles away, so this did not apply to me. But two Sundays a month were designated "long Sundays" (my father, with feeling, used to call them "very long Sundays") and the entire school was released after breakfast, wearing their own clothes.

Quite reasonably, my parents took turns with this chore and their methods of filling in this, to them, interminable day differed. Both were sensible enough to know that the main requirement was food, but after that the similarity ended. My father would take me, and later my sister, to the Kildare Street Club, an old Anglo-Irish establishment, located not surprisingly on Kildare Street. Lunch and dinner would be eaten there and the time between filled in with a walk around St. Stephen's Green or reading old copies of *Punch* and *Country Life*. Very occasionally we would go to the cinema in the afternoons. There was a school rule against this. My father was hardly a movie fan, but as usual he saw himself as being above the law. A minor rule which he could see as being, in principle, sensible did not necessarily apply to him. I remember him taking me to see *To Catch a Thief*, the first colour movie he had ever seen. The scene when Jessie Royce Landis, Grace Kelly's screen mother, stubs out her cigarette in a fried egg was, for him, the finest moment ever captured on film.

My mother did not have an establishment such as the Kildare Street Club on which to fall back. Once or twice we spent part of our day with Hector, the man who was to become our stepfather. I was fascinated by him. He was the son of Andrew O'Connor, who had been a well-known sculptor and whose work is still to be seen in Europe and even in New York on the edifice of St. Bartholomew's Church on Park Avenue. The frieze, now a familiar part of my New York landscape, I first saw in study form in my stepfather's flat. I remember it well; also some of his father's other work, most of it yellow with age, cigarette smoke and Dublin dust. It was the first time I had ever been in an apartment and I was fascinated by the tiny kitchen and the cups and saucers which didn't match, all of which were old and beautiful. My stepfather didn't go in for childish entertainment. My mother took me to the cinema, but if Hector had been along it would have been a foreign film, if such a thing happened to be playing in Dublin. He didn't ignore us; his attention was flattering, if a little disconcerting. He never tempered his opinions about politics or art to our conventional upbringing, nor his frequently cynical views on society or the relationship between the sexes. My mother would nervously interject: "Really, Hector . . ." from time to time and be ignored. I liked and respected him and found his opinion of my school identical to mine. This view did not always work to my advantage. I remember Hector insisting on a second cup of coffee after dinner one night when I was already disastrously late for my return to Hillcourt. It was my mother, of course, who had to face the headmistress when I was delivered at the exact hour of "lights out." My mother's "I know you won't mind, we usually bring her back early" sounded illogical to me, but the incident was so outside my headmistress's experience that I got away with it.

Both my parents wrote to me regularly while I was at school, providing the kind of support and affection which we all found hard to express face to face. At home, both my parents called me "darling," as they did my sisters and brother. And until things started to go wrong, or possibly until what had always been wrong began to surface, they addressed each other in the same way. But there was very little physical affection shown. Hugs and kisses came only at bedtime or when we had been separated for several days. We all found it easy to end a letter with the word "love," but I don't think I remember saying or hearing the words "I love you" as a child. I didn't, however, for a moment doubt that they did. Nor, I think, were other Anglo-Irish families more demonstrative.

Literature was not the only subject on which we were kept uninformed. To say that sex education was not part of Hillcourt's curriculum would stretch the meaning of the word "redundancy" beyond its normal boundaries. We didn't even learn biology, although the games mistress taught a class called Hygiene. We learned to name the different parts of the human anatomy in detail, except, of course, the breasts and reproductive organs. I achieved lower grades in this subject than my already abysmal average. My father, reading my school report, noticed that I had failed Hygiene and, looking over the tops of his glasses, asked: "Don't you wash?" It was a reasonable question, since the school had been so thriftily converted that there was an acute bath shortage. Baths were rationed to two a week, sometimes even necessitating a leave from "prep" (as study hall was called). Hair washing was officially performed only every other week, with half the school, in winter, trying to dry their hair around three banked-up fireplaces or tepid stoves. Hair dryers (other than the hooded kind one baked under at the hairdresser's), my children would be awed to know, didn't seem to have been invented then. The time-honoured tradition of cheap collective showers was not possible at Hillcourt, since the authorities waited, ever alert, for the epidemic of lesbianism which they dreaded and which existed only in their minds.

Not that there wasn't an opportunity for some research into the field of sex (which, I regret to this day, no one ever named the area of muddy grass where we played hockey), since those of us bored with swapping fairly familiar misinformation could always hit the hockey ball accidentally past the goalposts in order to have a good look at what the man in the lane was really doing. What he was attempting to do, as we all were aware, was to masturbate. Unfortunately, for him at least, he wasn't very good at it. In fairness, the extreme cold and our singularly unattractive school uniforms should not be underestimated. What we were supposed to do was to pretend we didn't see him and, in actuality, only one or two of the braver girls gaped openly. The rest managed to keep it down to a little muffled but inevitable giggling. About once a term the headmistress, backed up by the games mistress, both armed with hockey sticks, would put the run on him. Not only was this a richly comic spectacle but many of us realized that there was a certain poetic justice involved—the woman who dictated the repressive atmosphere in which our perfectly natural emotions and instincts were denied was being forced to face an unpleasant reality.

I have a few happy memories of my boarding school. A summer Sunday, mysteriously unsupervised, when I lay in the sun and read Bram Stoker; illicitly eating red currants in the garden; lying on the short dry grass beside the tennis courts watching a tennis match; eating my sweet ration while drying my hair, with the smell of coal dust and the sound of girls swapping women's magazines and gossip; lining up in the kitchen last thing at night to fill our hot-water bottles with not quite warm enough slightly cabbagey water. All of these moments are about warmth and food, or rather about a respite from cold and the choice of hunger or disgust.

These moments weren't enough. Although my lifelong fear of confrontation was already fully developed, I wrote to my parents and told them I wasn't prepared to stay at Hillcourt for my final year. The announcement was waved away as a problem not convenient for discussion at that time. I wrote back saying that if I was sent back the following term I would run away and added, as a clincher, that I had already sold my school uniform. The latter announcement did the trick, partly because it amused my father, partly because neither parent felt inclined or able to cope with me. The deal we made was that I should go to a crammer in England and at Christmas take the exams I should have taken the following summer. This was perfectly acceptable to me since I knew the amount of work involved was negligible. What none of us realized, though, was that the standards aimed at by my Irish school were so low that, even when achieved, they would not ensure any kind of decent job.

That summer at Ballinaparka a new pattern was perfected. I would come downstairs for breakfast, somewhat sluggish. After bacon and greasy fried eggs, tea and toast, I would return to my room and sleep. This part is perfectly understandable—a meal like that would now put me away for the rest of the day. Later I would wake up and try to study for the exams which would free me from being a schoolgirl. I had been so poorly taught that I didn't know how to study. But I knew that Shelley and Keats were on the syllabus. English, as it had been taught so far, consisted of compositions, learning by heart and destroying good books by reading them aloud around the classroom.

I used to read our set books in advance—mainly because I was still a big weeper and wanted to avoid a repetition of the singing-lesson humiliations at my previous school. It took a lot of advance preparation to get dry-eyed through *Wuthering Heights*—"Oh, Cathy! Oh, my life! how can I bear it?" was not intended to leave the reader unmoved. Nor was Heathcliff's speech of impassioned grief and rage on hearing of Cathy's death. This section got the attention of some of the rest of the class. I suspected that this momentary response contained the kind of sentimentality which Emily Brontë clearly despised and for which Isabel was so severely punished, and I was glad when we came to the passage where Ellen finds Isabel's pet springer hanged by Heathcliff. While appalled by the brutality myself, I was aware that the incident would separate the men from the boys and that I would be left alone with the book and the revolutionary message it contained. I was glad of this since I needed time to think. I was amazed that I seemed to be the only one who made any connection between a "school book" and real life—real life in the sense that we were all going to be, on some level, to some extent, living it. We all avidly read the fiction in the cheaper women's magazines. Did those stories seem to describe more valid human emotions or less farfetched premises? Did no one but me understand that the Cathy we read about had been not much older than we were when she gave her heart and soul to one man and her body to another? Did no one pause to consider that there might be a limited amount of happiness and passion out there and that some—many of us—weren't going to get our share? Why did no one wonder why we were reading about Heathcliff in an institution which went to great lengths to deny that "boys" were a legitimate field of interest?

So, that summer, I did the only thing I knew how to do in the circumstances: I learned by heart. By the end of the summer I knew hundreds of lines. I would memorize part of a poem and then sleep until lunchtime. This sleep served to leave the lines indelibly printed in my memory. Then a silent lunch. Then some more poetry and sleep. Tea and supper and more of the same. None of which interfered with the solid ten hours of nocturnal unconsciousness.

I am always surprised when a friend makes a reference to a favourite moment which I don't recognize in a book which I had thought, up to that moment, I knew well. I am equally surprised when I refer to one of my favourite lines (like "To make matters worse he has a toothache" in *Anna Karenina*) and a well-read friend looks at me blankly. Some books lend themselves to this kind of selective memory more easily than others. Almost everyone loves *The Catcher in the Rye* and thinks he knows every moment of it, but the same thing happens—one remembers and another looks blankly at the reference and quotes another passage. Those of us who love to read, and those of us who depend on books to give us the information we either can't or don't choose to look for in life, consume millions of words and enormous quantities of facts. Most of it, in my case at least, is forgotten. What I remember is telling and almost always unrelated to how recently I have read the passage in question. I have clearly read several hundred descriptions of parties, let alone the party scenes I have watched in the movies. The ones I remember immediately spring to mind. Natasha's first ball in *War and Peace*, Emma Bovary's visit to La Vaubyessard (some of the ladies didn't put their gloves in their wineglasses) and every tiny social gathering about which Jane Austen ever wrote. Since, on a basic level, social life is presumably one of the more civilized aspects of the mating ritual, sexual energy, sexual tension and expectation are the fuel which lights up a party. It is possible to spend a great deal of money, wear beautiful clothes, do exotic things with flowers and food and shiny things with silver and glass, make everything look warm and smell wonderful, assert one's taste or affluence or power—but without the possibility of a step in the dance of the sexes, nothing happens.

Jane Austen describes both the events where something happens and those where nothing does (dinner at Lady Catherine de Bourgh's is, I think, the ultimate literary description of a sterile display of power, where everyone goes through the motions but no one ends up any further along). My favorites are the evenings when someone counts up the available young people in the neighborhood and, after dinner, the carpet is rolled up, someone is coaxed to the piano and dancing commences.

It is not only the modesty of the arrangements which seems familiar, and the shortage of young people in a remote rural community, but also the complicity of two generations to tackle an important aspect of life while pretending to do something else. We belonged to a stratum of society which was more than waning, it was facing extinction. Clearly the next generation would have to adapt, but before it could adapt it would have to exist and for this it was necessary for my generation to procreate. Some procedure for marriage followed by breeding was necessary for survival but there were obstacles in the way. In addition to the obvious ones there were some subtle taboos to be overcome. As forbidden as the subject of sex was the subject of love. To feel it, to wish for it or, worse still, to need it was information best kept to oneself. I wonder now that either commodity managed to exist in this strange climate. It was as though we had a lunatic obstacle course to run if we were to avoid breaking the genetic chain. No wonder the small, very occasional dances and parties took on a survival atmosphere. Three or four times a year we would change into not particularly becoming dresses, and with home-curled hair, pale goose-pimpled arms and shoulders, we would have three or four hours to attract a lifetime mate. And, what's more, we were meant to do it while pretending that we weren't. Perhaps not surprisingly, these parties generated a Darwinian energy and in our dancing and banter we were like a small bunch of lemmings running around in circles pretending not to see the cliff.

I had my first party at Ballinaparka. We had a buffet supper, we danced to records and drank a wine punch concocted by my father. I saw him make it, but cheap white wine and soda water are the only ingredients I remember. There must have been others. It was relatively disgusting but I drank a good deal of it and felt wonderful. I danced with some young men who were staying with a neighbour. (A simple enough statement, one might have thought, and yet it reports the equivalent of a small miracle. This part reminds me of *Love in a Cold Climate,* in which there is such a dearth of young men for a dance that Uncle Matthew goes to London and rounds up a bunch of old codgers from his club to make up the numbers.) In Ireland hostesses were sometimes forced to resort to desperate measures such as including the occasional larger schoolboy who could find a dinner jacket that fit him. This kind of behaviour was considered unacceptable, but the condemnation always had an implied "there, but for the grace of God, go I" modification. At my party there were three perfectly viable unmarried heterosexual males, older than fourteen and younger than seventy, in addition to the usual suspects rounded up for these occasions. The music came from an ugly radiogram— a rare concession to changing times—which stood out among the otherwise antique furniture in the drawing room. Our selection of records, though supplemented by loans from neighbours, was extremely limited. I danced and reacted gauchely to unsubtle flirtations and completely ignored any of my guests who were not having a good time. One girl, I remember, sat disconsolately on the stairs, her unaccustomed stole wound round her neck like a rugger scarf. The evening seemed to go on forever and I felt as though I were living in a wonderful dream. But this was Ireland. I wasn't in love; I was drunk.

The next morning I felt horrible. I felt sick, dry-mouthed and, above all, guilty. I lied unconvincingly, said I was coming down with flu, had food poisoning, was exhausted. And yet I had done nothing wrong. I was seventeen, it was my first experience with alcohol, no one had warned me. There was nothing to be guilty about, but I was. And defensive. Looking back, it seems stranger still when I realize that I had never heard anyone express shame at having a hangover. Stories of drunkenness were always told with amusement or, if in the first person, bordered on bragging. I doubt that I fooled anyone, but my first lapse was never commented upon.

The lighthearted attitude toward alcohol and alcoholism, which we didn't then know to be a tragic disease, was shared by even the civilized and intelligent. I remember overhearing my parents and a friend discuss a mutual acquaintance's drinking problem or solution, depending on one's point of view. This unfortunate man had apparently ended a binge by passing out. His wife and presumably a servant or two had dragged him upstairs and put him in bed to sleep it off. The next morning he was still unconscious. They were surprised but not unduly concerned. However, the following morning he hadn't revived and appeared still to be drunk. Since he clearly had never been in a condition to get himself downstairs to the sideboard for a refill, it seemed worth a little investigation. Someone, a little more observant than the others, noticed that there was a narrow tube running along the skirting board of the room, attached to the wall, rather in the manner of a telephone extension cord. On further inspection it was discovered that one end of the tubing was concealed under his pillow, while the other disappeared through a carefully bored hole in the back of a chest of drawers. Inside, with the tube attached, was a now empty bottle of whiskey. This story was considered hilarious. Any suggestion that it was a little hard on his wife was dismissed. He was considered funny and earned some admiration for his ingenuity.

The morning of my first hangover brought good news. My father came into my bedroom with a letter which he'd received from a secretarial college in Oxford saying there was a space for me that autumn. The Oxford aspect of it, I'd manipulated. I had finished school and wanted to move on to the next place. No one made any suggestions about what might happen next, and when I trotted out the cliché that "a secretarial training was always useful," it was greeted with some relief. I'd worked out that London would be too big a move for me to make. Oxford might be more manageable.

I was duly enrolled at the Oxford and County Secretarial College. My mother delivered me to my lodgings and told me that she and my father were getting divorced.

Although I was sad and cried a little, the emotions I felt were mingled with new ones. I was concerned for my parents, hoped my mother would be happy, feared that my father would not—feared, selfishly, that I would witness his unhappiness. I was also guiltily aware that I would be the child least affected. My sisters and brother were still at home, while I was free, tentatively entering a world I had so far only read about.

I started life in Oxford knowing even less than the other girls at the boardinghouse where I lived. I didn't know how to drive, cook, play tennis or bridge, how to dance, dress or apply makeup, how to speak a second language, play the piano or sing, how to hold my liquor or balance a chequebook, sew, curl my hair or flirt. I knew enough to suspect that my basic outfit—a blue pleated skirt handed down by a neighbour and a yellow sweater I had knitted myself (knitting was also a skill I had not quite acquired)—would not, in the long run, do. I didn't know how to improve my appearance since I had very little money and lacked the taste to put together a look from my limited resources. Nor did I, in those days before hot rollers were invented, know what to do with my badly cut hair. Nor did I know that eyebrow pencils came in colours other than black.

I knew a few things that other girls my age didn't know, but I didn't know that I knew them and it was information that would not become useful until much later. I knew about figures on a Grecian Urn, though at seventeen the hard, cold, unsentimental message was not for me. I didn't know then that nothing is forever or that I wouldn't always be young. Love was then, as now, the central key. I had no idea how little power I had over those I hoped would save me, or how much power I had to do this myself.

This was the end of my childhood. It finished a period when it had seemed, although it was not true, that each moment up to then fitted a predestined pattern, shaped by someone other than myself. At seventeen it seemed that I could take control of my own life and choose from infinite possibilities. I was young and free and believed that I would be lucky.

It was not until I had passed forty and was newly separated from my husband, and with two affectionate and witty children, that I ever felt that way again. But the feeling, the sudden rush of joy and excitement, was identical. The similarity was as pleasing as the simultaneously sweet and painful homesickness I felt with those two children during a storm on a tropical island which took me back to the suspended time of childhood rainy summer afternoons by the seaside.

KINSALE

I THOUGHT I'd left home at seventeen. If I had, no one noticed. In the couple of years during which I suffered from this delusion, my father sold Ballinaparka and bought a house in Kinsale. For the first time his family, which now did not include my mother, lived in a house which was a practical size—two cottages knocked together on a hillside overlooking, to the right, the river Bandon and the old town of Kinsale, and to the left, the ruins of Charles Fort, the mouth of the Bandon and the open sea beyond. For the first time, also, my father was engaged in a business which ultimately showed a profit.

Kinsale is about twenty miles southwest of Cork, the second-largest city in the Republic of Ireland, and was at that time relatively undeveloped with a population of about fifteen hundred. Large fishing boats with foreign crews would sometimes put into the harbour to refuel, but most of the visitors were Saturday-night couples from Cork who would drive out for an evening's serious drinking at Acton's or the Harbour Bar.

Although Kinsale was tiny and without much to offer in the

way of day-to-day drama, there was plenty of evidence, mainly architectural, of a historic past. Within the town are traces of a seventh-century burial ground and southwest of Kinsale, near the Old Head, are the remains of a large three-ringed fort, also seventh century. St. Multose, our parish church, was founded in the twelfth century; the Carmelite Friary in the fourteenth. Desmond Castle was built in the fifteenth century and later used to jail French prisoners during the Napoleonic Wars. Most of the rest of the town is eighteenth century, with the usual modern additions, such as a small factory, some converted cottages, a jerry-built house or two and a small cinema. These disparate styles were not jarring; rather, they gave a layered feeling to the town. We found them no more incongruous than the sight of the occasional tourist, wearing shorts, passing on the street one of the older women wearing a hooded, ankle-length black Kinsale cloak.

To get to Charles Fort from our house, Ardbrack Cottage, one walked through a tiny village, down a steep street lined with the front doors of houses whose architectural differences suggested an uneasy combination of Beatrix Potter and Dylan Thomas. Charles Fort had been built in 1677 by the English to defend the harbour. It was a star-shaped structure with forty-foot-high outer defenses. The solid grey ruins stood partly overgrown with grass and wildflowers, a very pleasant place to walk on a summer's evening. It was where I experienced most clearly the call of the past, the sense that I was being told something important which would prove of value to me. There was also a sense of well-being which I now know was caused by the ruin's perfect proportions—a product of a time of clarity and clean straight lines, of freedom from sentimentality. I had no idea what Charles Fort was telling me although I had no doubt of the usefulness and value of the message. At that time I was longing for the material things which would, I thought, ensure and enhance the romantic, careless yet safe life I saw as my right. I wanted clothes, and fun, and enough money, and somewhere pretty and light to live and someone to love. I could not make a connection between these wants and the solid but unnamed, ungraspable thing I was being offered by the past. I do, to some extent, know now, and I don't blame my adolescent ignorance. At seventeen one is playing to win and it would not be healthy to allow for a fallback position. One should not be thinking: If all else fails . . . It is later that one learns to gather the resources which will see one through the thin times. Charles Fort and the past were telling me in a less personal or individual way what my grandmother and even my father had been showing me; a broader view, a sense of proportion. They took comfort from history and had a sense of being part of it, of being a link in the chain, of knowing the abstract pleasures. The message of the past that nothing is forever.

The French and English fleets fought outside Kinsale in 1380 and the English took the town in 1488. I had been taught about the Battle of Kinsale at school. I hated history as a child, but later, when I lived in England and was old enough not to weep over the fates of Mary, Queen of Scots, and Sir Walter Raleigh, I took pleasure from it. It took me a little time to realize that history should be written by the winners, that even the loyalist fan needs his team to score an occasional point. There are many true heroes in Irish history, but they are always outnumbered and out-weighed, and, when there does seem a real chance of victory, they are undone by treachery or bad luck or just sheer inefficiency. It's heartbreaking, but in time it wears you down. The Battle of Kinsale is a fine example of this kind of romantic waste.

Hugh O'Neill, the Earl of Tyrone, and his son-in-law, Red Hugh O'Donnell, led a largely successful revolt against Elizabeth I, a revolt which cost England a great deal of money and the Earl of Essex, the aging queen's favourite, his head. Spain, still smarting from the aborted armada of 1588, and spotting a potential winner in O'Neill, sent a force of three or four thousand men to help. The Spanish commander, del Aguilar, landed at Kinsale. Kinsale is about three hundred miles from where O'Neill was quartered in Ulster, a considerable distance to travel in winter over a country which was then almost without roads. Once in Kinsale, the obligatory snatching-defeat-from-the-jaws-of-victory sequence ensued. O'Neill wanted to lay siege to the heavily fortified town but was persuaded, against his better judgment, into a direct confrontation. He and the Spaniards were defeated by Mountjoy's army at the Battle of Kinsale on Christmas Eve of 1601. With their defeat died the last hope of Irish freedom for over three hundred years.

Alexander Selkirk sailed from Kinsale in 1703, on board *The Cinque Ports*—during this voyage he was left marooned on the Pacific island of Juan Fernández and immortalized as Robinson Crusoe.

But the event which had the most far-reaching historical significance took place at the beginning of this century. On May 7, 1915, a German submarine torpedoed and sank the *Lusitania* eleven miles off the Old Head of Kinsale. Half the two thousand passengers and crew were drowned. The sinking of the *Lusitania* and the death of 124 American citizens travelling on her was one of the key events which brought the United States into the First World War.

Among those who perished were Sir Hugh Lane, whose unsigned codicil to his will would start an English-Irish struggle over his paintings which lasted into my childhood, and Alfred Vanderbilt, the "millionaire sportsman," who did not know how to swim and is believed to have given his life jacket to a nurse. Also on board was an English student called Herbert Ehrhardt, who kept his head, helped those in distress, survived and later spoke of having had a conscious determination "not to do anything which I would regret or blame myself for in later life."

A few of those who drowned are buried in the graveyard of St. Multose Church. The *Lusitania* rests in three hundred feet of water. Many other wrecks lie in this area and they provide shelter for fish. Huge eels now live in the corridors and cabins of the *Lusitania* and smaller fish swim about her darkened ballroom— the furnishings and human remains now rotted and disappeared, the metal encrusted in barnacles. A friend of my family's, who had been part of a team of divers making a documentary about the shipwreck, gave us a brass trimming to a porthole, encrusted and corroded and unimaginable as ever having been part of something which moved fast and reflected sunlight.

The shallowness of the water, the wrecks and the warm currents make Kinsale a natural fishing ground. The lovely scenery and the beautiful old town make it a pleasant place to spend a holiday. My father realized that there was an opportunity to develop deep-sea fishing into a business. He approached the Tourist Board, found some partners, each with an area of expertise—an architect, an advertising executive and others—bought two boats, hired a couple of skippers and very quickly attracted deep-sea fishermen from England and the Continent. Unlike his previous business ventures, this one did well. There were, of course, problems along the way—storms, seasickness, the million and one mechanical difficulties which go with every boat. In the end there was some tension between him and his partners, partly, I think, because my father was right there and took a fairly professional and, for him, slightly humourless view of his responsibilities. Eventually the whole concern was sold to Trust Houses and everyone, my father included, got out of the fishing business with a healthy profit.

My father proved a self-sufficient head of household, although in a far from elaborate manner. He would shop for food, sticking to essentials and never indulging in an impulse buy nor attempting to build up a store cupboard. His housekeeper would cook him a meal based on these purchases, a "joint" of beef, for instance, which my father would eat hot on the initial day and then cold on the following days, accompanied perhaps by some chutney and a little lettuce. When the meat was finished he would shop again and his housekeeper would cook another simple meal. Although my father had always seemed adept at communication with working people, I once felt moved to ask him what arrangement he had made with his housekeeper as far as hours and pay were concerned. The very act of asking this question suggests that I was a little worried. His answer did nothing to reassure me. He told me that he didn't pay her on a regular basis, but gave her different sums of money at irregular intervals. I had been prepared to interfere on some minor level such as overtime or holiday pay, but the hopelessness of arbitrating a problem between two people who had voluntarily entered into such a bizarre arrangement deterred me from further action.

By this time I was living in Oxford and my occasional trips to London brought me into contact with two more members of my family. They were the first ones with whom I enjoyed my new, almost adult status.

Two of my grandmother's sisters, my great-aunts, lived in London. One other sister had died before I was born, and another lived in the North of Ireland. Although I must have met her, I don't remember her at all. Her name was Alice; she was the only one whose husband was still alive, and this gave her a different status from her three widowed sisters. She kept small dogs indoors, which would hardly make her remarkable in America but seemed a novelty to us. My father once had to stay overnight with her to attend a funeral. He had difficulty going to sleep in the strange house and each time he was about to doze off a clock would chime. There were three or four chiming clocks in the house. They chimed every quarter hour and, unfortunately, they were not synchronized.

The two great-aunts with whom I became close, while living first in Oxford and later in London, were Aunt Mollie and Aunt Frumpie. Aunt Frumpie makes an early appearance in my grandmother's memoirs:

What fuss all grown ups made about that baby. At times we felt like agreeing with the youngest of the Edinburgh Princesses. Princess Baby as she was known as, who, being upset by her nurse saying she was going to take the Scott baby [Aunt Frumpie] home announced promptly she would kill it. When explained to her how wicked it was of her to

*say or even think of such a thing, she thought for a mo-
ment and then said meaningly, "I will sing hymns to it,
sing hymns to it 'til it dies." Her brother Prince Albert was
much gentler because when he came to play with us, he
would take off the babies socks and kiss her toes.*

Aunt Mollie comes in a little later, again in the context of the
Edinburgh family:

*Molly, the youngest but one, was her [the Duchess of
Edinburgh's] god child and that day had to remember to
answer to her real name Marie. She was always called out
of the row and the Duchess kissing her gave her a small
velvet case which always contained some lovely piece of
jewelry. Later on we crowded round the sister gazing en-
raptured at the Jewel and wishing we had Grand Duch-
esses for our God Mothers.*

When Mollie and Frumpie "came out," my great-grandfather
and great-grandmother Scott had five daughters of a marriageable
age. Clearly it would have been counterproductive and almost
ludicrous for all of them to attend every social function. A roster
was devised and, two at a time, they took turns being the "official
daughters."

By the time I knew them, both my great-aunts were widows.
Aunt Mollie, who had been the most beautiful of the five, had
married a handsome and dashing young officer in the Brigade of
Guards. After a short time he had gone mad, leaving her with a
small son. She lived quietly near the private asylum in which he
was kept for many years. My father told me that my great-uncle
was perfectly rational most of the time and would write to him
occasionally, taking an interest in my father's career as an amateur
jockey. By the time I knew Aunt Mollie, she'd set up home with
her younger sister.

They lived in a large old-fashioned flat in Albert Court, overlooking the Albert Hall.

Aunt Frumpie was the rich one. She had also been wonderful-looking. Aunt Mollie was still a beautiful woman, and Aunt Frumpie, belying her name, was both very pretty and well dressed. Both women were elegant in a restrained way which did not involve much shopping. They both had dressmakers and I imagine that Aunt Frumpie's might well have been someone we would now call a couturier.

I don't know where they bought their groceries, or their needlework materials, but on most fine days they went to Harrods. They may have bought things there occasionally—Aunt Frumpie could well have afforded to—but a visit to the store was an outing, an adventure, a constitutional. It was from them that I first heard the hall on the ground floor of Harrods, full of sofas and armchairs, referred to as "the morgue."

If Harrods was their idea of a shop, then the Hyde Park Hotel, close by and overlooking the park, was to their minds the only place to lunch or dine. They thought of restaurants as new and not quite respectable; tinges of private dining rooms and the seduction of Edwardian chorus girls. My father, too, when in London, normally ate meals at one of the clubs to which a reciprocal agreement with his Dublin club gave him access, and referred to the conventional alternative as a "resterong." When we dined together at one of these newfangled places, there was a nervous moment at the end of a meal when he came to pay the bill. I was always a little afraid he'd imagine he'd taken care of the waiter with the Christmas fund.

I would visit my great-aunts once a week and have tea or an early supper with them. I remember these afternoons and early evenings with great fondness. I would come away from them with the virtuous feeling of a pleasant duty done and with that sense of security that comes from a dose of consistent well-managed family life.

We used to eat in the large, white, airy kitchen. Everything was very neat. They knew how to cook simple meals, although supper had usually been partially prepared by their maid earlier in the day. Afterward, while we washed the dishes, there would be gentle bickering about whose turn it was to dry and who'd put something away in the wrong place last time. The one who remained more serene was the one whose hearing aid was functioning less well. Sometimes this aid would be switched off deliberately. The garbage pail was always referred to as the *poubelle*, as though the object were too indelicate to be spoken of in English.

On the rare occasions I went there for lunch, after I was offered a glass of white port or Dubonnet, the meal was served in the dining room. Supper in the kitchen was cosy; lunch in the kitchen would have been "letting the side down."

The drawing-room windows looked out on the Albert Hall. My great-aunts used to enjoy watching the crowds pour in and out from concerts and were fascinated by those who lined up in advance for tickets, particularly students who would arrive with sandwiches, sometimes even sleeping bags. A glimpse of Sir Thomas Beecham, the conductor, was also a rare treat and it was a family joke that Aunt Frumpie had a mild, ladylike crush on him.

The flat was either owned or rented by Aunt Frumpie; she had the larger bedroom and had a bathroom with a lot of mirrors in it. Aunt Mollie would laugh about this bathroom, as if she thought it a little vulgar and mildly embarrassing. Aunt Frumpie would just smile. I was impressed by it. I had read enough Evelyn Waugh, Michael Arlen and Nancy Mitford to understand that such sinful luxury existed, but not for my great-aunt, who had to be nearly, if not actually, seventy years old. Was it a sign of vanity? Or the opposite? Surely a truly vain woman of her age would not wish to see herself at that disadvantage. Fully and elegantly clad in a bedroom mirror, yes; in the bathtub, no. It is possible, of course, that the mirrors had come with the apartment. But I don't think so.

Both my great-aunts had sons who had been divorced. This was hard for them to accept. Aunt Frumpie's son had been married in a rather grand way, but he'd managed to lose both his wife and his money. Later he'd married again, someone from a less exalted walk of life, and this second marriage had produced twins. Once when I was visiting, the entire family arrived, always a situation with a certain amount of strain attached to it. I mentioned something I had seen on the "telly" the night before. One of the twins repeated the word "telly" shortly afterward. His mother corrected him. "Television," she said. I was mortified by my carelessness as I slowly realized that, although it was all right for me to emulate the cockney accent and working-class slang which was popular among my friends and had been considered dashing by the Edwardian smart set of my great-aunts' generation, it wasn't the same for those trying to shake off traces of a working-class background and establish themselves in the upper middle class.

The women on both sides of my family lived longer than the men and seemed to be stronger in every way. At first I thought it was that, in those times and in those classes, women married men older than themselves, but both Aunt Frumpie and my grandmother Goff survived a son. With the deaths of both these sons, the problems inherent in these relationships were left unresolved. When my great-aunt's son died I made conventional and, I'm sure, clumsy attempts at condolence. She brushed them aside. I think that the women were better able to adapt to change, or that the society in which they lived did not make women responsible for the changes in their lives whereas the men must have felt inadequacy or shame that they could not make things stay the way they were. The women in my grandmother's generation just sat up straighter, spent less and maintained standards. The men didn't seem to be able to handle it.

Soon after I came to London I started work for a television company, initially typing postcards. Later I became a production assistant on a weekly news and documentary programme. My great-aunts used to have trouble, frequently of their own making, with their television reception. If this coincided, as it often did, with my visits, they were baffled that I was unable to make the necessary repairs.

They could never quite grasp, either, my perfectly conventional living arrangements. I was sharing, with two other girls, a furnished flat off the Earls Court Road. My great-aunts would inquire about my landlady, a woman who lived in the suburbs and with whom we communicated only by cheque, and ask whether she provided breakfast. They never accepted the real nature of the relationship. They preferred to believe that I had an adequate chaperone on the premises and refused to understand that this was not so.

A summer visit to Kinsale always worked better than a winter one, since my father kept the thermostat (a piece of equipment he had never seen before and didn't ever quite understand) in his more modern house at a level so low that it baffled the heating system and virtually precluded its working at all. Hair washing seemed suicidally irresponsible and I used to think twice even about taking a bath. Sometimes the presence of a large spider or two would serve as an additional deterrent.

After more than a year of very light shorthand/typing by day and total immersion in a newfound social life by night, I returned to Ireland, confident in my new makeup, fashionably short skirts, high-heeled shoes and an affected superficial attitude. A year of sub-Brideshead Oxford, a scurried visit to the public library for *Zuleika Dobson* in my first week, a couple of Commem balls (seventeen years old, dancing at dawn under the trees, in a light mist, as a steel band played "Yellow Bird"; a moment of romance rarely equalled, although the name and the face of my partner have long since been forgotten), a little punting, *Wild Strawberries* at the Scala Cinema, more curry than anyone's digestive system should have to deal with, a heart broken at least twice, followed by a shared flat in London, Saturday mornings on the Kings Road, cigarettes, nightclubs, bottle parties in South Kensington, the undergrounds, miniskirts, the Royal Court Theatre, standing in line at the Chelsea Classic, my first paycheque—all had, I thought, changed me beyond recognition. I was well aware of the favour I was doing everyone concerned when I attended my first social gathering in Kinsale.

Swanning into the room in a manner I thought Dietrich-like, and wondering to whom I would first condescend, I was welcomed home for the holidays by one of the many middle-aged spinsters present and asked how much longer I had at school.

BALLINAKILL

THERE ARE no surprises in a Church of Ireland funeral service. You get to choose a hymn or two and maybe a psalm, but the rest of it is there on the page. You follow the prayer book and line by line you get through it and then it's over. No one is going to get up to tell you his feelings or memories and break your heart or embarrass you. Privacy is implicit in the whole service. The words are beautiful and sad, but mercifully familiar; nothing special is required of the congregation. You sit phlegmatic, or crying silently, depending on your needs or ability to control your feelings. I wouldn't have it any other way. At my father's funeral I was more grateful for ritual than at any time before or since. I felt comfort in being told what to do, for having all responsibility taken away from me. Even the physical directions in the prayer book helped. "All stand," "all kneel," and the prayers and the responses, which generate their own rhythm and energy and speed, took us through the service and out the other end, out of the cathedral and into the pale sunlight. Even there, Anglo-Irish conventions carried us through. We shook hands, thanked people for coming, accepted condolences. Later, I was grateful for a moment, at that time rare in my life, when everyone concerned knew who the event was about. A moment of drama devoid of upstaging is a rare and beautiful thing. (At my wedding I was amazed to discover that there was at least one person who, while not getting married herself, thought she was the main event.) The funeral was my father's; the loss was the family's. Any private grief felt, or sense of loss from a non-blood relative, could be expressed, but the words had to be delivered without excessive emotion. I understood, as never before, that I am completely Anglo-Irish and that it is a good thing for me to be.

FOR PERHAPS six months before his death my father had been planning to visit me. He liked to travel and was quite adventurous in his later years. He had, for instance, gone by pony up the foothills of the Himalayas at an age when many would have been content with a leisurely stroll along the promenade. He'd taken a camera with him on this expedition and one of the photographs I like best had inadvertently included his pony's ears in the foreground.

He'd been planning an American trip, starting in Seattle visiting Goff relatives and then coming east by train to see the country and to stay with me. I'd welcomed the idea and told him to let me know the dates convenient to him. He hadn't and a later letter showed that he needed more urging. I didn't write back as quickly as I now wish I had.

Some time before, he'd given me a painting of an Arab horse by Herring senior and I sent him a catalogue for a horse auction which had the painting reproduced on the front cover. The letter and catalogue arrived before he died. Unfortunately, he was no longer in a condition to read and the letter was still unopened at his death.

My father's death left my brother, Robert, head of the family. Since Robert is thirteen years younger than I am, we'd never had any childhood in common. Born shortly before my parents' marriage finally crumbled, when my mother left to get a divorce, Robert stayed with my father. Since there is no divorce in Ireland, my mother had to go to Mexico to get divorced, then to France to establish residency long enough to be remarried. Even after she had gone through this complicated and expensive procedure she was, in the eyes of the Irish law and church, still married to my father and had no legal right to take Robert from my father's house. So my brother was, for a period of time, brought up by a father who had been a little over fifty when Robert was born.

My father did not wish my mother to see Robert, who was sent to a neighbour's house on the days when my mother tried to visit him. Fortunately, the neighbour was a sensible and compassionate woman and my mother, unknown to my father, used to see Robert there.

None of this made for a happy atmosphere, but it did not, all the same, generate enough heat for emotions to be verbalized or brought out into the open. We were living a life composed of scenes from both *Anna Karenina* and *Little Lord Fauntleroy*, but since no one ever said what was going on or what they felt, the feelings were repressed and, in my case at least, largely unexperienced. I increasingly retreated into the world of fiction, increasingly identifying with characters in literature, increasingly displacing my confused feelings into the misfortunes of tragic heroines such as Anna without ever making a conscious connection between her life and the not entirely dissimilar situation in which my mother found herself. I notice, too, that as I try to describe the parts of my childhood which involve painful memories or conflicting loyalties, I rely more and more on literary allusions or comparisons. To this day I search for answers in books, usually written years ago and not always in the same country as I am living. All of which makes it more bewildering that I could feel an appalled, horrified pity for my father's unspoken but clearly visible pain and have little or no imagination about what my mother was going through. It was not by chance that Tolstoy placed so much emphasis on the beauty, luxury and taste which surrounded Anna. We are constantly aware of the fineness of her clothing, the smoothness of her skin, the beautiful wrapping on the presents she brings her son, and these details both enhance and defuse the scenes. Thus he takes us into Anna's life, but does not make it possible for us to take Anna into ours.

My brother, against all the odds, managed to take all the good side of my father and ignore or remain tolerantly amused by the other aspects of his character. I always felt he'd been denied a real childhood, though I may be wrong, for he's much more adept at family life than are any of the rest of us. Robert has chosen to live in the Anglo-Irish tradition and has succeeded, with the help of hard work, humour and a perfect wife, in having a life which my father would recognize from his youth. At a time when the large houses of Ireland are being sold off or quietly disintegrating, Robert and Sheelagh are restoring theirs, clearing the grounds, re-creating the past. Their children help them pick raspberries and gooseberries in the walled garden.

My father had been born in outwardly enviable circumstances. His family was rich by Irish standards. They lived in a good, large house with beautiful grounds. His mother was very pretty and his parents were what would now be called "socially prominent" in America, but wasn't then in Ireland. The remote natures of his parents and the unpleasantness of his boarding schools (as a small boy he had nearly died of pneumonia) would not have been questioned by him. It was the way things were and in no way unusual in those days.

While my father was still a young man, his father lost his money in a celebrated financial disaster, had a heart attack and died. (Whether it was a cold-blooded swindle or the crumbling of a top-heavy financial empire, I don't know. My father once told me that it is not the innocent man but the hypocritically dishonest one who most easily falls prey to a con man, but his tone when he said it was interested and amused rather than bitter.) My father found himself head of a family with complicated money troubles and little potential for solving them. He had two younger brothers to look after, a sister and a mother who not only had no sense of the value of money but had never handled or been in charge of any. My grandmother had had no money of her own, and although my grandfather allowed her to charge anything to which she might take a fancy, he never gave her cash. My other grandmother, who'd known the family slightly, though not on terms of equality, said that one of my grandmother Goff's first reactions to hearing of the financial disaster had been to order a new car. She was also alleged to have told her bank manager—in reference to either this automobile acquisition or the general disastrous situation—that money was only a token.

Cars were a family hobby and there is an incident involving them which suggests a moment of rivalry between my father's and my mother's families. My great-grandfather William Davis-Goff owned the first car registered in County Waterford. Also the first car, probably the same one, officially to drive over the new Waterford bridge. Unofficially, a car driven by Jack Carew and containing my grandmother Woodhouse and my great-great-aunt Mollie Carew sneaked across before him. William Davis-Goff's license plate was WI 1, the number retained by his son and then by my father for many years. Eventually my father thought the ten-pound fee to retain the plate every time he bought a new car, which was not often, could be better spent elsewhere.

My father's life changed overnight when his father lost his money. Up to then his future had seemed to be clearly mapped out. The brewery, while not demanding much of his time, precluded the need for a more taxing career and allowed him to pursue his real interests, fox hunting and steeplechasing. He owned excellent horses and hunted twice a week in winter, as did all his friends. My father had been taught to ride by an unsympathetic army instructor on horses far too strong, and he once told me that he had taken no pleasure in riding until his first day's hunting. He won more than his share of the steeplechases he rode and I imagine these victories must have been another source of pleasure and pride. To ride well was obligatory. Even his sister, Dodo, tiny and not built for the sport, learned to ride well and hunted and rode point-to-points sidesaddle.

My grandfather died suddenly. My father was playing tennis when Dr. Walker, the physician who looked after all the Waterford Anglo-Irish families, arrived. He was not dressed for the game and called my father off the court. Apparently my father's face turned white. I imagine he experienced the same feeling I did, a generation later, when my brother telephoned me in the middle of the night to announce my father's death; a moment of knowing that something terrible has happened, of not knowing what it is. There is a desire to hold on to that moment, knowing that it is the last one before everything changes forever. And there is the realization that time cannot be slowed down. And again the tennis party. Tennis whites, grass courts, mild sunny Irish summer days, children, dogs, cucumber sandwiches. An evocative place to end an era.

I never heard my father complain about the change in his fortunes, although I knew that he was worried by financial pressures. His references to more affluent times were devoid of bitterness. What I heard instead were a series of anecdotes about times and places which had given him pleasure and the memories of which still did: an evening at the theatre in London, a C. B. Cochran review and supper with a pretty girl afterward. Races ridden and many of them won, hunt balls and ridiculous incidents which could still make him laugh. A misprint in a local newspaper—an advertisement which read "latest Parish fashions"—could make him happy for days. (Thackeray was equally overjoyed in 1843 by an advertisement he found in a Dublin newspaper which read: "To parents and guardians. Paris. Such parents and guardians as may wish to entrust their children for education in its fullest extent to Madame Shanahan, can have the advantage of being conducted to Paris by her brother, the Rev. J. P. O'Reilly, of Church Street Chapel," remarking: "which admirable arrangement carries the parents to Paris and leaves the children in Dublin.")

My father once told me that when he was a young man, in order to defer the moment when he would have to invest in a new suit, he'd taken an old one to his tailor and asked him to "turn it"—whether it was just the collar or a more extreme operation he had in mind, he did not say. After a preliminary investigation he was told, as was Tristram Shandy's uncle Toby (about his scarlet trousers), that this was a procedure effective only once.

After my father married he stopped riding races, but he attended race meetings regularly as a steward and was a member of the Turf Club. He continued to hunt until he was well into his sixties, although toward the end only once or twice a season and on a borrowed horse; not always with the finest pack of hounds. He was capable of looking a gift horse in the mouth, and once wrote to me after a disappointing day with a hunt which shall be nameless: "If I were master of the ———, which God forbid, those hounds which I could not give away as pets, I would shoot."

My father lived on his memories, his sense of humour and his belief that his life continued through his children. His disapproval of death duties (one of the Furies hastening the disintegration of the Anglo-Irish former ruling class) was based on his feeling that a man's main incentive to work hard was so that he might leave the benefits of that labour to his children.

Although my father's title was nothing grander than that of a baronet, and only in its third generation, a male heir was needed. My mother, I know, felt some pressure and I was aware that even I, to some extent, had an advantage over my sisters. To have been the first child and female when my parents were young and healthy was forgivable. Julia, as the second girl, was less enthusiastically received, and Alice, the third, was met with open commiseration. Not from the family, of course, but from society at large. Eight years after her birth, when my parents' marriage was already in trouble, Robert was born to great rejoicing. Soon afterward my parents separated.

Many of my father's opinions which might have seemed snobbish to others, I found, while not always agreeing with them, not offensive, since his views were always diluted by his sense of humour. He reacted to changing standards by making a joke of them. Soon after I left home, my sisters began to entertain a group of young people from Cork whose parents would never have met mine in the social setting of a previous generation, and my father told me of coming home one evening at a time when he might well have expected them to be leaving. After a roomful of guests melted away in a couple of minutes, my father found himself alone with one young man. After a minute or two of silence, my father asked him tactfully what he was waiting for. The young man replied: "My lady friend is in the toilet." Not perhaps since E. M. Forster's Jacky in *Howards End* have so many class-dividing words been crammed into so short a sentence.

Some of my father's prejudices were arbitrary. He used to sneer at my sisters' use of the word "cereal," pronouncing it in a long-drawn-out way which did, in fact, make it sound extremely common. What the acceptable word should have been was never made clear. The recently coined word "cornflakes" would only have covered one kind of cereal and would hardly have been more distinguished. My guess is that the eating of that kind of food was in itself unacceptable. How appalled and astonished and, at the same time, delightfully entertained he would have been by the myriad choices my children have. No one would have appreciated more a moment, soon after his death, when my children, staying in Texas, were presented with a choice of twenty miniature packages of what I, for want of a better word, have to describe as cereal. My daughter, pressed to make up her mind, announced that she would have "the porcupine poops."

Long after I had left home these tiny judgments followed me, making minor alterations in how I thought and spoke. Once Daddy wrote to me about some event which he thought might interest me and said: "the media . . . as people nowadays call the newspapers"—a word that has never since crossed my lips.

Sometimes it worked the other way. My brother tells of how he arrived at my father's house accompanied by the girl he wanted to marry. Even in the best-run households, such as the one in which Robert's intended lived, this kind of occasion can cause a little nervousness. Robert could not have been accused of disloyalty, by me at least, if he had been just a tad apprehensive about the domestic arrangements my father might eccentrically have made in anticipation of this all-important introduction. His worst fears were realized before they even got to the front door. As he led his bride-to-be through the garden they came upon a cluster of brightly painted plaster gnomes, given to my father by a local man. My father's sense of what was right had led him to display them in a prominent position.

American friends who know a little about my childhood sometimes assume it is a missing chapter from a Nancy Mitford novel, but they are mistaken. The eccentricity was there, of course, but I always feel the Mitford children knew that their childhood was a separate and temporary state which had a clearly defined end. At seventeen they would go to London, come out, get married and live the life of their choice. That several of them chose, not reactionary conformity, but rather more flamboyant lives than their parents', does not belie my belief. Literary, politically extreme or tragic, they were so in a way which was not an extension of their childhoods. When we were children we knew that if we wanted to change our lives it would require willpower, extreme effort and a good deal of luck.

My father was not at all Uncle Matthew but he had a touch of Jane Austen's Mr. Bennet about him; my mother was not vulgar and foolish, nor were his three daughters any sillier than other girls of their age, but he needed to retreat from a world changing too fast and in the wrong ways. Whatever disapproval he might have felt about events over which he had no control was concealed behind a sarcastic and ironic wit.

Recently I found a letter he'd written to me a year before he died. It is the only one I now possess, since he had made me believe that it is wrong to keep letters. I accepted this as a fact and, without questioning it, for years routinely destroyed witty and non-libelous letters from people of some interest (one eminent literary figure, I suspect, would not have taken the trouble she did when writing to me if she'd known just how limited her readership would be). This letter was saved by accident and it is a surprisingly complete picture of his life. It is typewritten, except for the opening and closing, which are carefully written in a shaky hand. It reads:

Darling Annabel,

I hope this will reach you in time to wish you a happy birthday and hope you will have many more. It's quite possible that you mayn't get it for ages as all our postal workers are going on strike.

I got back yesterday from visiting John and Julia [my sister and her husband] and found your book waiting for me. If the back of the cover had been put on the front it would be a best seller. It is a delightful picture of you. I have only dipped into it but will get to work on it when I have finished the book I am now reading.

I had a charming greataunt who often stayed at Glenville and used to "dip into" books I bought or got from the library. If there was a page with "bloody" or something worse she always opened it just there and put it down saying disgusting. I wonder am I in for some shocks.

All appeared to be going well at the Glebe. Julia has put up a little weight though how she has done it I don't know as she is always busy at something. John has got around to feeding the calves in the morning. He has done a tip-top job with the plumbing quite by himself. It is really good. Their children look well and I think will be tall.

Next week I expect to spend three nights with Robert and Sheelagh in Dublin. I have some things to do there and on the Saturday there is a good race at Leopardstown and we will go there. That is if the weather lets us. It has been horrible just lately. Snow and frost and we are not prepared for that. Our gossamer textured telephone and ESB [electricity] just collapse.

Let me know how the casino script goes. I have a very good book called Thirteen against the Bank by Norman Leigh and published by Weidenfeld. It is a true story. The author as a schoolboy used to be taken to Nice by his father where he watched father lose very heavily and as a result decided that when he grew up he could do better. He worked out a scheme—he had lots of time to do so while he was doing a year or so in gaol for something or other. Any how it worked and they did break the bank and were asked to leave. If you can't get the book but would like it I shall send it to you.

I have no news from Alice but when things settle down in England and the weather does too I am going to see them.

The only other news I can think of is that Cousin George is going to America for the first time. He is going to stay with the Bill Albertinis. "Where?" "Oh, somewhere in Georgia, I think, somewhere near a place called Atlanta." The fuss there is about a passport—his is out of date by about twenty years. "I don't know much about these bloody Yanks but I hear in the South they are very hospitable." I can see him already whooping it up on Rye and then spending a week or so with tummy trouble which is what he always did when he visited the Tonges in England.

No more now.

My love to all of you from
Daddy

It says it all to me. The shaky hand but no mention of his health; the only comment on the constant strikes and breakdowns of utilities is a humorous one in passing. He skates over the thin ice of my novel with a skill I could never emulate without, for a moment, avoiding the real issue. My two sisters, my brother and their families are touched on, a very large part of his life, and then he reveals the most interesting (a totally inadequate word but I'm trying to say it is the bit which interests me the most—is the most important, difficult to take hold of, the most elusive) aspect of his character. His sense of humour. I have enough humour to make me resilient but it requires the presence of another amused person. My father, alone, could have a mild laugh at a book which he undoubtedly enjoyed, and even makes me wonder why I didn't take him up on his offer of a loan.

He liked to read, sometimes books one would have thought he would have little identification with—Mark Twain, for instance. Toward the end of his life, when he was visiting me in Connecticut he came across some books by Scott Fitzgerald. He read several and loved them, although he seemed to find the descriptions of alcoholic self-destruction more amusing and less painful than I did. During the last years of his life he started to drink quite heavily. Little stigma is attached to drinking in Ireland, provided one does not become maudlin or fall to pieces. His small jokes about Cousin George were without malice. Jokes about drink or drinking were always of a high quality, perhaps another instance of his defusing yet one more painful area of his life with humour.

Clearly my father was going to get a lot of mileage out of Cousin George's American visit. Cousin George was a distant relative of my mother's. Since he was a contemporary of my father's, I don't know why he should have been designated "cousin"; there was no precedent for it—in our family you were either "Aunt" or "Uncle" or "Mr." or "Mrs." But he wasn't either "Uncle George" or "Group Captain Russell," and I wonder if the title of cousin didn't contain, somewhere, an affectionate, jocular lack of respect. He was my father's friend, a friendship based mainly on their shooting together—my mother can have had nothing at all in common with him, although I remember her being touched when he wrote to her after my father's death, touched and more than a little surprised, since her divorce had completely separated her from those friends of my father's whom she had entertained and, not to put too fine a point on it, put up with, during her marriage. My parents were never disloyal, and only rarely critical of their friends, and yet, as children, it was never concealed from us that some aspects of Cousin George's character were quite funny. An incident involving my sister Alice illustrated one of these.

Alice was, for some forgotten reason, alone at Glenville with the maids. Cousin George arrived for lunch, either on the basis of a too casual and then forgotten invitation or because he had been told to "drop in for potluck anytime." My sister acted with great aplomb, especially since she couldn't have been more than seven or eight at the time. The regular, predictable lunch was served; my sister presided. History does not record the content of their conversation, but I imagine it went fairly smoothly. Until dessert (a word we would never have used but it's hard to describe strawberries and cream as pudding—although we did) was served. Lunch was eaten at the large dining-room table with formal place settings, but one served oneself from a side table. The main course finished, Alice and Cousin George moved to the sideboard, where the picked-that-morning strawberries awaited them. Alice politely waved him ahead of her. Absentmindedly, Cousin George helped himself to the whole lot. Alice, bred for it, didn't bat an eyelid and later, bred for it, recounted the episode with deadpan glee to her delighted family.

There was also a running joke about dogs. My father was a very good shot (duck and snipe usually, deer and pheasant being in another class both financially and socially), and, while shooting was a comparatively inexpensive sport, there were certain costs incurred. You needed a good gun, and you might have to pay a share in a syndicate (I was an adult before I ever heard the word "syndicate" used in any context other than shooting or gambling) to shoot certain preserves, and you needed a dog. The dog had to be a well-bred Labrador and he had to be professionally trained. We normally had such a dog around, but outside the house. Cousin George most of the time did not. This tended to lead to unkept bargains of the "You bring the dog and I'll bring . . ." nature. My father could never have been accused of being a flamboyant or flashy spender himself, and was well aware that Cousin George would not always hold up his end of the bargain, but, characteristically, instead of being irritated or resentful, he was amused and not above enjoying a little mild teasing. The same attitude, in this case shared by our mother, applied to our honorary cousin's ludicrously right-wing political opinions, which they found funny instead of offensive.

My father and Cousin George both ended their days (to say their lives, which is what I really mean, implies, quite inaccurately, a suicide pact) at the same residential hotel. My father's joke about the amount of free drink Cousin George was likely to imbibe while enjoying the traditional hospitality of the southern part of the United States would not have been judgmental and would have included a tinge of envy.

AFTER THE funeral we drove out, past Glenville, past Ardkeen, where I had played with the de Bromhead children and which later became a tuberculosis sanitarium and is now a hospital, past the Bishop Foy's playing fields, to Ballinakill, where the graveyard is.

It was wildly overgrown, and we were all embarrassed to see that my father, characteristically, had never gotten around to getting a headstone erected for his mother. The family solicitor handed each of us an envelope containing the will. It is a sign of our venality that one of my sisters left hers, unopened, in the back of the car.

The coffin was lowered, earth shoveled on top of it. The other mourners left; we stayed until it was all finished. It seemed awful for us to drive away, to have drinks and the hot, comforting dinner that my mother was that moment preparing for us in Dublin, to fall asleep in a warm bed. And to leave him there.

The next day I was to return to the United States. My brother and I met briefly to discuss the will. It was a moment of light relief. For about fifteen years before his death, my father and I had enjoyed many good lunches and dinners and many a bottle of wine under the serious pretext of discussing his will. There had also been many letters on the subject, all designed to prevent inequity in the disposal of his modest estate. He was a very fair man. He had even gone to the length of buying a life insurance policy in my favour to make up for having given his other children furniture when he sold his last house. The will, despite all these discussions, was hopelessly vague and out of date. The first paragraph left Robert a house which had been sold some years before and a painting which he'd subsequently given to me. One paragraph read, more or less, "to be divided among you as seems fair."

Robert, growing more like my father by the minute, said, "I've told the solicitor that this will won't do; he'll have to try harder."

I did not go back to Ireland for several years after my father died. Now I make short visits; a christening, a stopover on the way back from Europe. But I haven't taken the children since my father's death. The holidays we took when my father was alive were strange and rewarding and fairly hard work. Ireland is not a large country, but we seemed to spend a lot of time travelling along narrow winding roads, our pleasure in the extreme beauty of the landscape marred only by the distress of carsick children. There was a lot of packing and unpacking and changing diapers and arranging meals which my American children would eat. Fortunately, in a sense, there is now a McDonald's in Dublin.

The children met their grandparents (and a great-grandmother) and aunts and uncles and cousins. Small, happy memories of these visits remain. Once we, three generations, were visiting Dublin Zoo. Jenny, a contented two-year-old, had never felt the need to speak a complete sentence. A noun, a look, a gesture would usually cause any need to be met or wish to be granted. But an unwitnessed event left her the sole possessor of a piece of information she wanted to communicate. Pink in the face, standing on tiptoe, hands outstretched, panting, she managed to articulate her first official sentence. Gradually we became aware that she had been bitten by an animal. Not one incarcerated in the zoo—this was Ireland, where nature is benevolent. She had been pecked by a local, Irish, freeloading duck. A painless, good-natured, curious nip. The event was tiny, sweet and unimportant except that it included my children for the first time in the communal memory of my family. If we are lucky and paying attention (the two are, I think, more closely related than most people imagine), we can take magical moments as they happen and incorporate them into our lives. With a little luck and by paying attention, we can, just occasionally, have our cake and eat it too.

My father's death cut a tie with the past. He had lived on the other side of an arbitrary generational date line. Perhaps what Anthony Powell calls "the hard line" of the Second World War, "after which nothing was ever quite the same again." I realized that there were many things about which we would never agree. He'd grown up with the values of a late Victorian society. We could never agree politically, for instance, and after one somewhat startling discussion I never mentioned the Theory of Evolution to him again.

His death also cut a tie with Ireland, with a way of life, a way of thinking. But it was a gentle cutting. His death was sudden and shocking. But despite the unopened letter, which still breaks my heart, it was a resolved relationship and was not without its place in the rhythm and pattern of my life.

THE JUDGES' CAVE

Y HUSBAND used to tell our children of a teacher who, in order to illustrate some natural law, stood with his back to a blackboard, holding a heavy object in front of him, just touching the tip of his nose. The object was suspended from the ceiling, and when he let go of it, it swung, a pendulum, in the opposite direction and returned, heavy and menacing, as though it would smash his face. He would wait, not flinching and holding the entire attention of his students. The weight would each time it returned, inevitably, fall short of his nose and swing once more in the opposite direction. Once the weight had swung back and forth a few times, demonstrably failing to strike him, each time falling short by an increasing distance, the experiment was over, the suspense broken. If the teacher and students had been patient enough, had sat still and watched, eventually the weight would cease to be a pendulum and would hang motionless beneath the hook from which it was suspended. If one were looking for a perpendicular line, it would be a true one. Given time, the wild swings subside and the truth emerges.

I was born at a time and in a place where certain assumptions were not questioned. In my adolescence these premises seemed to be predominantly about sex and, in fact, a great many of them were. The intrinsic value of virginity was unquestioned, as were the evils and dangers of fornication, adultery, homosexuality, or any kind of deviate, although unspecified, sexual activity.

Just a few years later and a few hundred miles east I was presented with a new set of self-evident truths. The other end of the pendulum's arc. The sexual revolution and the forerunning murmurs of incipient feminism extolled the virtues and values of sexual freedom, provocative clothing, foreign films, uninhibited language and behaviour and warned us against hypocrisy, inhibition, sexual frustration and the Establishment. None of these truths turned out to be absolute. A whole generation of young women, girls really, were caught between two conflicting half-truths and not all of us came away undamaged.

I was in my middle years by the time my personal pendulum stopped swinging. A comfortable time when some of the lessons I had learned years before started to make sense and some of the information stored away when I was a book-hungry schoolgirl could be unpacked (like a trunkful of clothes from the attic, suddenly back in style) and applied to the present day.

I was aware of losses—both of things I had once had and of things which I had never had and now never would. The most tangible gains were the human ones: my children; friends who had shared enough memories to be ensured tenure; a new level of attachment to my family in Ireland; and, for a time, a surprisingly successful marriage played by rules only visible to the two of us. There was also a feeling, a dispassionate one which contained some sense of pleasure, that the cast of characters in my life was almost complete. At the same time I was grateful that the circle was not yet quite closed, that the door was still open just enough for one or two more people to slide in. I understood that some of the losses were offset by, and coincided with, a newly recognized need for privacy.

Julia and I were divorced in the same year. Her marriage had lasted eighteen years, mine a little less. Two of my mother's three daughters had made the same choice that she had. A divorce sets the pendulum swinging, not smoothly, but with jerky and irregular movement. Loneliness is perhaps the most immediate price that one pays for that particular form of freedom. For me, next came doubts about previously unquestioned beliefs. The responsibility of making decisions without either the endorsement or the balancing dissenting opinion of another. All that I believed came up for reexamination and some of it was found wanting. I looked to my friends, to books, to the past, and found there a new cast of characters and set of influences.

I have told about being a child in Ireland and how my childhood was influenced by the previous two or three generations. Later, as an adult with children already the age that I was when most of the events I have described occurred, I found a new connection with the past. It was later in my life but the message came from earlier in my family's history. I had moved three thousand miles from where I was born, but it seemed that so had they.

WHEN I WAS a small child at Glenville, Julia and I would sometimes open a drawer in my mother's desk and look at one of the original copies of Charles I's death warrant. Each of the signers had a copy and the signature of one of our Goff ancestors, his handwriting strangely similar to my grandmother's, stood in fourteenth place.

The document was slightly torn and over the years it became more frayed and tattered. I was aware, even then, that it should have been more carefully looked after, and years later, when we had moved to Ballinaparka, the death warrant was accidentally burned by my father while destroying old letters and papers late one night. I did not learn of this loss until some years after it took place, and never spoke of it to my father. I still feel the pain of a link with the past lost, of the needless waste of something which should not have been ours to destroy.

As a child I heard very little about the man who had signed away his king's life, nor was I ever told that there were actually two ancestors' signatures on the document—talk about family history was not a form our particular brand of snobbery took. It was only after I had lived in Connecticut for some time that I began to learn about a moment when my family history and the history of New England overlapped.

I was sitting in the tiny public library in Bridgewater with my mother. Bridgewater is a very small village in Connecticut, about the same size as Aglish, where I spent part of my childhood. My mother was visiting me and we were fulfilling the extremely modest demands she makes as a houseguest.

This outing, which required nothing more than a two-mile drive, was to help her trace a man who might have brought dogwood trees from America to Ireland in the eighteenth century. She was writing a piece for an academic journal on Lord Charlemont's garden. She, too, had travelled a fair distance from the days when she exported china hens and pseudo-ancestor portraits. She is now an acknowledged expert in her field, Irish paintings, and the research she was engaged in was for a series of articles on the Dilettanti—their travels, their architecture, their lives and their influence on English and Irish taste and art.

While my mother was happily tracking down an eighteenth-century gardener, I was looking through some of the older books which the library had in its reference section. Some of them were from the nineteenth century and were, I assumed, rare. I started to glance through a history of Connecticut and came across my family name and an excerpt from a letter written in 1662 from a wife to her husband:

> . . . And, therefore, let us comfort ourselves with this, though we should never meete in this world againe, yet I hope, through grace, wee shall meete in heaven . . .

I spent the next year trying to find out more about the woman, Frances Goffe, who had written this letter and the man to whom she had written it. My fascination with this couple and this period of history was only partly because they were my ancestors. It was also because I am endlessly curious about the nature of love. I don't know anyone who could, were the circumstances similar, write or inspire such a letter.

An Anglo-Irish upbringing did nothing to spawn confidence in love. Although my family was a loving one, this love was never verbalized or demonstrated. Among the other families we knew socially there was a remarkable dearth of role models for an adolescent girl whose biological instincts were constrained by a society which provided no attractive alternative to marriage.

Having cast a very cold eye over the few Protestant males who were unmarried and in roughly the right age group, I could see how extremely unlikely it was that I would marry one of them. It also seemed very unlikely that anyone would ever want to marry me and, if someone did, I was unable to imagine a convincing wedding ceremony, let alone a lifetime together.

It occurred to me that perhaps the problem was Ireland. That the country, the people, the religion, the social order and, perhaps, the climate made it impossible for romantic love to flourish. Later, it became clear that although first London and then California could provide a great deal more fun than anything offered in the Republic of Ireland, the odds were still heavily weighted against one. There, love and sex were possible, probable and easily available on a temporary basis, but happy endings were no more common than at home.

For a long time I could find no way around the inescapable fact that as to live was to die, to love was to lose. I never realized that I had been given the necessary clue at school. Needless to say, by accident. In the same heedless, random way that I had been taught about passion in *Wuthering Heights,* I was given my first clue about endless love and the price it demands in "Ode on a Grecian Urn." That an unachieved love can be pure and uncompromised forever; that a great love ended by some random force is not a complete loss; that *Romeo and Juliet* has far from the saddest ending a love story can have.

As I learned about the Goffe family I came upon the kind of story I would go some lengths to avoid in an epic novel. It contained a family torn apart by the English Civil War, treason, fugitives with prices on their heads and a woman loyal to them through years of separation and deprivation.

FOR TEN YEARS, when I went to the theatre in New Haven, I would come down the hill on the northwest side of that city, drive the full length of Whalley Avenue to the centre, and then on to where the theatre in which my husband occasionally worked. Whalley Avenue is one of the main streets in New Haven but I never paused to wonder for whom it was named. Running at a slight angle to Whalley Avenue, and eventually joining it, is another street. If I had had occasion to vary my route, I would have shown more curiosity, since that street is called Goffe, an earlier version of my own name.

William Goffe and Edward Whalley had both signed the death warrant of Charles I. Whalley was Goffe's father-in-law. His daughter Frances was the woman who had written the letter which included the phrase I had found so moving.

I don't know if William and Frances Goffe's marriage was even a love match, but it is how a love affair endures rather than how it begins which allows us to judge it. The Goffes had six children and their married life coincided with a particularly volatile moment in English history, one in which William Goffe played an important part. His active participation in the affairs of his country and the upbringing of their children would be enough to tell us that this was not a relationship based on the kind of obsessive passion which precluded all else. But the marriage remained loyal, faithful and loving right up to the tragic end.

Both Goffe and Whalley bore arms against their king and

Whalley became the king's jailer at Hampton Court. Later he and Goffe were among the king's judges and Whalley signed the death warrant in the fourth place.

During the Protectorate, both men enjoyed nine years of power, privilege and responsibility, becoming members of Cromwell's House of Lords. Goffe was considered a contender to succeed Cromwell and to inherit the Protectorship. Nevertheless, Richard Cromwell, who was his father's heir and choice as the next Protector, trusted Goffe's loyalty and gave him land in Ireland—a gift confiscated as soon as Charles II came to the throne.

Richard Cromwell's trust was not misplaced. Both Goffe and Whalley supported him to the last and long after they both must have known that all of their days were marked.

Goffe was deeply religious and knowledgeable about his beliefs—he held a record for having invoked the name of God twenty-six times during one speech at the Army Council. There is something admirable in the fact that his belief never faltered during the long and hard years of adversity which followed his time of glory. Whalley when given charge of the local government of five counties showed a more human side and, breaking Puritan tradition, allowed the Earl of Essex to run a horse race, for a cup, at Lincoln.

As the Restoration became imminent, it was clear that the regicides, as those who had signed the death warrant were called, were in danger. My two ancestors left their families, their homes, their country and quickly sailed for America on a ship appropriately named the *Prudent Mary*. The ship left before Charles II was proclaimed king, and Goffe and Whalley were among the seven "judges" who were excluded from the general pardon in the Act of Indemnity.

Whalley and Goffe arrived in Boston in July 1660. They were warmly welcomed by John Endicott, the governor, and the prominent citizens of that city. Neither the Bostonians nor the fugitives themselves thought of them as anything but devout, serious and distinguished visitors. News, of course, travelled slowly in those days and it was the end of November before the governor realized that a reward of one hundred pounds was being offered for each of his distinguished visitors, dead or alive.

On October 13, the first of the regicides who had remained in England was executed. Pepys wrote:

But my Lord not being up, I went out to Charing-cross to see Major-Generall Harrison hanged, drawn, and quartered —which was done there—he looking as cheerfully as any man could do in that condition. He was presently cut down and his head and his heart shown to the people, at which there was great shouts of joy. It is said that he said that he was sure to come shortly at the right hand of Christ to judge them that now have judged him. And that his wife doth expect his coming again.

Thus it was my chance to see the King beheaded at White-hall and to see the first blood shed in revenge for the blood of the King at Charing-cross.

Not put off his food by the events of the morning, Pepys took two friends to the Sun Taverne for oysters. Living in a world where people tend to be dramatically better at handing it out than taking it, I am impressed by the strength of the Harrisons' faith. The Goffes appear to have taken similar comfort from their beliefs.

Harrison's execution was followed by those of other regicides—mercy being defined as permission for the relatives to dispose of the bodies afterward instead of having their heads "set up for a traytor" in public.

Endicott was the first New England governor to find himself embarrassed by the presence of Goffe and Whalley. Not to arrest them and deliver them to the English authorities was treason, and yet to do so conflicted with personal and religious principle, the laws of hospitality and the sympathies of the people he governed.

He chose, as later did the governors of Connecticut and New Haven (then a separate colony), to make an energetic and highly visible search for the regicides while, at the same time, taking care not to find them.

My ancestors travelled through Connecticut unscathed and arrived in New Haven, where they were hidden in the house of the Reverend John Davenport. On the first Sunday after their arrival, Davenport preached a sermon, giving as his text Isaiah 11:3–4:

Take counsel, execute judgement, make thy shadow as the night in the midst of noonday, hide the outcast, betray not him that wandereth. Let mine outcasts dwell with thee: Moab, be thou and convert to them from the face of the spoiler.

Goffe and Whalley hid at Davenport's house for a time and then, for their safety and for his, moved on. They spent a couple of nights in a mill in the woods and later in a hiding place which has ever since been called "the Judges' Cave." This cave, which in reality is no more than a few huge rocks, was a very inadequate shelter for two men, one no longer young and probably beginning to lose his health. Hiding in a cave has, in fiction, a certain dramatic appeal, but in reality these two men lived without running water, sanitation, cooking facilities, a roof over their heads or any of the rudimentary necessities for keeping themselves and their clothing clean.

At the same time that they lived in such physical discomfort they had very little to look forward to. They could never hope to be incorporated into any American community or to move on to a safer country. The best that they could wish for was that they should remain concealed—prisoners really—until they died. They must have been aware not only that they would remain in danger for the rest of their lives but that neither would ever see his family again.

Fortunately, neither seems to have ever doubted either the

wisdom or the correctness of his acts. They lived in hope of vindication on earth and certainty of it in heaven.

At night the two men were kept awake by wild animals and eventually a catamount or panther grew bold enough to thrust its head into the mouth of the cave, which was no more than a few feet from where they lay. The next day Goffe and Whalley moved on to Guilford.

According to a letter of Davenport's, they left the Judges' Cave with the intention of giving themselves up. They could not survive on their own and wanted to spare their friends the danger of aiding them. They travelled to New Haven, where, according to Governor Thomas Hutchinson, "some persons came to them to advise them not to surrender." It appears that while officials in New Haven were obliged, perhaps even more than those of securer colonies, to make an outward show of loyalty and obedience to the Crown, no one wanted to be the man who arrested the regicides and returned them to England to be hanged, drawn and quartered.

Legend and several historians have it that Davenport argued them out of surrendering in a cellar while Governor William Leete ate his dinner in a room above. As the historian Hollister has it: "unseen by the governor though fed from his table." As with many other colourful stories about my ancestors, there are several versions, all of which can be traced back to the right period, though none to a reliable source.

Goffe and Whalley hid in Milford for two years, not once able to leave their room, since their presence there was not known to the entire family in whose house they were hidden. Certainly not to the daughters. It seems that they were visited by a friend who entertained them (and the two men concealed in the room directly overhead) with a new Royalist ballad which had just arrived from England, little knowing that the objects of their ridicule were within easy earshot.

In 1664 it seemed wise to leave Milford, and Goffe and Whalley moved to Hadley, Massachusetts, where Whalley died fourteen years later. They were sheltered there by the Reverend

John Russell. Again they lived in concealed quarters, in a room behind the kitchen which had a hidden trapdoor that allowed them to hide in a small cellar below in case the house were searched. William Goffe kept a journal, which I would give a great deal to see. There are references to it in several history books, but I assume the writers had merely seen excerpts in previous books. It seems almost certain that the journal and other papers were destroyed when a mob rifled the house of Governor Hutchinson in 1765.

Fortunately, some copies of a small part of the Goffes' correspondence remain. Governor Hutchinson, who had access to most of Goffe's papers, wrote in 1764: "There is too much religion in their letters for the taste of the present day: but the distresses of two persons, under these peculiar circumstances, who appear to have lived very happily together are strongly described."

Copies of two letters from Frances Goffe, one complete, one nearly so, survive. They were written ten years apart, one in 1662 and the other in 1672. The first, which contained the excerpt that so moved me, was written before the Goffes adopted the subterfuge of addressing each other as mother and son, and allows Mrs. Goffe to write with some passion, though never leaving the name of the Lord uninvoked for more than a line or two:

> *I do hartily wish myselfe with thee, but that I fear it may bee a meanes to discover thee, as it was to ——— and therefore I shall forbeare attempting any such thing for the present, hoping that the Lord will, in his owne time, return thee to us againe. . . . And, therefore, let us comfort our- selves with this, though we should never meete in this world againe, yet I hope, through grace, wee shall meete in heaven, and soe ever be with the Lord, and it will not be in the power of men to part us. My dear, I know you are confident in my affection, yet give me leave to tell thee, thou art as deare to me as a husband can be to a wife, and, if I knew any thing I could doe to make you happy, I*

should doe it, if the Lord would permitt, though to the
losse of my life.

In their later letters she assumes the name of Frances
Goldsmith and he of Walter Goldsmith. After her husband and
her father fled to America, Frances Goffe and her children went to
live with a family called Hooke. Mrs. Hooke is referred to in the
letters as Mrs. Jane or "my aunt." They lived somewhere in the
country and, as Frances Goffe wrote, "have no wante of food or
rayment, though in a meane way."

It is not clear how Frances Goffe managed. There was
evidently some money, since several historians mention that
Goffe and Whalley received money from England. They even
seem to have carried on some business—probably owning cattle
with a Captain Daniel Gookin—and the Reverend John Russell
was well enough rewarded for his assistance to be able to send two
sons to Harvard. But the Goffe estate in Herefordshire and their
land in Ireland had been confiscated at the Restoration, and
although the "meane" food and clothing to which Frances Goffe
referred may have been temporary, hers must have been a
wretched and fearful existence.

One complete letter of Goffe's, almost four thousand words
long, survives—it was included in a book of Hutchinson's papers.
Written in 1674 from his secret, shared room, it contains a great
deal more than his wife's letter from London two years before. It
is a curious letter, beautifully written but oddly paced. He writes
in August (although unsure of when he will be able to send it) in
reply to a letter of hers sent in March. She lets him know that she
still hadn't received one that he had sent to her the previous
October. The time lapses between writing and receipt and the
unsureness of successful delivery make Goffe seem even more
remote from his family. Whalley was by this time failing and
Goffe must have been lonely, which is perhaps the reason for his
detailed journal. The leisurely way he approaches his subjects, in
this case death and a marriage, seems at first a little cold-blooded.

But this letter was intended less as a telegram of condolence or congratulation than as a concrete thing for Mrs. Goffe to keep and read; to give her a sense of an ongoing marriage with a man she knew she would never see again. It starts slowly with a few lines about letters sent and received, which at first seems trivial but was, of course, vital information in a correspondence as complicated and potentially dangerous as theirs. Then he comments on the marriage of his daughter Frances to a man of whom he knows nothing and the imminent birth of her first child. He moves on to comfort his wife since one of their other daughters had died. There is a certain amount of "the Lord knows best." I find it hard to imagine that anyone would want to hear this at a time of grief, but it is possible that my Puritan ancestors really did find comfort in it.

Next he writes a brief paragraph about her having moved from where she was living with a hope "that the Lord guided you to that notion." It sounds a little bossy but in light of what happened later, his fears turned out to be well founded.

Then he gives her news of her father, whom he refers to as "Your old friend, Mr. R.," and tells her that he is still living, though failing. Again, he seems a little cold-blooded with his descriptions: "not being able, of a long time, to dresse, or undresse himselfe, nor to feed, or ease nature either way . . ." But I don't think his directness is unkind. Any questions on these important topics could take up to a year to be asked and answered, if at all. It makes sense for him to anticipate and answer his wife's questions as fully as possible. She wants to know the state of his health, both mental and physical, and is reassured by reading that her father is being well looked after by her husband and that her husband is a man who gives the help willingly:

> . . . and it is a great mercy to him that he hath a friend that takes pleasure in being helpful to him, and I bless the Lord that gives me such a good measure of health and strength, and an opportunity and a heart to use it in good and necessary a worke.

Just over halfway through this letter, which was written over several days, a letter comes from Mrs. Goffe, and although it negates some of the contents of his first few pages, he replies to it as though the previous letter had already been mailed or could not be revised. I think he didn't want to do her out of a letter, with his considered reactions to her news, just because a letter from her had arrived. Again, his reply starts with dates of letters sent and received before he addresses himself to the news that his daughter Frances's baby had died. Goffe, now having to offer comfort for a second family death in the same letter, does not waver: " . . . and tho' it hath pleased the Lord so soon to transplant him from the militant to the triumphant church."

Despite the references to God's will, each with chapter and verse, and the constrictions of writing as from a son to a mother, William Goffe manages to show loving concern for his wife's well-being and ends with a postscript from which I think Frances Goffe must have derived comfort and strength:

> But oh, my dear mother, how could you feare such a thing
> from me? Yourselfe knoweth I never yet spake an angry
> word to you, nay I hope I may say (without taking the
> name of God in vain) the Lord knoweth I never conceived
> an angry thought towards you, nor do I now, nor I hope I
> never shall, and so saying I do not commend myselfe, for
> you never gave me the least cause, neither have you now,
> and I believe never will; therefore, dear mother, the whole
> praise belongs to yourselfe, or rather to the Lord, who,
> blessed be his name, hath so united our hearts together in
> love that it is a thing scarce possible to be angry one with
> another.

Goffe's missing papers would have answered many of my questions, among them the date and circumstances of Whalley's death and the place of his burial. But perhaps the most interesting information would have been his account of the "Angel of

Hadley" incident. Or his lack of such an account, since it is by no means certain that such an event ever took place.

This is a story which has a firm place in the history of Hadley but for which there is no confirmation from that period. In 1676, during King Philip's War (settlers versus Indians: King Philip was an Indian), the inhabitants of Hadley were attacked by Indians. The Indians had an immediate advantage since they not only were greater in number but found the community observing a fast in their meeting house. The settlers fought bravely and desperately but were getting the worst of it when a stranger, old and odd-looking in both dress and appearance, started giving directions and organizing with such skill that the Indians were routed. Afterward the stranger disappeared and was never seen again. Some of the villagers thought that the man was an angel sent to deliver them, but it is more likely, if true, that it was General Goffe's last military campaign. Both Sir Walter Scott and James Fenimore Cooper borrowed this incident and used it in novels.

After Whalley's death, Goffe, freed from his obligation to his father-in-law and friend, moved to Hartford, where he had every expectation of a freer and more satisfying life. What happened next was cruel and ironic. It was at this time that he lost his family.

Goffe wrote to the Reverend Increase Mather, whom he and his wife had used as an intermediary, in August 1678, telling him of Hooke's death ("That heavy word has been spoken") and saying:

My mo: writes that he being dead she hath written to her Friend (by whom I suppose she means yourself) to send her letters to another place, but did so far forget herself, as not to inform me either of name or place.

Mather does not appear to have replied to this letter, and Goffe wrote to him several times again, each time with increasing desperation. There is no evidence to suggest that Mather ever acknowledged his pleas or that either William or Frances Goffe ever received another letter from each other or, it is likely, ever again knew if the other were dead or alive. The last recorded letter of Goffe's is an impassioned plea to Mather to help him find his family, of whom he once wrote: "This world hath indeed nothing in it more Desirable than such faces."

Goffe may have died in Hartford, but New Haven and Stow, Massachusetts, also lay claim to his grave. My guess, based on a little wishful thinking, is that he returned to Hadley, maybe even had some correspondence with his family, and died among friends. He may even have been buried with Whalley. The accounts of the bones in the basement vary from a few small human bones, to the skeleton of a large man, to two skeletons. Clearly Whalley was secretly buried there and it seems likely that Goffe was also.

I don't know what happened to Frances Goffe, but her son, Richard, turned Royalist and regained the land given to his father by Richard Cromwell. My family lived at Horetown until the end of the last century, when our branch moved first to Maypark, then built Glenville, where I was born.

There are American Goffs, but they came later. Some of those who lived in Seattle were family-conscious and used to make visits to Ireland. They would visit my father, whom they considered the head of the family. A nineteenth-century male Davis, whose mother was born a Goff, succeeded his uncle Jacob Goff and added his mother's maiden name to his and assumed the Goff arms by royal licence in 1845—so the line isn't entirely unbroken. My father would go on trips with these distant cousins, only slightly discouraged by their teetotaling ways when they stopped for liquid refreshment.

AT FIRST I assumed that the Judges' Cave didn't exist anymore or that its whereabouts was unknown. Everything else in the story was gone—my father's copy of the death warrant destroyed by fire; Goffe's papers lost in an eighteenth-century riot; the house under which Whalley was buried now marked only by a plaque. And I knew that the cave had been only a freestanding pile of rocks rather than the traditional, more durable dwelling place hollowed out of the side of a cliff.

The search was a ludicrously easy one. An all-purpose road map of Connecticut showed West Rock marked clearly, and I realized that it was the large red meat-loaf-shaped cliff which caught the setting sun on the many summer evenings I had driven to New Haven to go to the theatre there. So one September afternoon toward the end of my children's vacation I piled them and an extra child who happened to be loitering in the kitchen into a station wagon and we set off for New Haven.

The first clue was somewhat bigger than a bread box and found within minutes: the Three Judges Motor Inn, located just off Whalley Avenue. I'd driven past it countless times without questioning the name.

We turned off the main road and struck up a couple of side streets toward the huge red rock. Each time we hit a dead end in either a residential street or the chain-linked boundary of a small light-industry plant. At last I stopped and asked a young woman exercising a dog if she knew how we could gain access to West Rock and if she had ever heard of the Judges' Cave. She told us that she used to visit it but that it was quite a walk. The directions she gave us were clear (the landmarks she chose to mark the way were all fast-food outlets) and I expected the information about its being a steep climb to be equally accurate. I hoped that the late summer vegetation and scrub would not prove impassable, although I had already resigned myself to coming back alone at a later date if it looked too ambitious for the rest of the group, who were, after all, only along for the ride and a meal at one of the junk-food establishments we had passed.

I therefore felt more than a little foolish when the Judges' Cave turned out to be not only less than an hour's drive from the home I had lived in for thirteen years, but the centre of a National Park with a parking lot at the base and a nice smooth blacktop road leading up to the cave.

We did at least walk up. The smooth tarmac road looped back and forth to allow for a reasonable gradient and on either side the hill looked old. Trees had fallen and rotted where they fell. No one had interfered with Nature's erratic but efficient scheme. The uncleared woods were the usual mixture of weedy trees and crippling and suffocating scrub so often the reality behind the evocative description "virgin forest." It was through identical brambles and saplings that my ancestors must have made their way up the side of the rock. And far older than woods were the smooth eroded rocks and primeval ferns, unchanged since long before any man or even warm-blooded creature had passed that way.

It was a warm day and the walk up was steep despite the undulating road. The children didn't complain—they weren't very interested in the outing but managed clearly, though wordlessly, to acknowledge that what we were doing was important to me. It was a long way up.

It was a long way up on a sunny afternoon on a smooth and clearly defined road, wearing shorts and sneakers, rested and well fed, carrying nothing, pursued by no one. With families and homes to go to and warm beds with clean sheets, with hot and cold running water and cooked meals eaten in comfortable surroundings. And books and music and freedom.

In 1661 these woods were not friendly. The rocks and boulders which I admired had to be scaled; the woods, full of wild animals, were the hunting grounds of Indians.

The process of renovation which had restored the blacktop had not yet reached the crest of the hill where the cave stood. The ground had once been paved and the paved area bordered with stone, but time and Nature had reclaimed and modified the intrusion. The cave stands clear of the surrounding woods, and apart from its historic associations, it is an object of curiosity in its own right. It consists of several huge slabs of rock, some of which lean against one another to form a small sheltered area. It is difficult to imagine what forces could have brought these immensely heavy pieces of stone together, especially since they are at the highest point of the hill. The rocks around them, apart from those rearranged to form the parking area, are smooth, ancient, weathered, half concealed by moss, with grass growing at the edge and ferns and the odd resilient tree attempting to sprout from their shallow dirt-filled cracks.

The children clambered over the rocks and into the cave itself. Their size made the barren rocks seem more accommodating, but still one could see how inadequate a shelter it had been. There was room, just, for two men to sleep, at an angle and not on a flat surface, with some degree of shelter from the elements. Nothing more. The shape and space would have made a better grave for these two outlaws than it made living quarters.

Although there was an encouraging lack of litter, the cave itself was predictably adorned with linked names of those promising eternal love or the single names of those who had decided to go it alone as far as a temporary immortality was concerned. The Judges' Cave seemed a curiously inappropriate place to stake a claim to either.

It seemed to me, also, that the message of the two men who had hidden there—more than three hundred years ago and still remembered and honoured—is that there are no shortcuts to anything of value, no unearned grace, no easier and softer way. That action defines character, that courage is grace in the face of adversity, that a losing hand has to be played out as bravely as a winning one, that it is never permissible to whine, that it is futile to show or even feel self-pity, that principles are more important than personalities, that a life of value is ruled by loyalty, courage, truth and that most loosely used and misunderstood word, honour.

The old Indian trail along the ridge of West Rock to the site of the cave still exists, part of it incorporated into an abandoned road; overgrown, mysterious, romantic and with the stones ambiguous as to whether man or nature had placed them in almost symmetrical order. The trail, too, was ambiguous, dividing and then dividing again, each time making one unsure which was the real path, aware there would be another decision to make at the next fork. Each fork offered a partly covered path which constantly threatened to peter out and seemed both excitingly full of unknown promise and familiar in a way I did not quite understand. Not pausing to consider genetic memory or anything smacking ever so lightly of reincarnation, I kept walking, trying to clear my mind of the effort to recognize or remember, and to concentrate on the narrow strip of beaten earth, on the evergreen shrubs, on the partly buried stones, the roots, the ferns, the formation of the hillside which suggested a ruined and buried fortification. Then I suddenly knew why I had had the feeling of having seen this before. If I had stooped enough to have looked from a viewpoint perhaps eighteen inches lower it would not have taken me so long. The woods at Glenville were like this. The lines and landscaping of man modified and improved by time and weather and growing, living, dying vegetation.

Through the trees I could see the brightly coloured shorts and tee shirts of the children coming to look for me. I could hear their laughter and the sweetness of their voices. For a moment I could feel the gentleness of a summer evening at Glenville, I could see the dragonflies hovering over the ponds, the once carefully landscaped but now ruined walks which I had run along with my sister. Glenville—the house where we roller-skated in the corridors, saw a ghost in the stable attic, ate strawberries under the nets, shelled peas and topped and tailed gooseberries in the large, light, tiled kitchen. Glenville, where on an evening such as this we wandered through the woods cracking open beechnuts and watching the mail boat start down the river.

I went to meet the children, confused by the mixture of my ancestors—strong, uncompromising, brave; Glenville, a house and a life that no longer existed but made me, in part, who I am, and the traffic and noises of New Haven below, fast food, neon lights, advertisements—an easier but thinner life.

We started down the hill together, and it seemed to me it was possible, if we were lucky, took the broader view, respected our memories, paid attention, showed a little faith, that we could have it all.